A LIFE OF JOHN WILKES

JOHN WILKES

After a print by Carrington Bowles in the Guildhall Library

A LIFE OF
JOHN WILKES

By OWEN AUBREY SHERRARD

BOOKS FOR LIBRARIES PRESS
FREEPORT, NEW YORK

First Published 1930
Reprinted 1971

INTERNATIONAL STANDARD BOOK NUMBER:
0-8369-5910-8

LIBRARY OF CONGRESS CATALOG CARD NUMBER:
77-164627

PRINTED IN THE UNITED STATES OF AMERICA

PREFACE

"I HAVE been much misrepresented", said Wilkes on one occasion, and on another, "the nation and posterity I trust to". Hitherto the nation and posterity have betrayed their trust. Wilkes has been represented as utterly vile or at best as an amusing scoundrel, though the evidence is unsatisfactory. Facts compel the admission that his opinions were invariably right, and because it is unseemly that a man should be at once persistently bad and consistently right, the goodness in him has been placed to the credit of Government's badness—Wilkes was made by the folly of his opponents.

It is time that posterity paid its debt. Wilkes was no saint, but no more was he an inhuman monster. His views and actions were his own, and the folly of Government did nothing but delay the fruition of his ideas beyond his death.

. Wilkes had two failings—he was naturally coarse and he had inordinately strong passions. These two failings would certainly not have given him his reputation in his own lifetime had he not added three cardinal sins. He was inveterately independent in an age of "connections"; he was deplorably honest in an age of shams; he was not a born gentleman in an age when an aristocracy of birth was everything.

Yet even for these sins he largely atoned by the brilliance of his wit and the geniality of his nature. Most of his contemporaries ran him down only while they knew him by hearsay. When they came to know him personally, they succumbed to his charm and went about declaring loudly that he was a gentleman, thereby paying him their highest compliment—and incidentally telling a lie.

But their tardy repentance could not wipe out the hard things they had said before; and even if they praised his manners they were still averse to his politics. So he had no recognized champion among his contemporaries, and the judicious pearl of praise was lost to sight in the huge heap of abuse when a succeeding age came to assess his character.

After it had once been decided that Wilkes was a profligate and libertine, a demagogue and debauchee, the Victorians thought it best to leave him in his unclean sty. And no doubt it would have been, if he had ever been in it.

The following pages are an attempt to see him as he was, neither straining his virtues nor defending his vices. The evidence has been culled mainly from the original MSS. in the British Museum, supplemented by the numerous printed journals, letters, diaries, and histories of the times. If the Wilkes of fact proves no less interesting than the Wilkes of imagination, it will be all that the author dare hope. That he will be less lurid is a foregone conclusion.

———————

CONTENTS

ILLUSTRATIONS

A LIFE OF JOHN WILKES

CHAPTER I

A COMMON DOMESTIC EVENT

(1)

ON the 17th of October, 1727, the wife of a wealthy distiller,
living in St. John's Square, Clerkenwell, gave birth to a child
who was destined to go through life with the monosyllabic
and unmelodious name of John Wilkes. The event caused no
stir in the world. To the family a third child and second son
was something of an anti-climax. As for Society, the news
never reached its ears, for Society, and in fact the world at
large, was too much occupied with another event.

Three months earlier an elderly, uninteresting gentleman,
German by birth and English by adoption, was driving across
Europe when he was suddenly struck down by apoplexy. His
attendants, seeing his condition, wanted to stop at a small
wayside town, but the obstinate old gentleman insisted im-
patiently that he should be carried to Osnabrück. The coach
rumbled on and bore the elderly gentleman's body to its
destination—but his spirit had escaped on the way.

When the news reached London its effect was electrical.
Peers and prelates began writing letters to a certain James
Stuart, better known as the Old Pretender, who galloped
hurriedly from Italy to France, and then as hurriedly galloped
back again. Another Englishman, who was neither peer,
prelate, nor pretender, but a stout, good-humoured country
squire, also set about galloping in a hurry, but only from
Chelsea to Richmond Lodge, where he announced himself as
Sir Robert Walpole, Prime Minister of England. He demanded
to see the owner, a fiery little bantam of a man, who was asleep
after dinner, and in no very good humour to see visitors. None
the less the Prime Minister came in and announced that

George the First, King of England and Elector of Hanover, had died four days before at Osnabrück. "Dat", retorted the bantam fiercely, "is one big lie." Sir Robert insisted, not only that George I was dead, but that the little bantam prancing about before him was at that very moment George II. Convinced at last, his new Majesty began his reign by depriving Walpole there and then of the premiership, and giving it to an inoffensive favourite of the name of Compton.

The excitement was not confined to the King or to the upper classes. Everyone was agog from the highest to the lowest, and while the sober citizens shook their heads and glanced fearfully at the family blunderbuss, the rabble, picturesque in tarnished lace and ragged wigs, gathering into knots at the street corners and lurching round the doors of coffee-houses, demanded to be told what the fuss was about.

The more knowing feared or desired a Jacobite rising, but not a single man of them knew the real meaning of the ferment. It was not due to the death-throes of the House of Stuart, but to the quickening of democracy; and among the events leading to the coming change none was to prove more potent than the common domestic occurrence in St. John's Square, Clerkenwell.

(2)

Walpole's genius was sufficient to restore him within a few weeks to power, where he remained for the next fourteen years to lead the country in the paths of peace and prosperity, and thereby establish for good the Hanoverian dynasty. It was this atmosphere of growing wealth and budding loyalty that formed the serene background of Wilkes's youth, and possibly had some share in confirming the sunny optimism of his temper.

The family in which he found himself was plebeian to the core, very eccentric, and equally vulgar. His father was a self-made man, with a quaint sense of humour and a strong pride in his own achievements. He knew that it was useless to thrust himself upon Society, and while he shrugged his shoulders, gratified a lurking envy by cutting a dash in his own end of the town, and proving by his display that he was richer in money, if poorer in blood, than many a lordling of Court and Parliament. Perhaps the same envy and pride mingled with his paternal desire that one of the family, at least, should grow up a gentleman. Perhaps, too, something of the sardonic humour mingled in his choice; the eldest sons of the gentry succeeded to the titles and estates, while the cadets were foisted into the Church or thrust into some other semi-inferior calling. Just so the distiller would breed his eldest boy to the trade, while young John should be destined for the poor profession of gentleman.

John's mother was a strong-minded woman, at once good-humoured and hot-tempered, devoted to her husband and proud of her children. But above all she was a Nonconformist of rigid principles and strict morals. She led her family to Presbyterian meetings, where the young John imbibed a lasting contempt for humbugs and a deep respect for saintly lives.

The elder Mr. Wilkes left religion to his wife, occupying himself with trade and politics. Political feelings ran high at the time because they were based upon personal loyalties. Whigs and Tories were nominally fighting a constitutional battle: the former defending the right of the people to govern themselves and the latter upholding the divine right of kings. By a fiction that was none the less strong because it was false, the Glorious Revolution was supposed to have transferred power from the King to the people. Actually it had achieved much less, merely substituting a close oligarchy of magnates for a single despot. The people had no influence on the course of government, but they took their choice between the Old Pretender and the reigning King, and on that basis fiercely argued constitutional points they did not understand and were in no position to support.

In general the Tories had their stronghold in the country

among the fox-hunting, hard-drinking squires who, like Squire Western, refused to have their acres sent over to Hanover. The Whigs looked for their support to the commercial classes of the towns. This natural division between trade and agriculture, emphasized by a clash of personal loyalties, was still further enforced by a cleavage of religion: the Tories, roughly speaking, belonging to the established Church, while the Whigs were Nonconformist.

The elder Mr. Wilkes, as a trader with a Nonconformist wife, must have been, and was, a vehement Whig. So vehement was he that he even made politics the touchstone by which to settle John's education—a fact amusing in itself and still more significant for the light it throws on Wilkes's life. Although he never showed the least skill in parliamentary practice, he did display at all times a thorough grasp of constitutional principles; and it was no doubt at home and by his father's Whiggish sermons that the seeds were sown.

However this may be, it is the fate of fathers never to do right, and Wilkes thought poorly of his father's choice of schools. Certainly it was out of the ordinary, considering that Wilkes was to be made a gentleman. Society then, as now, sent its offspring to the older public schools and the two universities, and if John was to be a gentleman the obvious course was to push him through the same mill. But Mr. Wilkes would have none of it. His robust plebeian soul contained a large measure of contempt for the Society he envied from a distance, and though he meant his son to enter it, he was equally determined that his character should be formed on wholesome lines and his principles firmly grounded before he was thrust into the glittering cesspool of magnificent corruption. So from the time he was seven to the time he was twelve, John attended a humdrum middle-class school at Hertford where, for all his injured complaints in later years that the school had taught him nothing, he was given a sound education in the classics.

Towards the end of these five years the serene period of

peace became clouded in one of those bursts of patriotic Jingoism which spring naturally out of heavy purses and large paunches. Walpole had been too successful. In Parliament he had grabbed every scrap of power to himself, and by refusing to share it had driven everyone into exasperated opposition. Outside Parliament his policy had produced inflated notions as the direct result of unending prosperity. The merchants, waxing daily more rich, grew impatient of restraint and began to clamour for war with Spain merely to sweep away restrictions on their South American trade. Here was the opportunity of the Opposition, and they seized it with considerable ingenuity. Wilkes was eleven or thereabouts when all England was stirred by the story of Robert Jenkins and his ear. Jenkins was the master of a trading sloop, who at one period of his life had been foolish or unlucky enough to fall into Spanish hands while engaged in smuggling. Now, trusting to a large wig which covered both his ears, he produced a piece of mummified flesh, wrapped in cotton-wool, which he declared to be his own ear, torn off by his captors and flung to him with the taunting command to carry it to the King. He was asked what his feelings had been at the dreadful moment, and his reply rang through England like a trumpet-call: "I recommended my soul to God and my cause to my country." A year later war was declared amid the ringing of bells and the lighting of bonfires. In another year the whole of Europe was convulsed by the war of the Austrian Succession. Jenkins's ear and his famous reply were enough to inflame the imagination of a high-spirited boy just entering on his teens, when the glamour of war is unchecked by experience, reason, or fear.

In the midst of this upheaval Wilkes was taken from the school at Hertford and placed under the care of Mr. Leeson, an elderly dissenting minister at Thame with a penchant for heresies. The general ferment in Europe seems to have reproduced itself in the old gentleman's mind, for barely twelve months later he discarded the Presbyterian for the Arian faith, and the care of his flock for the protection of a rich widow,

B

Mrs. Mead, who gave him the light of her countenance and a free house at Aylesbury. Mrs. Mead and Mrs. Wilkes were bosom friends, worshipping in the same conventicle, and it was probably this fact rather than his own religious Odyssey which enabled Mr. Leeson to carry his pupil with him. At all events, to Aylesbury Wilkes came, and more important still, not only to Aylesbury, but often enough to Mrs. Mead's house, where he always found himself a welcome visitor.

When the boy was rising seventeen, his father began to think of universities. He would have nothing to say to Oxford or Cambridge for fear of "the possible contagion of a political stain", but Leyden offered greater hopes. It was then affected by both the English and Scotch, but better still, it was situated in Holland, whose glory it was to have produced William of Orange. So to Leyden John went in September 1744, still accompanied by the ineffable Mr. Leeson. Two months earlier the *Centurion* had dropped anchor at Spithead, and Wilkes must have left England with his head full of Anson's almost incredible voyage round the world, a richly romantic story of four years' battle with Spaniards, elemental storms, and the ravages of disease.

John's university career lasted for something under two years, but he made excellent use of his time. Besides putting the coping-stone on his classical studies, he became conversant with French—an accomplishment which was to prove useful later on. At the same time he made the most of his social opportunities and became popular, though more with his elders than with men of his own age. Indeed, throughout his early years Wilkes's friends were generally much his senior. The fact suggests that Wilkes was taking pains to ingratiate himself with the exalted world for which he was destined. But with his own generation, half jealous, half contemptuous, and at bottom wholly antagonistic, he would find it no easy task to storm Society, nor would he be secure even when within. One slip, and the latent hostility would break out. Wilkes was essentially a "foreign body", and the turmoil of his career can be likened to nothing so aptly as to the formation of a pearl in an oyster.

He returned to London in July 1746, to find the Jacobite rising of '45 just crushed and ended, and no doubt a jubilant father itching to explain its constitutional significance.

CHAPTER II

MARIAGE À LA MODE

(1)

Now that his education was complete it was time for him to set about his career. His family had no idea of what was entailed by "being a gentleman", but as it appeared to consist of doing nothing on a comfortable income, they decided that he must marry money. They had, indeed, discussed the matter while he was abroad, and fortunately had not far to look. Mrs. Mead had long since succumbed to the pleasing manners of her schoolboy friend, and was also growing anxious about her daughter, now verging on thirty and, in spite of the half-hearted nibbles at her fortune, likely to remain in single blessedness. The little plot matured in an atmosphere of mutual satisfaction, and Mrs. Mead undertook to pave the way into her daughter's heart.

All was ready by the time of Wilkes's return. It was only necessary for him to learn of his good fortune and to go through a decent pretence of storming the lady's heart. No one seems to have doubted his compliance, though the lady was ten years older than her intended mate, without vivacity or charm, and as unsuited to him in nature and character as well could be. Wilkes, who had spent the last two years trying hard to please, went down to Aylesbury without demur. Whatever the lady's feelings may have been, she was likely enough to succumb to her suitor. It is true that nature had given him a face that was more than usually ugly, but he was bubbling over with wit and his manners were fascinating. Moreover, he had made it his business to develop his natural gift of entertaining—to such effect that, as he used to boast, he could talk away his face in half an hour. The wooing progressed without a hitch, and the couple were married at St. John's Church, Clerkenwell, on the 23rd of May, 1747.

There is nothing to be said for this sorry business except that there were precedents in plenty. Marriages of convenience were the order of the day, which thoroughly understood how to overcome their inconvenience. "Love", remarked the *Connoisseur* some five years later, "is, indeed, a very rare ingredient in modern wedlock." But while that might be true, it was not a thing to be deplored. "The great convenience of expelling love from matrimony is very evident. Married persons of quality are never troubled with each other's company abroad, or fatigued with dull matrimonial discourses at home; my lord keeps his girl, my lady her gallant; and they both enjoy all the fashionable privileges of wedlock without the inconveniences." The *Connoisseur*, as a popular Society journal, was pleased to exaggerate; but it is none the less a fact that from one end of the social scale to the other marriage was regarded as a means of procreating fortunes as much as children. At the one end of the scale were the plausible villains who entrapped heiresses into runaway matches, and the still greater scoundrels who indulged their appetites cheaply by means of bogus unions, while at the other end were the calculating machines, parents and children alike, who regarded marriage as an arithmetical sum in compound addition. Wilkes was merely following his appointed task of doing as Society did, and one can only regretfully add that he was the less perturbed because he had no intention of keeping his marriage vows. Little was expected of the bride beyond her money, which certainly had its uses. As her dowry Mary Mead received the Manor of Aylesbury with the house attached to it, and it was as a country gentleman that Wilkes first decided to make good his footing.

In the eighteenth century a favourite pastime with landed proprietors was to "improve" their estates—a process which often consisted in reversing nature; hills were levelled, dells filled up, and waterfalls created where no water could possibly fall. When the soil had been thus "improved", its surface came in for attention; classical temples were erected for no particular reason, and ruins built of entirely modern stone. It is to the credit of Wilkes's common sense that his efforts were turned in saner directions. If fashion demanded a tinkering with the estate, then fashion should wed utility, and both work for the common good. He saw to such things as drains, made shrubberies and lawns, and bought up some cottages that spoilt the view. His improvements were mainly practical, and as such wholly in keeping with the more important side of his character.

Besides busying himself about the estate, Wilkes took pains to cultivate his neighbours and to show an intelligent interest in local affairs. Both were pursuits entirely to his taste. As a racy, jovial young man, full of sparkling wit and a host of good stories, he would have been the best of company in any capital in the world. It was natural that he should want to take his share in such society as there was, and still more natural that the county magnates should have welcomed him with open arms.

The interest in local affairs was equally in keeping with his nature. Wilkes had excellent administrative brains, which were barely exercised by the small estate of which he was master. He needed wider fields in which to give his talents a chance of shining, and he found them in the sphere of local government. Here once more he was indebted to his wife for his opportunity. To take his seat upon the local bench he had himself to be a landowner. Accordingly he persuaded his wife in January 1752 to settle the Aylesbury estate upon him by deed of gift, whereupon he at once became a magistrate. As such he was most assiduous in his duties, obtaining an insight into the law which was to prove of material assistance in the future.

(2)

Such in outline were his early activities at Aylesbury, and for the most part they were confined to the summer months. The winters were spent by the young couple with Mrs. Mead in one of the dull, dark houses of Red Lion Court, behind St. Sepulchre's Church, Holborn. Here Wilkes threw off his reforming, magisterial self, and indulged the lighter side of his

character, as a general rule deserting his mother-in-law's house
and entering eagerly into the ways of a man about town. He
would have been wiser to insist on a house of his own from the
beginning. He did at last—and the step has been condemned as
a proof of extravagance and riotous living; but it has all along
been Wilkes's fate to have his sanest and most obvious actions
twisted into proofs of villainy and self-seeking. As long as he
could, Wilkes endured the muffled drabness of his gilded cage,
and when endurance snapped, slipped unobtrusively out to
happier haunts.

Not that his endurance was a feeble growth. On the contrary, it seems to have remained in full flower for at least two
years. Wilkes was determined to storm Society, and if at
Aylesbury this was to be done by making drains and dispensing
justice, in London it was to be achieved by becoming a member
of the various associations to which Society belonged. Wilkes
may have had his eyes mainly on those more uproarious clubs
which tried to startle or amuse the world by their names, such
as the Beefsteak, the Dilettanti, or the Hellfire Clubs, but he
seems to have realized that progress must be slow if it is to be
sure. He began operations with an assault on the Royal Society,
of which he became a Fellow in 1749. It was, of course, easier to
obtain the honour then than now, but even then it was not
thrown at the heads of profligate young libertines.

He had to be nominated, and six eminent gentlemen, including a future president of the Society and a future curator
of the British Museum, declared solemnly that upon their own
personal knowledge he was a gentleman of distinction and
learning, well qualified for the honour he desired, and likely to
become a useful member of their body. Truth compels the
admission that Wilkes was content with election; thereafter he
had no dealings with the Society except that many years later
he was in the habit of dining annually with it at the "Crown
and Anchor" in the Strand—a measure of conviviality that
smacks more of Wilkes than of the learned Fellows. None the
less the six eminent gentlemen afford proof that Wilkes was

an outwardly respectable member of society, whose expeditions beyond the purlieus of Red Lion Court were discreet even if they were not entirely reputable.

Having "bagged" the Royal Society, Wilkes went ahead with his schemes with the acquiescence, if not the whole-hearted approval, of Red Lion Court. He became by degrees the admired centre of a small coterie of brilliant men. The earlier friends of John Wilkes were mostly men of eminence in their individual lines, and all men of strong literary tastes. To shine in such a circle is proof of considerable parts; and if the members of the circle enjoyed Wilkes's rather profane and certainly coarse wit—as indeed they did—the fact must be borne in mind when assessing the weight to be attached to their subsequent attacks upon his character and morals.

(3)

The course of conviviality on Wilkes's side and apathetic dullness on his wife's was interrupted in August 1750 by the birth of their daughter Polly. It was a landmark never to be forgotten. Whatever love Wilkes failed to give his wife he more than made up for by the devotion he lavished on his child. His unvarying tenderness to Polly and his many acts of self-denial for her sake are proof, if proof is needed, that Wilkes was quite capable of strong and deep feelings, perhaps more capable than most. That no woman with whom he came in contact raised these feelings was more his misfortune than his fault, and the result was that his attitude towards womankind was wholly sensual and the reverse of elevated. But, for the proper appreciation of his career, there is much significance in the fact that his finer and truer love should have been paternal—entirely void of all grosser feelings and entirely altruistic.

CHAPTER III
NEIGHBOURS

(1)

WILKES pursued his twofold career of rake and magistrate with monotonous regularity. In London and Bath he was regarded as the embodiment of pleasure, profanity, and good company. "This place", wrote one of his friends from Bath, "continues yet pretty much the same as when you saw it. I perceive no other difference but that of course it is grown some degrees duller. With the spirit of infidelity, you have carried away, I think, all other sort of spirit too."

Aylesbury was a different matter. At Aylesbury, if he shone, he also toiled; and his genuine hard work not only brought him more closely into touch with the local magnates, but convinced them of his abilities. It was here rather than in Town that his future was determined, and it was determined by the type of men around him.

By far the most important of his neighbours was Earl Temple, the wealthy owner of a magnificent seat at Stowe. Temple was nineteen years older than Wilkes. He had lost his father while still a youth, and grew up self-willed and cantankerous, something of the spoilt child with too good an opinion of himself. He might have been even worse if he had been completely his own master, but fortunately it was not till 1752 that he succeeded to his title and estates, which came to him through his mother. When he was twenty-three he entered Parliament, sitting for the Borough of Buckingham, and at once fell under the influence of the elder Pitt, becoming, as Walpole said, "the absolute creature of Pitt, vehement in whatever faction he was engaged, and as mischievous as his understanding would let him be, which is not saying he was very bad." His alliance with Pitt was cemented when in 1754 Pitt married his only sister.

Wilkes met Temple soon after going to Aylesbury. Considering his ambition to enter Society, it was natural for him to cultivate so influential a neighbour, at whose house he was likely to meet all the leaders of Society. The two became intimate and gained a real affection for one another. At Stowe, which was the headquarters of the Pitt party, Wilkes found himself in a hot-bed of political intrigue, and it would not have been surprising if he had thrown himself heart and soul into political affairs. But Wilkes was quite content to admire the great men who came and went at Stowe without wishing to emulate them. There is not the least trace of a desire to meddle in politics, a fact which puzzled some of his friends. "I hope", wrote one of them in kindly remonstrance, six months before Wilkes first stood for Parliament, "I hope I shall live to see you as good as you are agreeable, as religious as you are sincere, and as much inclined to serve the publick as you are capable of it, if you please to give your mind to business."

This lack of interest was in keeping with Wilkes's character. By birth and upbringing he belonged to the executive part of mankind, preferring to administer the law rather than to make it. Even when the duty of framing a political programme was finally thrust upon him, it was towards reform that he turned rather than to any purely original scheme. There was, however, another reason. Wilkes did not merely lack interest; he positively disliked the utter corruption of politics. More than half a century had now passed since the Glorious Revolution and its inevitable fruits had had time to mature. In theory the Revolution had invested the people with power through their representatives in Parliament; but it was only in theory, since Parliament, owing to the minute electorate and the large number of rotten boroughs, was far from representing the people. Actually the Revolution had placed power in the hands of a small and irresponsible body working in secret. It was hardly surprising in the circumstances that the bolder spirits should have learnt to corrupt the House. With the advent of corruption came a swarm of attendant ills—intrigue, treachery, backbiting, and abuse. The picture presented was the reverse of pleasant, and Wilkes felt the disgust of an honest man. "I have",

he wrote in 1756 to Temple's younger brother, George Grenville, "religiously observed your commands, and have sent it
[a political pamphlet], but I really pity you who have to wade
through so much dirt, and thank Heaven it is well over
with me."

At the outset Temple left him to his own devices, conscious
that "you have from your youth upwards been in *actual service*
all over the whole district of the good town of Aylesbury".
But Temple was the type of man to ignore private preferences
and even the public good when they stood in the way of his own
schemes. Directly he needed Wilkes, he would not hesitate to
use the whole of his influence to bring Wilkes into line with
what, after all, Society regarded as its duty.

Perhaps it was natural that Wilkes should have felt a tinge
of awe for the statesmen and nobles so much his senior who
flocked to Stowe. At all events, the one member of the circle
with whom he became most intimate was a much younger
man, though still nine years older than Wilkes himself. This
was Thomas Potter, son of the Archbishop, who had recently
died, leaving him a more than ample fortune. Potter was a
great deal more handsome than is good for a man, and was
blessed with brains of an uncommon order. The combination
proved too heady a draught, especially when fortified by a
large income. His genius tended towards perversion, his wit
was Rabelaisian, and his excesses certainly hastened the early
death which his delicate health made probable. At this time,
however, he was a brilliant member of the circle with a splendid
future in front of him. Pitt was enthusiastic, declaring that
"Mr. Potter is one of the best friends I have in the world",
although he must have known the sort of reprobate that Potter
was; Potter had already killed one wife by his bad treatment of
her, had married another solely for her fortune, and was prevented only by ill-health from rivalling Don Juan in the number
of his rapes and seductions. In public affairs he was resolute, clever, and brave; in private, he displayed a mind that
resembled a cesspool of all that was profligate and profane.

Superficially Wilkes and Potter had much in common—brains, wit, courage, and a strong propensity to amours. But there was an essential difference. Potter was utterly cynical and utterly carried away by the prevailing belief of Society in its own superiority; to him the common people were dirt, and patriotism a matter of political advantage. Wilkes was fundamentally a reformer, with a heart that was capable of being touched by suffering and a pride in his country that was as genuine as it was strong. They enjoyed each other's company, however, and understood their respective bents. Wilkes helped Potter, who was a member for Aylesbury, in his parliamentary elections; and Potter used his influence to get Wilkes appointed High Sheriff of Buckingham—a post he obtained in January 1754. A few months later, to Potter's great surprise, Wilkes was standing as a candidate for Parliament. The key to this unexpected move is to be found in the development of the political situation and the part which Pitt played in it.

(2)

The Spanish war of 1739, which may be said to have issued out of Jenkins's ear, had first been merged in the war of the Austrian Succession, and then had overthrown Walpole—a statesman eminently fitted for peace and eminently unsuited to war. He was succeeded by Carteret, whose natural bent was directed towards foreign affairs, and whose aim was to combine Europe against the menace of a united France and Spain. Carteret, in the prevailing manner of the times, was at once an unaccountable, high-spirited drunkard and a statesman of wide views and commanding abilities. At one moment he would read love-letters to his embarrassed colleagues and at the next electrify them with bold and decisive schemes. "He is never sober," wrote Horace Walpole, "and his rants are amazing, but so are his parts and his spirits." Unfortunately for himself his eyes never lighted upon anything between the tankard or the mistress beneath his nose and the far-distant horizon of European politics. He neither could nor would apply himself to the corruption of Parliament, which he was clever enough to know was necessary and frank enough to admit in public. "What is it to me", he said to an applicant for a post, "who is a judge and who a bishop? It is my business to make Kings and Emperors and to maintain the balance of Europe." With such notions he was riding for a fall, and it came quickly. The rumour was bruited abroad by his enemies that he was sacrificing English interests to the King's Hanoverian whims. It was caught up and spread amazingly. The merchants who were ready enough to fight Spain for trading privileges were in no mood to fight France for the security of a petty German state, and one, moreover, which they regarded with jealous eyes. They raised an outcry, and Carteret, finding that Parliament had only too certainly deserted him for the men who made a business of bribes, fell unmourned, to make way for Henry Pelham. The new administration bungled the war, which nobody minded, and were temporarily embarrassed by the Jacobite rising of '45. In the end, however, their very embarrassments proved an advantage; the Jacobite rising completely effaced the Tory opposition, and the failure of the European war led in 1748 to the peace of Aix-la-Chapelle, which was accepted with relief, though it was neither advantageous to England nor likely to endure. With the extinction of the Tories and the end of the war Pelham had nothing to bother him and nothing to propose. Politics pursued a placid, uneventful course of offering and accepting bribes, until Pelham's sudden death on the 6th of March, 1754, threw the political world into a fresh ferment. Who was to succeed him? His brother, the Duke of Newcastle, had little difficulty in stepping into his shoes as First Lord of the Treasury, but this merely complicated the position. The Duke was an amiable, fussy gentleman who loved power simply for the opportunity it gave of dispensing bribes; and precisely because he was nothing more, the choice of the new Secretary of State became a matter of tremendous importance.

If merit were a consideration, there were three possible candidates: William Murray, afterwards Lord Mansfield, the Solicitor-General; Henry Fox, afterwards Lord Holland, the Secretary at War; and William Pitt, afterwards Lord Chatham, the Paymaster of the Forces. The various intrigues which at once began are more bewildering than edifying, and in any case irrelevant. More to the point is the fact that Newcastle, unable to come to terms with either Fox or Murray, hit upon a mild nonentity of the name of Robinson. Pitt was not so much as offered the post. His chagrin was obvious; yet if he paused to look back over his career he ought not to have been surprised. His life had been stormy enough.

William Pitt was born on the 15th of November, 1708. For all practical purposes the family had been founded by his grandfather, Governor Pitt, a rough diamond who had made a fortune in India by his wits and want of scruple. Hence Pitt possessed little of the aristocrat by blood, and, as a younger son, handled little of the family's newly acquired wealth. All that he inherited from his forbears was violent gout and a turbulent temper. He went to Eton and then Oxford, whence he was driven by ill-health before he had obtained a degree. A tour on the Continent completed his education, and at twenty-three he became a Cornet in the Blues with the princely income of £100 a year. Four years later, on the 7th of February, 1735, he found himself a member of Parliament, having been elected by that mound of earth known as Old Sarum—a rotten borough, which Governor Pitt had bought on his return to England. That the future "Great Commoner" should represent exactly nobody and not much even in the way of Mother Earth is one of those diverting strokes that Fate enjoys. Apparently she astounded even this hot-headed Cornet of the Blues, for it was well over a year before he ventured on his maiden speech. On entering the House he found Walpole's long day beginning to wane, joined the opposition, which arrogated to itself the name of "Patriots", and paid his court at Leicester House, the residence of

Frederick, Prince of Wales, whose main merit was that he died before he became King.

Pitt's delay in opening his mouth made his first speech the more effective. It created a sensation. Nominally it was a speech of congratulation on the approaching marriage of the Prince of Wales; actually it was a fiercely ironical attack on the King. George II was more than annoyed, and from that moment, 29th of April, 1736, may be dated his antipathy to the rising statesman. Walpole was dismayed and is reported to have said, "We must muzzle this terrible Cornet of Horse." As the usual method of bribery had no effect, Walpole tried severity. Pitt was cashiered from the Army and reduced to greater indigence than ever. This touch of the whip had the effect of heightening Pitt's talent for invective. He lashed everyone high and low with his tongue, and found especial delight in pouring scorn on the King's favourite projects. Needless to say, he did not become a *persona grata*, though he earned, and amply earned, a frightened respect and grudging admiration. The wholesome horror which the King felt for him and the mixture of dread and dislike which he inspired in the reigning oligarchy kept him out of office until 1746, and the small sop then given him was only extorted by his obvious powers. The main interest of these probationary years is the evidence they afford of Pitt's inconsistencies and the gradual development of his dominating principle—the idea of a British Empire founded on supremacy at sea.

The fulfilment of his dream was to come later. For the next ten years, up to 1756, he was gradually learning the bitter truth that genius without birth was a galling irritant. The magnates were too strongly entrenched in their monopoly to give way to an outsider. Pitt suffered one disappointment after another, and the rebuff which Newcastle administered in 1754 was only one of a long series.

By this time, however, Pitt's patience had snapped, and he determined to wrest for himself the prize which no one would give him on his merits. As a first step he wrote a long letter to Newcastle in which he spoke of "the mortifying situation of Your Grace's humblest servant", "the repetition and multi-plication of most painful and too visible humiliations", and "my degraded situation in Parliament"; he declared that "things standing as they do, whether I can continue in office without losing myself in the opinion of the world is become matter of very painful doubt to me", and threatened that "my mind carries me more strongly towards retreat than towards courts and business". But though talking of retirement, Pitt was in fact meditating the best method of opposition. He had told Temple his "whole poor plan", which included the intention "to look out and fish in troubled waters, and perhaps trouble them in order to fish better", and he added towards the end of March 1754 that "the place of importance is employment".

The task which he had set himself was by no means easy. When everything was done by "connections" it seemed im-possible for an unconnected man to build up a party. There was no material with which to start. For many years the Tories had been practically extinct. All that remained were the number-less Whig factions, none of them with more policy than can be found in allegiance to an individual, based on corruption and cemented by hope of preferment. There was no opening here for Pitt, who refused to knuckle down to the leaders, and had nothing with which to seduce their followers.

Confused as the position was, it was worse confounded by the probability of the King's early death. He was an old man, and it might be wiser not to seize office at the moment, but to curry favour with the Prince of Wales, in the hope of riding into more permanent power when the new reign began.

With so many cross-currents Pitt thought it best not to break outright with Newcastle, but merely to threaten to with-draw. This would give him an excuse for moving in either direction later on, as events should decide. Meanwhile it was essential to begin building a party of his own. His alliance with the Grenvilles gave him a sound nucleus, and his few other personal adherents, such as Potter, added to his strength. But above all he wanted new men—brilliant and resolute young-sters, who were not bound by any ties to the Whig magnates.

Such men were not easy to find, but in his many visits to Stowe Pitt had discovered his ideal recruit. Wilkes had shining talents and outstanding courage; better still, he was fascinated by Pitt's conversation, and for years past had been all un-consciously framing his political creed on the ideas that Pitt flung out. While Pitt was condescending towards this agreeable young squire, who treated him with such obvious respect, he was also making a mental note of his capacities. He must have discussed Wilkes more than once with Temple, and perhaps at this crisis in his affairs may have urged Temple to influence the young man directly. At all events, Temple brought pressure to bear. At the last moment, and obviously in a hurry, Wilkes was persuaded to stand as candidate for Berwick-upon-Tweed. Pitt's letter to Newcastle was written on the 24th of March, and the elections were to take place in April. There was little enough time to spare, but Temple was prompt and Wilkes too much under his influence to refuse, without counting his desire to please and his ingrained love of a "lark". By the end of March Wilkes had agreed, and a few days later he was on his way north.

(3)

At Berwick he enjoyed himself thoroughly, catching salmon, making love to the lassies, and strolling along the banks of the Tweed. He regarded the whole trip as a holiday, and except as pleasing his friends, was quite uninterested in the result. Electioneering he can hardly be said to have taken seriously, though he is credited with a practical joke of great dimension and greater daring. His opponent, so the story runs, had arranged for a number of his supporters to be brought up from London by sea, and Wilkes bribed the captain to land the bewildered voters on the coast of Norway. The story may quite possibly be true, since it is entirely in keeping with Wilkes's character and the spirit in which he went north. For the rest, he issued an election address, and thereafter left the purely political work to others, contenting himself with being generally agreeable. His methods were on the whole surprisingly successful, since although he was not elected he gained 192 votes.

More interesting is the address issued by this young and wholly inexperienced candidate. He informed the electors that he had embarked in the cause of liberty; he was thoroughly sensible of the excellence of the Constitution, and would use his utmost efforts to preserve it; he regarded the laws as sacred and the happiness and security of every man as depending on their observance; his sole ambition was to serve his country, and he offered himself as the faithful representative of the electors.

To the twentieth century there may seem little in this beyond the ordinary highflown sentiments of a would-be member. But they meant much at the time, and more as interpreted by Wilkes. Liberty was then a mere word, and the Constitution very much in the melting-pot. As for representation, it was scouted, and the laws were sacred only when they shielded the interests of the mighty. It was to be the glory of Wilkes that he gave a real meaning to these pious aspirations, and left as his legacy to England a new conception of liberty, the Constitution, the sacredness of the laws, and the meaning of representation.

His brief and excellent address was delivered on the 16th of April, 1754, and has been held up to derision ever since. In order that the derision may be justified, exactly two sentences are quoted: "Gentlemen, I come here *uncorrupting*, and I promise you I shall ever be *uncorrupted*. As I never will take a bribe, so I will never offer one." This, of course, was a barefaced lie. But it is worth noting that the lie was all on one side. While Wilkes spent some £4,000 in bribes at Berwick, and a great deal more at subsequent elections, he remained himself uncorrupted throughout life. But there is something more to be said than that. Before branding Wilkes as a common, and one must add unskilful, liar, it is as well to remember that in

1754 bribery was the normal method of obtaining a seat in Parliament, and the least reprehensible part of the political corruption. The sale of boroughs was perfectly open; they were hawked about like pedlars' trinkets; they even put themselves up to auction, knocking themselves down to the highest bidder. Indeed, this very election is mainly memorable as having given rise to Hogarth's four "humours of an election", the second of which deals with nothing but the methods of bribery then current. All candidates practised the art; everyone knew it. Wilkes's remark was more in the nature of good manners than a lie, and did not deceive anyone, least of all the electors who were the happy recipients of his money. From the purely moral point of view his action in spending his own money is to be preferred to the methods of Pitt, who accepted the gift of a pocket borough—Aldeburgh—from Newcastle, or, in other words, took a bribe from the very man he was intending to desert.

But whatever view may be taken of this palpable lie, the speech as a whole stands out in refreshing contrast to the speeches of other candidates. They were not concerned with fine sentiments, still less with their true beliefs; most of them were occupied in attacking three Acts recently passed, two of which were wholly desirable and one innocuous—the Act for adopting the Gregorian Calendar, the Act to prevent the scandal of mock marriages, and the Act to permit the naturalization of Jews. Wilkes might have harped on the three with the best, but he preferred to leave well alone and stand for liberty, order, and common sense.

(4)

Wilkes returned from Berwick in no way distressed to continue the life he most preferred. It was summer, and Aylesbury was a pleasant place in which to read the classics and enjoy good company. He invited some of his friends to come and share the combined beauties of nature and of literature.

"You needed not", one of them replied from Bath, "for my
temptation, in the account you give me of the wonderful
verdure of the rich vale of Aylesbury, and the fragrance of
your bean-fields in full blossom, to have described Arabia
Felix; for I could readily have waited on you in the very
deserts." It is a pity the description of the bean-fields no
longer exists, for in the scanty remains of Wilkes's own writings
the most charming passages are those describing scenery. He
was well in advance of his age in his appreciation of nature,
whether it were the grandeur of the Alps or the sweetness of a
bird's song. It was a true lover of nature who could write "My
cherries are the prey of the blackbirds, and they are most
welcome".

But whatever Wilkes may have wanted to do, he found that
his escapade was not to be an isolated *jeu d'esprit*. As High
Sheriff of Buckingham he had gained a respectable position;
as the nominee of Lord Temple for a parliamentary career he
was launched on Society. The door was open, and his friends
expected him to pass through it. He received other letters with
none of the fragrance of the bean-fields about them, and
among them one from Potter. If Wilkes was to become a
member of Parliament, which was a new idea to Potter, why
had he been sent on such a wild-goose chase? Potter, had he
been consulted, could have secured a safe seat. So he wrote out
of a genuine vexation, "From the moment I saw your letter to
Lord Temple until now, I have uttered more blasphemies than
a drunken parson at a bawdy-house. Sure there never were such
idiots as your friends, Temple and all the raggamuffin herd who
call themselves the principal voters of Berwick. . . . Had it
not been for that damned Berwick, you might have been
member for Bristol with Nugent."

These friends did more than lament over the past, they
pushed Wilkes along the well-trodden path of disappointed
candidates. When elections were a matter of bribery, no one
liked to feel that he had flung his money away. The first and
almost automatic step was to appeal from the electorate to

their representatives. By a happy inspiration it was laid down that the House itself should decide disputed elections. Needless to say, a corrupt House exercised its grave judicial functions in the best tradition of party warfare. Unless the scandal was too open and obvious, right somehow or other was always on the side of the Government's supporter.

Wilkes was persuaded to play out the game and lodge a petition. It was a forlorn hope, since a Pittite would have been suspect from the beginning, and rather more than suspect by the time the petitions were considered, some seven months after the elections. Wilkes himself was largely indifferent; he looked upon the petition mainly as an excuse for another tour in Scotland, nominally to collect evidence, but actually to escape from his wife and amuse himself among the society of the Scottish capital. It was on this tour that he sought out David Hume. Although his taste in ladies was catholic, he preferred his male friends to be men of sense and learning. If they combined spicy living with their high thinking, so much the better; but brains appealed to him more than brawn or birth, and he could if necessary heartily despise the company which social ambition forced him to keep.

The tour provided an example of another side of Wilkes's character. He had many friends from Scotland, and a partiality for all things Scotch. Perhaps it was for this reason that he chose a Scottish barrister to conduct his case. Whatever the reason, he chose badly; the barrister was a rogue who pocketed the retaining fee and refused to do the work. Wilkes appeared in person to demand his money back, and was told with a sneer that he could go to law about it. Wilkes was generally prepared for all eventualities. On this occasion he was carrying the law at his side, and forthwith proceeded to draw it out of the scabbard. A few minutes later he was being bowed out with his money in his pocket.

The petition came on for hearing on the 25th of November, 1754, and was remarkable as the occasion of one of Pitt's most famous speeches. The sitting member, being sure of success as a supporter of the Government, treated the whole affair as a joke, and kept the House in a continual roar of laughter. Pitt, who was in the gallery with Wilkes, came down to the support of his friend and follower, and, as Henry Fox informed the Marquis of Hartington, "took it up in his highest tone of dignity". He made a slashing speech which reduced the House to quaking terror, and wound up by taunting the House with degenerating "into a little assembly, serving no other purpose than to register the arbitrary edicts of one too powerful subject".

Pitt's speech has been attributed partly to his friendship for Wilkes, but mainly to his indignation at the thought of bribery. Remembering that Pitt had been in Parliament for nearly twenty years, and in that time must have had innumerable opportunities of expressing his indignation, it is not unreasonable to suppose that other motives played some part. The sting of the speech, as all allowed, was the contemptuous reference to the "one too powerful subject", who was no other than Pitt's professed leader, the Duke of Newcastle. In a word, Pitt was throwing down the gauntlet, admitting the breach between himself and Government, and by championing Wilkes's petition raising a standard around which his own followers might rally.

Apart from these incidents, Wilkes's petition is of little interest. It dragged on till the 5th of February, 1756, when Wilkes himself withdrew it.

(5)

His expedition had another result. The marriage which had begun so inauspiciously some seven years before was growing daily less tolerable, and the loss of £4,000 on an unsuccessful election did nothing to ease the strain. Finding little that pleased him at home, Wilkes absented himself as much as possible. About the same time that he became High Sheriff, he also became a member of the Sublime Society of Beef Steaks, and he neglected his wife to consort with those more congenial spirits. The result was that the two drifted steadily apart, until two years later, in 1756, they decided to separate. Under the deed of separation Wilkes allowed his wife £200 a year.

In such a marriage failure was almost a foregone conclusion, and there is little, therefore, to be gained by apportioning blame. Wilkes, of course, was mainly responsible. He expected nothing of his wife beyond her money, and offered her nothing in return but a cold civility. To use his own words, he was "an extremely civil and complaisant husband; rather cold, but exactly well-bred"—which means that he left her entirely to her own devices. Cold civility is a poor basis for married life, and Wilkes made it no better by notorious infidelity, neglect, and a crowd of disreputable friends.

It is hard to say what Mary expected of her marriage or what were her original feelings. The fact that she gave her husband the Manor at Aylesbury suggests affection or at least a faith in his abilities. To say that she was dull is perhaps beside the point in a marriage of convenience, and if it is not immaterial, reflects as much discredit on the suitor's discernment as on the bride's disposition. That Mary's friends were as distasteful to Wilkes as his were to her will not be accepted as an excuse, however true it may be. But it does emphasize the glaring fact that the two ought never to have married. There was only one chance of a common tie—their daughter Polly, and it is part of life's irony that this tie should have bound Wilkes more than usually fast while it left his wife more than usually free. When the inevitable separation came, Mary gladly washed her hands of a child in whom she took no interest.

There is only one other point worth mentioning. As history is determined to paint Wilkes one unrelieved black, his wife has been drawn in pathetic colours as a woman so outraged that she consented to live on a mere pittance in order to escape from the misery of her position. The picture is hardly true. It is impossible to pretend that Wilkes treated her well, but however much her feelings may have been lacerated she never suffered a moment's want. She was the acknowledged heiress of her mother, a rich woman, and of her uncle Sherbrooke, a rich man. When she left Wilkes she returned to a style of life beyond anything Wilkes could offer. If anyone lost financially it was Wilkes, who forfeited the prospect of his mother-in-law's money—Wilkes, and the innocent Polly, who remained beneath his care.

His marriage had no effect upon him beyond the advantage gained by Mary's money. The separation was to have greater results. Henceforward Wilkes proved himself an extensive, rather than a great, lover, making up in sensuality what he lacked in pure affection. It was this vice which was to give his enemies and critics their opportunity to blacken his character beyond redemption. The ironical point is that Wilkes was free from the two vices most characteristic of his age—drunkenness and gambling; the particular vice he affected is common to all ages and not least to his own.

CHAPTER IV

SCRIBBLER'S ITCH

(1)

DURING these idle years between 1754 and 1757 Wilkes contracted that young man's complaint—the scribbler's itch. In its first form—verse—it soon passed off, but it was destined to have remarkable results.

It was in October 1754 that Wilkes sent Potter a couple of poems. Potter was staying with Pitt at Bath, and still grumbling over the Berwick episode. "I cannot", Potter replied, "begin my letter as you do; nor indeed can I carry it on and conclude as you do. But I am in no good humour; no, tho' I have this moment read your parody for the 99th time and have laughed as heartily as I did at the first, I am still not in a good humour. This cursed B[erwick] sticks in my gizzard." However, he read the verses to his host—at dinner, of all extraordinary times—and his host chuckled over them immensely. "He [Pitt] bid me to tell you that he found with great concern you was as wicked and agreeable as ever. In my conscience I think you exceed yourself."

One may hope that Potter was right. The effusion which delighted Potter and Pitt was one or other of two short poems called the *Veni Creator* and the *Universal Prayer*. Both are quite unprintable, being extremely obscene parodies of well-known hymns. The hectic bravado of youth produces a feeling of great-souled defiance at twenty-six, but rather overwhelms thirty-five with a sheepish feeling of regret. When in 1763 these parodies came to light, Wilkes suffered from a very real and very shamefaced regret at ever having perpetrated them, and never quite lived the feeling down. In his *Letter to the Electors of Aylesbury*, written in 1764, he did his best to put a good face on an impossible position. "In my own closet", he remarked, "I had a right to examine, and even to try by the keen edge of ridicule, any opinions I pleased. If I have laughed pretty freely at the glaring absurdities of the most monstrous *creed*, which was ever attempted to be imposed on the credulity of Christians, a creed which even great Tillotson *wished the Church of England was fairly rid of*, it was in private I laughed. I am not the first good Protestant who has amused himself with the egregious nonsense, and silly conceits, of that strange, perplexed, and perplexing mortal, that *saint* of more admirable swallow and more happy digestion than any of the tribe, *Athanasius.*" If this account suggests a great deal more of weight and a great deal less of obscenity than can possibly be justified, it still contains an element of truth, and very obviously betrays the twinges of anger and annoyance.

What made the sting of their publication rankle the more was that on the strength of these silly exuberances Wilkes was charged with blasphemy. *Prima facie* there was good ground for the charge, but in fact Wilkes intended no more than to be funny at the expense of a dogma in which he disbelieved. The charge of blasphemy came as a shock, and he was always extremely touchy about it. Twice he protested in Parliament that he was innocent of blasphemy, on the first occasion demanding an alteration of the records which proclaimed him guilty, and on the second occasion exacting an apology from a member who had dared to tax him with it. Many years later his memory was still sore at the recollection.

Soon after he had penned these parodies he set to work on another effort known as the *Essay on Woman*, which also came to light in 1763. The authorship is supposed to be doubtful, some authorities holding Wilkes responsible, some Potter, and yet others asserting that the two collaborated. The point is hardly worth the ink that has been spilt upon it. As Wilkes undoubtedly wrote the two parodies, he is not going to be much blacker or whiter because of the *Essay*. The probabilities are that he did most of the work, though Potter may have made suggestions.

Being the longest of the three, the *Essay* has become the best known. Wilkes himself was rather pleased with it, and there is no doubt that it displays a certain ingenuity. It consists of Pope's *Essay on Man* altered so as to give a frankly indecent turn to practically every line with the minimum of verbal change. Notes are added purporting to be by Dr. Warburton, Bishop of Gloucester. A piece of this type could only be produced by a coarse-minded young man to whom sex was still a novelty and the display of obscure learning still a matter of pride. There is nothing in the least remarkable about it except the obscenity, and precisely for this reason Wilkes was not much concerned at its publication. Obscenity never worried Wilkes, nor for that matter did it very much worry the age, which was as gross as any age can hope to be. Wilkes claimed that his vices were "natural" and his own affair. He was quite willing to admit that he would be better without them, but he could not see how they concerned other people. So he would neither defend nor excuse himself, and in his *Letter to the Electors of Aylesbury* dismissed the *Essay* in an offhand manner, vastly different from his irritable defence of the parodies. The *Essay*, according to him, was "a few portraits drawn from warm life, with the too high colouring of a youthful fancy, and two or three descriptions, perhaps too luscious, which tho' Nature and Woman might pardon, a Kidgell and a Mansfield could not fail to condemn". The example of his reticence may be fitly followed.

A curious set of chances made these effusions important factors in his career, not as literary landmarks, but as dynamite to blow up his character. His prose writings were in every sense more important, setting their mark on the political and constitutional history of England. He may also not untruthfully be called the father of modern journalism. For many years he had been in the habit of writing snippets, which in these days would have made his fortune as a paragraphist. He wrote them purely for the amusement of himself and his friends, spending much more time and thought upon their polish than they deserved. Hitherto, however, he had not thought of publishing them. It was in 1755 that he first appeared in print with a skit based on the statement in Dr. Johnson's newly published Dictionary that "the letter H seldom, perhaps never, begins any but the first syllable". The quip, which spread all over the town, was short, amusing, critical, and perhaps one may add ruthless—four characteristics which can be found in most of Wilkes's writings, and which largely accounted for his popularity.

2

These same years, 1754 to 1757, which sowed the seeds of Wilkes's career, were sowing the seeds of mightier events in the field of the world.

For some time there had been bickerings between the French and English settlers in America, mostly cloaked under the semblance of Indian feuds. But by 1754 the disguise was wearing thin. In Nova Scotia a body of French fugitives was routed by Major Lawrence. At Great Meadows in Ohio, George Washington, whose career as an Englishman scarcely gave promise of his career as an American, signalized his appearance on the pages of history by defeat and surrender. Meanwhile Lord Albemarle's feeble handling of the situation as Ambassador in Paris served to inflame the ill-feeling between the two nations, and his death in December 1754, though sudden, was yet too late. War had begun, though it had not been declared.

Newcastle and his Cabinet showed all the folly of irresolution, giving pinpricks where they should have given smooth words, and withholding orders that were undoubtedly wanted. In April 1755 Boscawen received the farcical order to follow a large French armament and attack it if designed for the Bay of St. Lawrence. When the leading British ship under Captain (afterwards Lord) Howe came within hailing distance, the French commander asked if it was peace or war. Howe was obliged to reply that he did not know until his Admiral signalled, and the two waited patiently while Boscawen was making up his mind. In July more trouble followed. Braddock was defeated near Fort Burgoyne, while Johnson gained a victory near Lake George, and Monckton captured Beausejour in Nova Scotia. At almost the same moment the Cabinet were debating the weighty question of what to do with the fleet under the command of Sir Edward Hawke. Some were for striking a blow, some were against, and Newcastle solved the difficulty by suggesting that Hawke should have no instructions at all, but merely take a turn in the Channel to exercise the fleet. If that did not meet the views of the Cabinet, he could be ordered "not to attack the enemy, unless he thought it worth while"!

However, it is an ill wind that blows nobody good, and this pitiful indecision had the effect of clearing the political atmosphere. As the people were growing more and more discontented, Newcastle made Fox Secretary of State and Leader of the Commons. The result was that Pitt moved farther over to the Opposition, and flouted the Prime Minister to such an extent that in November 1755 he and his friends were summarily dismissed.

About this time Wilkes emerged again definitely as a candidate for Parliament. The reshuffle due to Pitt's dismissal seemed likely to involve a by-election at Aylesbury, and Wilkes prepared to contest the seat. "I am determined to oppose him," Wilkes wrote to a friend on the 24th of November, 1755, "and will attack him with the utmost spirit, particularly the true Aylesbury way of *palmistry*. Be assured I will at any expense carry my point." The date is significant. Hitherto Wilkes had shown no desire to follow up Potter's suggestions, and had taken no steps at other by-elections; he had failed to press forward his Berwick petition; he had been engaged more in pleasure than in canvassing. But the moment Pitt went definitely into opposition, Wilkes came forward again; recruits to the new party were more than ever necessary. As it happened, no contest took place.

Meanwhile the friction in America was having its counterpart on the Continent. For many years France and Austria had been sworn enemies. In this rivalry France had looked to

Spain as an ally, Austria to England. But not long since a fresh Power had arisen to disturb this nicely adjusted balance. Frederick the Great had moulded Prussia into a kingdom, and snatched Silesia from Maria Theresa. The loss rankled, all the more because the Empress was a Catholic and Frederick— so far as he was anything—a Protestant. At this juncture Prince Kaunitz became the leading light in Austria, and threw the whole weight of his influence into a break with the traditional Austrian policy. Why, he argued, should Austria and France exhaust one another merely to let Prussia scoop the spoils? It would be better for France and Austria to unite, and with overwhelming force crush the upstart and divide his kingdom. The plot gathered strength because both had much to gain. France, trembling on the verge of war with England, was anxious to avoid a break with Austria; and the latter, afraid of Prussian aggression, was only too glad to keep France quiet. The negotiations progressed smoothly, and were extended till in May 1756 the Treaty of Versailles united France, Austria, Russia, Sweden, and Saxony for the pleasant, profitable, and apparently easy task of dismembering Prussia. In August the Seven Years War broke out.

Meanwhile Frederick had not been idle. A traitor, Menzel, had betrayed the whole design to him, and with his accustomed promptness he at once began counterplotting. His first step was to secure allies, and as the only one left was England, he made up his ancient quarrel with George II.

In May France began the war with England by a descent on Minorca, then a British possession. Newcastle bungled badly, and to add to the general dismay Admiral Byng failed to relieve the island. Throughout the winter the fear of a French invasion had kept the country on tenterhooks, and the obvious incapacity of Government added fuel to the smouldering discontent. When news arrived first of the Treaty of Versailles and then of the loss of Minorca, the discontent became ugly. Newcastle, who was always in a state of terror at his own responsibilities, and was only induced to bear them by the greater terror of losing office, was almost gibbering with fright; and instead of using such brains as he had to repair the military situation, began feverishly plotting to unload the odium on to others. Byng was the most obvious scapegoat, and Byng was not only recalled to stand his trial but hanged in advance. "Oh, indeed," cried the Duke of Newcastle to a deputation from the City, "he shall be tried immediately—he shall be hanged directly!"

So backboneless a Ministry was bound to fall now that war had actually broken out, and the coming fall cast its shadow before. During the summer Leicester House, the residence of the Prince of Wales, became busy, and Bute, who was to play so large a part in Wilkes's career, was appointed Groom of the Stole to the young Prince, contrary to the King's wishes and in spite of his disgust. In October Fox resigned, and Murray seized the double opportunity of the Duke's distresses and the death of Sir Dudley Rider to slide out of the political storm into a peerage and the shoes of the dead Lord Chief Justice.

Searching round desperately for help, Newcastle appealed to Pitt, who told him sneeringly that so unimportant a man as himself could not presume to be the associate of so experienced a Minister as the Duke, and then made haste to let the King know through Lady Yarmouth that the exclusion of Newcastle was his first condition of accepting office. To apply to the King's German mistress was a trifle shabby and more than a trifle ruthless, but at this point Pitt's schemes were near fruition and he was in no mood to compromise. A few more futile struggles, and on the 11th of November Newcastle resigned. The King realized that Pitt was next door to inevitable, and after a little hopeless manœuvring Devonshire became First Lord with Pitt as Secretary of State and Temple at the Admiralty.

The measures Pitt proposed were vigorous enough and thoroughly patriotic, but his overbearing temper and proud attitude made everything impossible, and whatever corns he overlooked were trampled on by Temple. Everyone was irritated. "Pitt used to call me madman," exclaimed Carteret, now

Lord Granville, "but I never was half so mad as he is." "The Secretary", complained the King after a few weeks' trial, "makes me long speeches, which possibly may be very fine but are greatly beyond my comprehension; and his letters are affected, formal, and pedantic. But as to Temple, he is so disagreeable a fellow that there is no bearing him. When he attempts to argue he is pert and sometimes insolent; when he means to be civil he is exceedingly troublesome, and in the business of his office he is totally ignorant." A few more weeks and the King could stand it no longer. He commanded Waldegrave to approach Newcastle. "I know", said the King, "he is apt to be afraid; therefore go and encourage him; tell him that I do not look upon myself as King whilst I am in the hands of these scoundrels; that I am determined to get rid of them at any rate; that I expect his assistance, and that he may depend on my favour and protection." When Newcastle hesitated, the King took matters into his own hand and dismissed the two offenders. For several months England had no Government, though she was at war with France and Europe was in a vast upheaval.

This remarkable interregnum was fraught with such obvious dangers and difficulties to England, to Europe, and to the world, and its end so clearly depended upon the attitude which Pitt and Newcastle were pleased to adopt, that the friends on both sides felt bound to intervene, and on the 29th of June, 1757, the famous Newcastle-Pitt administration came into being.

(3)

Pitt had not been idle during the lull, and his activities had a profound effect on Wilkes. His claim to power did not rest upon the same foundation as that of his contemporaries. He was not a Whig magnate in the accepted meaning of the term, and boasted that his hands were clean from corruption. He based himself partly on the broad ground of popular favour, partly on the broader ground of his own genius. Unfortunately, as things then stood popular favour carried very little weight, and his own genius carried too much envy; the more inevitable he became, the more the magnates loathed him. For that very reason he thought it essential to make as big a parade as possible and collect around himself a cohort of brilliant young men. The parade was not very difficult. Directly their idol was dismissed, the cities of England began with one accord to confer their freedom upon him: "for some weeks", said Horace Walpole, "it rained gold boxes".

But the brilliant young men were a more ticklish task, because after all brilliance is a rare commodity. Pitt's circle had proved rather disappointing. Temple, on closer inspection, proved an overbearing ass; Lyttelton a knock-kneed *littérateur*; Legge a humdrum economist; George Grenville a narrow-minded formalist. There were two exceptions—Potter and Wilkes, and the latter was not in the House. He must be brought in, and Pitt was going to leave the matter neither to chance nor to Temple. This was not the moment for escapades at Berwick. What actually took place is not known. Almon says mysteriously that "there was a good deal of manœuvre and trick practised on this occasion". Outwardly there was a sort of game of consequences. Pitt received and accepted an invitation to stand for Bath, bequeathing his own seat to Potter, who in turn bequeathed *his* seat to Wilkes, presumably on the ground that Aylesbury was more appropriate for Wilkes. Anyhow, the expenses of this general post amounted to £7,000, which the two elder men very neatly transferred to the greenhorn Wilkes. But where their own pockets were not concerned they were lavish of wire-pulling and advice. "Mr. Pitt", as Potter wrote, "has done what he could to prevent the Duke of Newcastle sending down any opposition to you." Potter himself kept guard at the Duke's front-door and wrote triumphantly a day or two later: "I have saved you a scouring, at least I hope so, from Admiral Knowles, whom by great accident I met at Newcastle House with his bags in his chaise ready to set out for Ailsbury if the Duke of Newcastle did not forbid him.

D

I talked to him in such a manner that he promised me to carry his bags home again."

Meanwhile they instructed him in the gentle art of winning elections. The messenger of the Great Seal was to be bribed—price ten guineas—to deliver the writ to the under-sheriff at a given time; the under-sheriff was to be bribed—price unknown—to proclaim the election for a Saturday morning. "By this means", Potter explained, "you will avoid two inconveniences, the seditious conversations of the market people on Saturday and the day of leisure for hatching iniquity on Sunday."

Everything went on oiled wheels. The three conspirators were all elected; Wilkes paid up his £7,000, and when this huge expense for a seat in the fag-end of a Parliament landed him in difficulties, Potter added to his former favours by introducing him to the Jews.

So Wilkes became a Member of Parliament, and because it is invariably asserted either that he was always burning with ambition for a political career or that his ambition arose out of a desire to mend his broken fortunes, a recapitulation may perhaps be pardoned. His first attempt, at Berwick, coincided with Pitt's determination to oppose Newcastle; his second, at Aylesbury, coincided with Pitt's dismissal from Newcastle's administration; his third and successful attempt coincided with Pitt's dismissal from the office of Secretary of State. This series of coincidences is too striking to be overlooked, especially when Wilkes's utter indifference before and after Berwick is borne in mind. The fact is that Pitt had a great idea of Wilkes's talents, and, being in need of able lieutenants, urged him on. His failure to make a name and his apparent indifference to oratorical success came as a surprise and disappointment to most of the party. Temple put it down to laziness. "Give yourself up", he wrote in 1762, "to parliamentary labours, and let applauding senates give testimony to the excellent talents of the gallant gay Lothario. I wish you had been, and were, deprived of pen, ink, and paper for some time, that all your ideas might concentre in the great object of eloquence." As

Wilkes was doing yeoman service at the time with pen, ink, and paper, the extract proves the short-sightedness of Temple as well as the good opinion he had of Wilkes's powers—but that is by the way. Pitt was at first equally misled, but soon came to have a truer grasp of Wilkes's natural bent.

As for mending broken fortunes, the Berwick episode cost Wilkes £4,000 and lost him the prospect of his mother-in-law's money; the Aylesbury election cost him £7,000 and delivered him over to the Jews.

Wilkes was elected on the 6th of July, 1757, and Potter made haste to put him wise as to the next step. "You will", he wrote, "doubtless leave your name at Mr. Pitt's door in St. James's Square. If you intend to make one among the friends of so inaccessible a Minister, you will go farther, and by letter signify to him your election and your disposition to enter into his connexion." Wilkes took the hint and wrote to Pitt on the 14th of July. After a decent interval to mark his importance, Pitt replied on the 20th: "I was not a little mortify'd to lose the pleasure of seeing you when you was so good as to call at my house, and of having then an opportunity of congratulating you very sincerely, as I now do, on your being placed in a publick situation of displaying more generally to the world those great and shining talents which your friends have the pleasure to be so well acquainted with. The favourable sentiments and kind disposition with which you are so good to honour me, I shall always rank among my best possessions, tho' conscious I have no title to keep them, but the same partial friendship that gave them." It would have been a friendly letter whoever had written it; from Pitt, whose letters were "affected, formal, and pedantic", it was positively gushing, and was thanks in advance for the loan of the "great and shining talents".

(4)

Before Wilkes entered on his parliamentary career he had one final brush with his wife.

Shortly after the separation Polly contracted smallpox, and Wilkes, easily allowing his affection as a father to overcome his indifference as a husband, besought Mary to go at once to the child. But Mary, who had never been much interested in her daughter, took absolutely no notice, a fact which Wilkes bitterly resented, and which effectually killed whatever chance there may have been of reconciliation. Wilkes and his own mother tended Polly, and Wilkes nursed her during the convalescence, though it coincided with the fret and hurry of the election. The scare was over just about the time that Wilkes was faced with the costs of his election—the £7,000 with which Pitt and Potter had saddled him. Whilst wondering how to pay his way, he remembered the annuity of £200 settled on his wife, and determined to get it back. At first he tried to persuade Mary to give it up voluntarily, and when that failed, tried to frighten her by suing for restitution of conjugal rights, with no better success. Henceforward she disappears out of his life.

CHAPTER V

JOHN WILKES, M.P.

(1)

FIRST impressions are always important, and the first four and a quarter years of Wilkes's parliamentary career coincided with Pitt's great administration. Every day was a festival and feast of glory prepared by Pitt, and Fortune, with her wonted liberality towards her favourites, flung into the plate an endless stream of extra and unexpected dainties. Clive won the battle of Plassey a week before Pitt became Minister, but the news reached England months later to form part of Pitt's glory. Frederick the Great won the victories of Rossbach and Leuthen, unaided by England, within the first six months of Pitt's ministry, thus enabling Pitt to repudiate the Convention of Closterseven. But these adventitious aids have rightly been absorbed in the sun of England's splendour. It was Pitt who found an England restless, depressed, discouraged, who infused into it his own glowing optimism and high faith, who roused the half-drugged spirit of the country and led it to the pinnacle of achievement. It was right and proper that the blaze of his advent should be heralded by beams of light.

The details of these four years are too well known to need recounting: the conquest of America and India; the abasement of France and the expansion of England; the rebirth of the Navy and the supremacy of the seas. It was enough to dazzle the most keen-sighted. It blinded even Pitt's colleagues, who were content merely to ratify his wishes and carry out his commands. Opposition, doubt, disapproval were swept aside by his vigorous decision, and the whole administration centred in himself. It was easy to have confidence when such results were daily proving the skill of the master-hand. "You would not know your country again," wrote Walpole to Sir Horace Mann; "you left it a private little island, living upon its means. You would find it the capital of the world; St. James's Street crowded with Nabobs and American chiefs, Mr. Pitt attended in his Sabine farm by Eastern monarchs, waiting till the gout had gone out of his foot for an audience. I shall be in Town to-morrow, and perhaps able to wrap up and send you half a dozen French standards in my postscript." The cool certainty of that last sentence, founded on experience, represented the feeling of England, and explains the confidence with which Ministers and Secretaries of State could put their names to documents which Pitt presented to them for signature, not for perusal.

When one man was all and opposition had gone, Parliament had nothing to do but acquiesce in the Minister's proposals and cheer the news of each fresh victory. "Our unanimity is prodigious," Walpole told Sir Horace Mann; "you would as soon hear 'No' from an old maid as from the House of Commons."

Here was no picture of a normal Parliament, but it seemed to be a complete vindication of the new ideas which Pitt had for years been distilling at Stowe and pouring into Wilkes's ear. In the fewest words these new ideas were government based on patriotism and popularity. Pitt had been driven to them by the fact that the existing system barred him from office. Not that he meant exactly what he said, nor that he disapproved entirely of the system then in vogue. Pitt was as imperious as any Whig magnate, and a system which enabled one man to become an absolute ruler suited him down to the ground. No one had ever been so regal in his outlook, no one more confidently arrogant in his pretensions. "I know that I can save this country", he boasted, "and that no one else can." It was not the system which disgusted him, but the thought that he lacked the cards of entry. He did not belong to the close corporation of Whig magnates, and he had no hope of competing in the stress and surge of bribery. It was essential for him to find some other support than "connections", some other lever than money. So in his grandest manner he opposed patriotism to corruption and popularity to birth. In reality he was little affected by his own preaching; he merely turned a blind eye to the shady transactions at the Treasury, and in his private conversation expressed his contempt for the common herd. But whatever reservations he may have made in his own mind, patriotism and popularity had their obvious meanings, and acquired a golden, if fallacious, aura from the splendours of his own administration.

The effect on Wilkes is not hard to imagine. He had sat at Pitt's feet at a time when he himself was impressionable, both because of his youth and his desire to enter Society, and when Pitt was more than usually in earnest because he had not yet succeeded. He had entered Parliament as Pitt's firm supporter, and there saw the ideas he had been imbibing at once produce the most dazzling results. Moreover, he was Pitt's friend, and supposed to be marked out for a brilliant career. In such circumstances it was inevitable that he should believe implicitly in patriotism and popularity, even if his natural bent had not been in the same direction. But there was this difference between the teacher and his pupil—Wilkes had no *arrière-pensée*; he accepted patriotism and popularity in their most literal meaning; and when in due course Pitt fell and the miserable system of corruption and intrigue resumed its old incompetent way, Wilkes first of all worked without hesitation for Pitt's recall, and failing in his endeavours, very soon realized the need for fundamental reform. Thenceforward he was its steady champion. This, however, is anticipating.

(2)

For the moment Wilkes found Parliament an idle place. So far as he could see his only function as a member was to deal with the begging letters which inevitably followed his entrance into public life.

Whatever the interest of such correspondence, it was a poor day's work, and Wilkes, as an energetic man, had no sooner felt his feet than he discovered, as he had always known subconsciously, that his interest in Parliament was of the slightest. Before long he was seeking for more congenial work and discovered it easily in one of Pitt's schemes.

During his short administration the previous year Pitt had found England in a state of war without troops and in fear of invasion without a defence force. His first step was to meet these two needs. He raised troops for foreign service by the brilliantly successful expedient of recruiting Highlanders. For home defence he had recourse to a national militia—with less success, because the worthy English farmers had a sturdy faith in their pitchforks as the best means of expelling foreigners. The need, however, was pressing, and the gentry were entreated to do their best. In Buckinghamshire Lord Temple took steps to raise the necessary quota. Sir Francis Dashwood was appointed Colonel and Wilkes the next in command. The work was arduous and not without danger, and the bulk of it was borne by Wilkes. In the first months of his parliamentary career in particular he was kept busy. Riots broke out, especially in the inland counties, where the people felt themselves far removed from danger. "On the day of meeting," the Duke of Bedford wrote to Pitt, "Sir Roger Burgoyne and Colonel Lee, the only two gentlemen there present, were informed by some of the constables that they had passed a mob of 1,000 persons who were coming to Biggleswade to murder the gentlemen and prevent the lots for militiamen being drawn, upon which these two gentlemen thought proper to retire."

This matter of the militia caused a good many gentlemen to think "retirement" proper. But Wilkes was an exception—as, curiously enough, was Potter—and his services were uncommonly useful. Long after the preliminary tumults had died down he was still showing a courage and firmness that contrasted well with the pusillanimous thoughts of others. As late as May 1762, after boldly issuing warrants against the servants of two peers in connection with militia duties, he reported that "Sir William [Bowyer] and Mr. Mason did not join in granting the warrant, from prudential motives".

The Buckinghamshire regiment was quartered at Winchester, and was employed in guarding a camp of French prisoners. Wilkes spent much of his time there, and in one of his letters gives a vivid account of militia life and the troubles he had to face. "On friday night there was a great alarm at the King's House. Twenty four of the prisoners had got into a large drain, and about eleven at night were making their escape from the bottom of the hill near the ditch. The Sentry challeng'd, and on no return being made, fir'd. One Frenchman has been wounded in the head, endeavouring likewise to escape. Four have escaped; all the rest were brought back. The night was very dark, and from the neglect of the turnkeys, the lamps were not lighted till an hour and a half after the usual time. All our men shew'd the greatest vigilance and spirit. As the Frenchman who has had his arm cutt off, is in a very dangerous way, I have given the soldier who shot him, one Aplethorp of Captain Osborne's company, leave of absence for three weeks, till the event is known. Our laws are remarkably deficient in this case, and the conduct of some of the Colonels here, particularly Sir G. S. as unaccountable. The Bucks were on guard that day, and exerted themselves in retaking those who had escap'd into the fields. The Hampshire beat to arms in the town, which alarm'd the inhabitants so much, that when I came here on saturday noon, they had not recover'd their consternation."

The letter brings out two traits in Wilkes's character which go a long way towards explaining and justifying his career. The first is the care he took of his men as individuals, showing not only interest but sympathy. The second is the precision with which he put his finger on a weak spot in the laws.

(3)

Wilkes diversified his perfunctory attendance in Parliament and his more prolonged efforts with the militia by bouts of strenuous and disreputable conviviality.

His Colonel, Sir Francis Dashwood, was a Buckinghamshire

magnate whom he may or may not have known before, but
with whom he now reached terms of familiarity. Although
Dashwood was nothing but a good-natured ox with more
physical energy than he knew what to do with, he was in some
ways a dangerous man to know. He was nineteen years older
than Wilkes, and had had the misfortune to lose his father
when he was sixteen. Coming into a title and large estates at
this immature age, and having no one to control his super-
abundant energy, he plunged forthwith into a whirlpool of
pleasure. An incurable itch for adventure led him into all sorts
of escapades on the Continent, where he gained something of a
European reputation for the madness of his pranks. On his
return home he tried to find an outlet for his misguided energy
in the more notorious gatherings of excited youth, and finding
them insufficient, proceeded to found clubs with more startling
aims and objects. The first was the Dilettanti, for which,
according to Horace Walpole, the nominal qualification was
having been to Italy, and the real one being drunk. About the
same time he entered Parliament, and four years later, at the
age of thirty-eight, married. The combined dullness of legislation and domestic duties spurred him on to his final effort in
the direction of picturesque depravity. Somewhere about this
point he founded a "brotherhood", known occasionally as the
Franciscans of Medmenham, but more generally as the Hellfire
Club. The brotherhood rented and renovated Medmenham
Abbey, a spacious old house near Marlow, which was the
scene of their private debaucheries. Being a graceless set of
hardened old sinners, verging on the sober forties, their jaded
appetites needed more stimulating than in their lusty youth,
and accordingly they spared no pains or money in making their
abbey as artificially suggestive as possible. All the pictures,
statues, and trappings were as grossly improper as perverted
ingenuity could invent, and the orgies as succulent as wealth
could procure.

Dashwood invited his gay lieutenant to become a member
of the fraternity. Wilkes jumped at the opportunity, and

extracted all possible pleasure out of his membership. "I
feast my mind", he wrote from the camp at Winchester, "with
the joys of Medmenham on Monday, and hope to indemnify
myself there for the noise and nonsense here."

From Wilkes's point of view this invitation was the most
unfortunate he ever received. His membership offered a ready
confirmation of the stories to his discredit, and indeed his
subsequent reputation was founded largely on the wild tales
connected with the place. Being by far the most notorious
member, all its sins were heaped on his head, and Medmenham
became practically synonymous with Wilkes. It is almost
impossible to exaggerate what this meant. Although the Abbey
was nothing but a private house of ill-fame, the luxury of the
surroundings, the reputation of the members, and the secrecy
of the proceedings—the one sign of grace in this otherwise
graceless crew—gave rise to all manner of ridiculous stories,
and long before Wilkes joined membership was regarded as
tantamount to selling one's soul to the devil. Hence its popular
name of Hellfire Club—to be spoken in deadly seriousness.
Some of the more melodramatic tales were spread by a novelist,
one Charles Johnstone, who declared amongst other things
that the object of the Society was to destroy religion. The fact
that this fantastic theory was accepted is but another proof
of the credulity of the age. It had about as much foundation as
the lurid prophecies of a demented soldier who foretold an
earthquake which was to swallow up London and its wicked
inhabitants, and so terrified the population that most of them
spent a ghastly night in the roads and fields, tremblingly
awaiting the extremely ordinary dawn of the next day.

But if Medmenham was nothing but a haunt of very ordinary
vice, it did represent a trait in Wilkes's character, for which
the best that can be said is that he never allowed his passions
to interfere with his work or sap his genius. He himself gave
a very candid account to a friend who expressed the fear that
he would allow himself to be distracted by an Italian courtesan.
"I never expected", Wilkes replied, "to have been reproach'd

with constancy to women. My life will confute that too as to the Italian girl you have heard of. That amusement, however, I must have, and it is almost the only one I take."

Wilkes enjoyed Medmenham because it was luxurious and whole-hearted, and at the same time completely cut off from the pursuits of everyday life.

(4)

Meanwhile, however much he might be benefiting his friends, and however useful he might be on militia duties, Wilkes was finding his own affairs sufficiently difficult. Having entered Parliament in the middle of its life, he had to prepare at once for the next election. Canvassing was an expensive hobby, but Wilkes was forced to do as others did, and once a fortnight he was in the habit of giving dinners to his constituents, besides dispensing the usual "gratifications".

As time went on, careless though he always was over money affairs, he saw that a political life on the present lines was beyond his means as well as contrary to his bent. Accordingly he tried to amend his position. As a measure of thrift he determined to avoid wholesale bribery. "Select three hundred men", he wrote to his agent, "and bid the others do their worst." Nor would he bid very high even for this restricted number; he was not so urgently desirous of re-election. "I declare", he told his agent in another letter, "they shall have five guineas or else I desire no vote, but I will never be trampled upon, and I would as soon sell my estate at Aylesbury and quit the borough now as hereafter."

He also kept his eyes open for an appointment where his administrative abilities could be usefully employed and the salary might improve his finances. In 1760 the British Minister at Constantinople retired, and Wilkes applied unsuccessfully for the post. Early next year he asked Pitt for an appointment on the Board of Trade. "I am very desirous", he explained, "of a scene of business, in which I might, usefully I hope to

the public, employ my time and attention. The small share of
talents I have from nature are such as fit me, I believe, for
active life; and if I know myself, I should be entirely devoted
to the scene of business I was engaged in." He asked that, if
the request were granted, he might be appointed "in the interval
between the two Parliaments to avoid some very disagreeable
circumstances attending on re-election at Aylesbury"—a
dignified reference to the low state of his finances and the high
cost of elections, which should have touched a sensitive spot in
Pitt's memory.

He failed to get the job because Pitt had other views for him.
Canada had recently been conquered, and the pacification and
settlement of this vast new province was one of the hardest
and most important of the tasks before Pitt. It obviously
needed the best man he could find—a man at once tactful
and resolute, broad-minded and prepared to take responsibility.
Pitt had a wonderful knack of picking the most suitable man
for a difficult task, and it therefore speaks highly of Wilkes's
capacity that Pitt had fixed upon him and would have sent him
but for his own fall from power. It is a thousand pities that the
project failed. Wilkes would have made an excellent Governor,
just as fourteen years later he made an excellent Lord Mayor.
Not long afterwards Wilkes described his views of the work
to be done. His ambition, he said, had been "to have gone to
Quebec, the first governor; to have reconciled the new subjects
to the English; and to have shown the French the advantages
of the mild rule of laws over that of lawless power and despot-
ism". It was no mean ambition, and might have had a profound
influence on the course of American history.

The events which led to Pitt's fall, and so kept Wilkes from
Canada, also led up to the great struggle for reform with which
Wilkes's name is indissolubly linked. They began with the
accession of George III and even before.

CHAPTER VI

THE RISING STORM

(1)

HAD he been listening, Pitt might have heard the first distant mutterings of the storm shortly after his rise to power. Under the first four Georges it was customary for the Prince of Wales to head the Opposition, and so it had come about that Pitt, who was perpetually in opposition, open or disguised, had long paid his court at Leicester House. It was largely as the nominee and through the influence of Leicester House that he had become Minister. As such he was in a peculiarly favourable position to enforce his pet theory of uniting all parties under his own guidance. But office produced its invariable effect, heightened in Pitt's case by an imperiousness which refused to take orders from either the King or the Prince. George II had the good sense to issue none, contenting himself with a Minister who could do no wrong. But the Prince, and Bute as his trustee, felt their influence waning and grew annoyed. At the outset Bute had congratulated Pitt wholeheartedly. "Thank God", he wrote, "I see you in office." But a coolness arose; his "dearest friend" became his "worthy friend", and then degenerated into "dear Sir", and the coolness was heartily reciprocated by Pitt. Not that he broke definitely with the Prince or Bute. He could hardly wish to create an opposition, when his whole theory was founded on a united England and an absence of parties. But he was too much wrapped up in his own royal notions, too much carried away by his own success, perhaps too big a man to enter fully into the feelings of jealousy he aroused, to pay much attention to the hints of trouble. He thought a little condescension, a touch of sweet reasonableness, was all that was necessary, and contented himself with a few soothing words. He thought he was striving to maintain a happy family spirit, when in fact he was attempting to placate rivals. It was laughable enough to consider Bute or the Prince,

or even the pair of them, as competitors to be feared. The
Prince was merely an uneducated boy and Bute a barber's
block. Yet the two of them together were to overthrow the
greatest man in England—through his own defects.

(2)

In October 1760 George II died suddenly, and was succeeded
by his grandson. The new King was twenty-two years old.
His education had been hopelessly neglected in all that pertained
to literature, art, science, or general knowledge. It was not much
better in any other direction. "Was there ever", he once said
to Fanny Burney, "such stuff as great part of Shakespeare?—
only one must not say so! What! is there not sad stuff?—
What?—What?"—a remark that was typical both of his thought
and his manner of speech. He could hardly be blamed for his
ignorance. When he was twelve years old his worthless father
died, and thenceforward his mother, a narrow-minded,
intriguing woman, had matters entirely her own way. "His
education", she once confided to Bubb Dodington, "has
given me much pain; his book-learning I am no judge of,
though I suppose it small or useless, but I hope he may have
been instructed in the general understanding of things."
The tutors engaged to give him this desirable understanding
pursued a method that was as simple as it was original. "I
once desired Mr. Stone", the Princess Dowager told Dodington, "to inform the Prince about the Constitution, but he
declined it, to avoid giving jealousy to the Bishop of Norwich. I
mentioned it again, but he still declined it as not being his
province." "Pray, Madam," inquired Dodington, "what is his
province?" "I do not know," the Princess replied, "unless it
is to go before the Prince upstairs, to walk with him sometimes, seldomer to ride with him, and now and then to dine
with him."
However, if the method was original, it seems to have

imparted some of Mr. Stone's obstinacy to the young Prince. But for the respect due to Kings, George III might certainly be called pig-headed. Moreover, by one means or another, he was primed with a very convenient theory of the Constitution, nominally founded on Bolingbroke's *Patriot King*, but actually a rehash of the old theory of divine right. It was summed up by the Princess Dowager in a slogan short enough to stick in the young Prince's memory and enticing enough to thrill him: "George," she kept repeating, "be a King." For the carrying out of this arduous task he possessed by nature or upbringing almost all the desirable, and none of the necessary, qualities. He was born to the position; and, better still, as he reminded his subjects in his first speech, he was born an Englishman; but unfortunately he had not been born kingly. He was virtuous in himself, but had collected the drawbacks alone and none of the advantages of virtue, being humdrum, hard-working, abstemious, and dull. He lived on thin gruel and took an incredible amount of exercise, but only for the same end as does a society beauty—to keep down his natural corpulence. He poked his nose into every department of State and wrote orders innumerable in his own hand, but simply to further his own intrigues. He was blessed with the unbending courage of an obstinate man, but employed it for unreasonable ends. He recognized genius in others, but chose his Ministers for their subservience to himself, and applauded their want of scruple if it was used on his own behalf.

Yet ,dull as his intellect was, he was no worse than the Whig magnates, and had it not been for Pitt he would have been quite justified in striving to regain for the Crown the power which the magnates had stolen in the name of the people. At all events, with his mother's slogan ringing in his ears, he set to work indomitably, using the precise methods that the magnates had elaborated for themselves. He entered the arena to bid with Fox, Bedford, Rockingham, and the like against Pitt, and conducted his campaign uncommonly well. After all, he was in a better position than anyone else to bribe, and owing

GEORGE III

After a painting by A. Ramsay in the National Portrait Gallery

to the convenient theory that the King can do no wrong, was able to work his will without the risk of being brought to book. His only requisite was a Minister who would subordinate himself entirely to his Royal master. Finding just such an instrument in John Stuart, Earl of Bute, he proceeded to make utter chaos of the political system by secretly building up a party of "King's Friends". This active, and yet hidden, participation in affairs was wholly unexpected, and so long as the King did not appear openly, apparently irresistible. Taken by surprise, and angry at his defeat, Pitt confided to Wilkes that "the King is the falsest hypocrite in Europe".

(3)

John Stuart, Earl of Bute, through whom the King worked, was not worthy to be either Pitt's friend or his enemy. After a wholly undistinguished youth he had been noticed by Frederick, Prince of Wales, at some private theatricals, and on the strength of a telling representation of Lothario in *The Fair Penitent* was invited to Leicester House. Frederick was not remarkable for his sagacity, but even he could say no more for his favourite than that he "was a fine showy man, who would make an excellent ambassador in a Court where there was no business". Nobody had a good word for him. Walpole remarked that he "had passed his youth in studying mathematics and mechanics in his own little island, then simples in the hedges about Twickenham, and at five and thirty had fallen in love with his own figure, which he produced at masquerades in becoming dresses, and in plays which he acted in private companies with a set of his own relations". Shelburne was even more biting. According to him Bute was "proud, aristocratical, pompous, imposing. . . . Added to this he had a sort of gloomy madness." He prided himself upon his devotion to literature and when in power aped the Mæcenas, but as Walpole says, his "letters grew a proverb for want of orthography",

E

and his patronage was only redeemed from its wholesale want of discrimination by the fact that he gave Dr. Johnson a pension—though this was to buy his pen, not to reward his genius. When Frederick was dead he gained a great ascendancy over the Princess Dowager, and began early to pave the way for the Prince. In the last few years of George II's reign he started interfering, quite arbitrarily, in elections, and tried to dictate to Pitt who should be appointed to embassies.

At the same time, criticize as one may, Bute must have possessed a very pretty talent for intrigue and a dogged determination not easily to be discouraged. On George III's accession he found a Ministry deeply entrenched in popular esteem and strongly bulwarked by a series of magnificent victories; he found a Ministry which comprised every man of ability in the House, and was backed not only by the rank and file, but also by the populace; he found a blank where opposition might have been expected, and enthusiasm where he might have hoped for war weariness or depression at the load of taxation. On his side there were only the King, an inexperienced, obstinate boy of twenty-two, and the remnants of the old Jacobites, who had no leaders and less ability. Yet in spite of these seemingly overwhelming odds, within little over a year he was completely master of the situation.

From the outset he realized that different measures should be employed in different quarters. In the Cabinet he followed with deadly success the old maxim of *divide et impera*; in the world at large he tried the effect of slanderous tongues. He began vilifying Pitt and his administration, partly by an army of detractors who hung about the coffee-houses to spread ugly rumours, and partly by a horde of paid scribblers who sent abusive paragraphs to the papers.

Meanwhile George III pursued the methods of the cuckoo, laying Bute in Pitt's warm nest, and encouraging the interloper to eject the rightful occupant. It was clear to everyone that so long as the war lasted Pitt must remain in full control. The first object, therefore, must be to secure peace at all costs and on any conditions. Bute set himself to work to create a peace party. Two days after the King's accession he was elected to the Privy Council and prepared the King's speech, in which the King was made to talk of "a bloody and expensive war" and of obtaining "an honourable and lasting peace". Pitt, more annoyed than alarmed, remonstrated with Bute and changed the printed version. After this preliminary skirmish, Bute continued to edge himself into the Cabinet and sow the seeds of discord among its members. It was not hard to do. Pitt shared with Wilkes the disadvantage of lack of birth; the great magnates put up with him because they had to, but they were always suspicious and had begun to jib at the haughty arrogance of his manner. They were ready to leap at the chance of getting their own back, without in the least realizing where "their own" would land them.

Parliament met on the 18th of November and was treated to a speech in which the King professed entire concurrence with the policy adopted during the last few years of his grand-father's reign. It was too early to use any other language; yet intrigue was already at work to overthrow his Ministers and reverse their policy. Eleven days later Dodington pressed Bute to oust Holderness and take his place as Secretary. Bute admitted the concoction of a plan by which Holderness was to throw up his post "in seeming anger", and the murky business actually took place on the 25th of March. Meanwhile Bute had been interfering right and left in the all-important matter of "managing"—to the intense dismay of Newcastle, who protested, "whenever I ask an explanation of these and other matters, the constant answer is, the King has ordered it so". Pitt made the process too easy. In his ostentatious neglect of patronage he left his friends an easy prey to the brazen Bute. In March Legge was summarily dismissed and two of Bute's supporters, Charles Townshend and Sir Francis Dashwood, received promotion. So the merry game went on, and still Pitt remained wrapped in his foreign affairs, regardless of the rapid undermining of his position at home.

(4)

Whether because of Bute's intrigues, or out of real necessity, or for some other reason, 1761 had not proceeded far before France began negotiations for peace. Pitt was prepared to listen, but the terms he demanded were not light. England was to receive Canada, Senegal, Goree, and Minorca; the four neutral islands in the West Indies were to be equally divided; Dunkirk was to be reduced; and the French conquests in Germany were to be given back. In return England would surrender Belle Isle, Guadeloupe, and Marie Galante.

Fearing that the terms might be too hard, France was carrying on secret negotiations with Spain, and on the 15th of August signed the "Family Compact", which was in effect an offensive and defensive alliance aimed at England. Pitt got wind of this compact and in the middle of September not only broke off the negotiations with France, but decided on immediate war with Spain. More than that, he conceived the idea of stripping Spain of her South American colonies and adding them to the British Empire, for which purpose he prepared plans for the conquest of Panama, Havannah, Manilla, and the Philippine Islands. "If any war", he declared significantly, "could provide its own resources, it was war with Spain."

The Council, torn by internal dissensions and bemused by Bute, held back in dismay. As Pitt said scornfully, "the Council trembled". But if it trembled with fear at his proposals, it trembled with eagerness for his departure, and when Pitt, growing more and more imperious as obstruction increased, threatened that "he would no longer remain in a situation which made him responsible for measures which he was no longer allowed to guide", the Council promptly took him at his word. So Pitt was manœuvred into the wilderness, and on the 5th of October he and Temple resigned. Egremont succeeded Pitt, and Bute became master of the field. More than that, he managed very adroitly to damage Pitt's reputation in the one quarter where it was still supreme—the City. On Pitt's retirement the King offered him any reward he chose to name, and Bute eagerly plied him with temptations. Pitt refused all sinecures, but accepted a pension of £3,000 and a title for his wife. The result was a severe slump in his popularity. There were murmurings, discontent, and open gibes at "Lady Cheat'em", and the indignation was not confined to the populace. It was so widespread and strong that Pitt was obliged to defend himself in a letter to a City friend. This letter had some effect in restraining the prejudice, and on Lord Mayor's Day he received an ovation at the Guildhall so much more enthusiastic than the King and Queen that George III was seriously annoyed. But what did still more to revive his popularity was the fact that all his anticipations were verified. He had scarcely laid down office before Spain adopted a new tone, and on the 4th of January, 1762, Great Britain was forced to declare war.

CHAPTER VII

DUELS—PAPER AND OTHERWISE

(1)

PITT's fall created very little stir in parliamentary circles; only two men followed him into retirement—Temple and James Grenville, while the remainder of the world turned eagerly to Bute's rising sun. But it had one surprising and never-to-be-forgotten result: it galvanized Wilkes into sudden life, so that within a few months this gay idler, who was known only as a profane wit and frequenter of Medmenham, became the moving spirit of public opinion, and was openly described by the Duke of Devonshire as the heart and soul of the Opposition.

He showed not a trace of hesitation. The news appeared in the *Gazette* of the 10th of October, together with details of the pension which aroused such discontent. This snapping by the people at the hand that had fed them disgusted Wilkes, and he at once wrote to condole and comfort. His letter is lost, but Temple's answer remains: "Your generous and discerning spirit felt as it ought the indignity done to a man who had deserved far other treatment from the public, than to be condemned on bare suspicion, and rolled in the kennel."

Private sympathy was easy, but public support while the tide was running so strongly needed greater courage. Wilkes was equal to the occasion. Parliament met on the 3rd of November, and at once this hitherto silent back-bencher stepped forward to nail his colours to the mast and do his little best to restore his leader. His oratorical powers were small and his influence smaller, and as a parvenu he was particularly shy of appearing foolish. But this was not the time to let the fear of ridicule keep his mouth shut. For the next few months he was not infrequently uttering short, pithy speeches, more in the nature of angry statements than harangues—all of which passed unnoticed in a House where eloquence alone received attention, and that only as an entertainment. Wilkes had a knack of facing facts and soon realized that his laboured efforts would do no good. But if he was not a fluent speaker he possessed one talent which might well be of even greater service. He could write, and as it happened events offered him a theme admirably adapted to his pen. Pitt had fallen definitely on the question of a Spanish war, and Bute had taken good care to insert a soothing report from Madrid in the *Gazette* announcing Pitt's departure. Yet within three months England had broken with Spain. The Opposition were fully justified in demanding all the papers, and Government were obliged to produce a selection, which they did on the 29th of January, 1762. They chose those which they hoped would be innocuous, and edited them with a view to obscuring the facts as far as possible.

Wilkes examined them with meticulous care, and on the 9th of March published anonymously a pamphlet entitled *Observations on the Papers Relative to the Rupture with Spain*. The *Observations* rested on three main texts: Pitt had been absolutely right; the Government had been absolutely wrong; and the Ministers were deliberately hiding the facts. The first two points were self-evident; the third he had no difficulty in proving from the omissions and inconsistencies of the papers themselves. On the basis of these texts he held up the Government to ridicule, pouring scorn on their inexperience, their bungling, their incompetence: "Two Secretaries of State in these dangerous times become Ministers by inspiration." Over against this picture he set Pitt and the splendours of his administration: "I speak with the honest warmth and pride of an Englishman, who really feels with his Sovereign the *great and important services* of Mr. Pitt, and glories in seeing his country recovered from the most abject state of despair to such a pitch of grandeur and importance as to hold the first rank among the Powers of Europe."

The pamphlet was well written, soundly argued, and quite unanswerable. It was a telling blow, and caused a great commotion. Wilkes, ever a practical joker, followed it up with one of those bursts of irresponsible mischievousness which always delighted him. Happening to meet a time-serving parson, one James Douglas, in the Park, Wilkes solemnly told him that Douglas himself was supposed to be the author. Douglas, in a frenzy of perturbation, spread the rumour by trying "to trace this groundless story to the fountain-head", and failing dismally, implored Wilkes for further information. His tormentor promised to "contradict so groundless a rumour". "I shall be strenuous", he added, "in contradicting the report; for, undoubtedly, the author of the *Observations* has no chance of favour from any of the present powers"—a remark calculated to worry his victim still more, and also proof of Wilkes's knowledge that he was burning his boats.

(2)

In spite of Wilkes and his *Observations*, in spite of the Spanish war, Bute went steadily ahead with his twofold plan of monopolizing power and securing peace. By the end of May he had driven Newcastle out of office, become Premier himself, and promoted Lord Halifax to the vacant post of Secretary of State. At the same time Sir Francis Dashwood, to his own astonishment, was appointed Chancellor of the Exchequer. As a result of this unexpected promotion he resigned the colonelcy of the Bucks Militia, to which Wilkes succeeded.

Meanwhile, on this full assumption of power, Bute turned more vigorously than before to the vilifying of Pitt. It was essential to crush the deposed Minister entirely before the peace proposals were mooted. At Bute's instigation, and in his pay, Smollett produced a weekly paper, known as the *Briton*, and an Irishman, Arthur Murphy, a second paper known as the *Auditor*. These were the official organs of Government, and as such were legitimate, but their methods were deplorable. Instead of explaining or defending the actions of Government, they simply abused Pitt, his administration, and anyone connected with him.

The publication of the first number of the *Briton*, on the 29th of May, 1762, gave Wilkes his second opportunity. The next Saturday, June 5th, an opposition paper made its appearance under the name of the *North Briton*—a paper which ran for forty-five numbers and was destined to make Wilkes the best-known man in England.

The object of these weekly papers was to support Pitt and to attack the Government. They were frankly partisan, and the choice of subject was dictated by the prospect which it offered of forwarding the main object. No one expects a paper of this type to be impartial, and no one need be surprised if popular prejudices were exploited. At the moment there were two such prejudices very much to the front—a dislike of Bute and consequently of all things Scotch, and a deep distrust of the influence of the Princess Dowager—prejudices which were combined in a very prevalent belief that Bute and the Princess were guilty of illicit connections. Wilkes exploited the personal scandal and the Scotch prejudice for all they were worth. It is not perhaps very profitable to inquire whether the scandals were justified. Probably they were not, though it is only fair to add that the two persons concerned were indiscreet. The Scotch prejudice was another matter altogether. The Scottish invasion of England has always been fair game. Wilkes, for the most part, treated it jokingly, and merely as an adjunct to the trouncing of Bute. It provoked most of his Scotch friends to betray their proverbial lack of humour, but Boswell was an exception. "The truth is," he remarked, "Wilkes is a most agreeable companion. He is good-humoured and vivacious, and likes the Scots as well as anybody; only he considers the abusing that nation as a political device, which he must make use of. Whether or no this can be esteemed fair, I am really at a loss to say. Wilkes and I are exceedingly well, when we meet."

But because Wilkes made the most of foolish feelings and passing fancies it must not be supposed that the *North Briton* was mere sensational journalism. Generally speaking, Wilkes preferred sound argument of the type which he used in his *Observations*, but he found, as other editors have, that the supply of "meat" is not as constant as journalists would like. Indeed, for the eighteenth-century newspapers the whole year was one continual "silly season". Parliamentary reporting was not allowed; news agencies did not exist; police-court news was scanty, and official statements reserved for the *Gazette*. Journalists had to make bricks without straw, and this fact largely accounts for the poor and abusive quality of the political pamphlets of the time. The striking features of the *North Briton* were its comparative freedom from mere scandal, its comparatively steady flow of news, culled from Parliament by Wilkes himself, and the large proportion of soundly argued papers. Still more striking were the wit and courage displayed— courage especially. Political writers were liable at any moment to be imprisoned, fined, and even pilloried for their productions, and consequently avoided trouble by a liberal use of blanks and asterisks. No names were ever mentioned, and even such harmless words as Minister, Government, and Administration appeared with only their first and last letters, joined by a dash. Wilkes swept the whole clumsy contrivance aside, and his action seemed like a fresh wind blowing across a sultry plain.

Wilkes would have found it difficult to keep the paper going by himself, occupied as he was with parliamentary and militia duties, not to mention his moments of relaxation. But he had fortunately about this time fallen in with a new acquaintance, Charles Churchill, who was ready and able to help. Churchill was a congenial soul—a beefy, blustering giant, who had entered the Church at his parents', and left it at his Bishop's, request. His life was scandalous, being one long riot of drunkenness and debauchery; but it was redeemed by a savage power, both physical and mental, and a gift of devastating satire not unmingled with poetry. He poured out an unending stream of verses which took the town by storm, and might have placed this wild bacchanal in the ranks of great poets, had they not all been dedicated to passing political events. They are full of allusions, which were pointed enough at the moment but almost unintelligible a week later. His poetical works can be summed up as a powerful defence of Wilkes and a bludgeoning of all his enemies. Churchill was as devoid of fear as Wilkes, and as strongly partisan. He agreed readily to correct proofs and do other donkey-work, and when it was necessary he wrote the articles himself. It is impossible now to divide the papers between the two, but those which are definitely known to be by Churchill are less interesting, less argumentative, and more abusive than those known to be by Wilkes.

Whoever wrote them and whatever their contents they sold by the hundred, and Wilkes's rivals were reduced from their high estate as moulders of public opinion to penning frantic diatribes on Wilkes himself. Since it is sometimes said that all these papers were equally scurrilous, it may be as well to give short examples of the abuse each poured on the other. Smollett in the *Briton*, true to the silly practice of the day, attacked Wilkes under far-fetched names. "Of all these children of perdition", he wrote, "the most wicked and abandoned was Jahia Ben Israel Gin, a being of such an unhappy disposition, that it was commonly believed his soul was confined to its present prison, in order to do penance for some atrocious crime, unexpiated in its former state of existence. His external form was such as happily expressed the deformity of his mind. His face was meagre, sallow, and forbidding, as if he looked pale and haggard from the consciousness of guilt. His eyes were distorted, with such an hideous obliquity of vision, that the sight of him alone had frightened some matrons into mis-carriage, and made such an unfortunate impression on the imagination of others, that instead of children, they brought goggle-eyed monsters into the world." The description con-tinues on these lines for two more pages.

Wilkes's methods were different. "This author", he wrote of Smollett, "only gives himself out for a *Briton*. I have heard of a paper called the *Free Briton*; why has he dropt the title of

Free? I am sure it never could be more properly applied, according to that famous verse

> Nunquam libertas· gratior exstat
> Quam sub rege pio.

But it is not for *freedom* that this writer chooses to draw his grey goose-quill. As little pretensions has he to the title of *True* Briton. Conscious of this, he only gives himself out as a *Briton*; a circumstance equally common to him and *Buckhorse.* I wish the *Briton* had given us any clue to unravel what his real views, besides pay or pension, could be. He only declares his design to be to detect the *falsehood of malice*: mine shall be to detect the *malice of falsehood,* of his in particular." The rest of the paper is mainly devoted to refuting statements in the *Briton.*

It will be obvious that Wilkes's abuse is much less personal, more restrained, and concerned with Smollett's views rather than with his physical defects—in a word, is infinitely to be preferred. It was also much less frequent.

(3)

But the career of the *North Briton* was exciting enough without taking into account its excellencies and defects.

The first excitement began with the issue of the twelfth number on August 21, 1762. This particular paper was devoted to the question of pensions, and a good deal of play was made over Dr. Johnson's definition and the fact that he had himself accepted one. Then came the turn of two peers— Litchfield and Talbot. Talbot was one of the minions introduced to Court by Bute. At this point he was the Lord Steward. No one pretended that he had abilities, but he was a handsome, well-set-up young man, who passed his time pleasantly enough between boxing and the ladies. That and a somewhat engaging freedom of speech won him a measure of popularity sufficient even to survive his plan of reducing the expenses of the Royal Household by cutting down the breakfast allowance of the

Maids of Honour. In his boyish enthusiasm he had specially
trained his horse to walk backwards, so that he might make a
proper exit at the King's coronation. Unfortunately, the horse
insisted on entering, instead of leaving, the Royal presence
backwards. Talbot, with equally boyish shame, was very touchy
over this incident—and Wilkes had the temerity to refer to it.
Bursting with indignation, the hot-headed young peer demanded
if Wilkes were the author of the paper. "My answer", Wilkes
replied, "is, that I must first insist on knowing your Lordship's
right to catechise me about an anonymous paper. If your
Lordship is not satisfied with this, I shall ever be ready to give
your Lordship any other satisfaction becoming me as a gentleman." A few more letters followed on either side, and then
Talbot sent a challenge. The two combatants, accompanied by
their seconds, arrived at the Red Lion, Bagshot, on the afternoon of the 5th of October, intending to settle this knotty
question with pistols early next morning. But Talbot was
nervous and excited, had worked himself up into a passion and
insisted on fighting there and then. Wilkes, cool, collected, and
politely sarcastic, demurred at this sudden change, but finally
agreed. He had first, however, some private business to transact,
business which, like an idle man of pleasure, he had postponed
to the last minute. Would Talbot wait whilst he wrote a letter?
Talbot would, and Wilkes proceeded to write to Temple,
asking him to look after Polly if anything should happen to her
father. Meanwhile Talbot's nerves became fretted, and when
Wilkes suggested that the door should be locked and the matter
settled in the room, he became almost hysterical—it was
butchery, and Wilkes was seeking his life; he would kill Wilkes,
and then Wilkes would be damned; Wilkes was trying to
murder him, and he hoped Wilkes would be hanged; Wilkes
was an atheist and wanted to die—and altogether the wretched
young man was half off his head with nerves and excitement.
He was not made any happier by Wilkes's cool sarcasm.

At about seven they stood opposite each other in the garden,
eight paces apart, armed with horse-pistols and lighted by the

moon. The signal was given; two shots rang out and two bullets whistled harmlessly through the night. Having satisfied honour at a great expense of nerves, both suffered a pleasurable reaction. Wilkes admitted writing the paper, and Talbot swore that Wilkes was the noblest fellow God had ever made. The two enemies, momentarily fast friends, returned to the inn with their seconds, and all four sat down to a bottle of wine, highly seasoned with an intense feeling of relief.

Wilkes wrote Temple an amusing account in a letter which was to have its own history. But there was one immediate result. Litchfield, who was equally interested in the paper, hearing that Wilkes had admitted authorship, instructed his solicitors to prosecute for libel. But Wilkes was not disposed to allow Litchfield to scoop the spoils when Talbot had done the work. Accordingly he wrote that in avowing the paper "it was never in his idea to suffer such a trifle to be made the serious subject of a wrangling litigation of attorneys, and that the morning after his Lordship commenced any kind of proceeding in Westminster Hall, Mr. Wilkes would oblige him to decide the affair by the laws of honour". Litchfield did not pursue the matter, for reasons that he wisely kept to himself.

(4)

Before this duel had come to a head, Wilkes was involved in fresh trouble. Finding his host of scribblers routed, Bute tempted Hogarth, and found him ready to sell his pencil. Hogarth was an old friend, and Wilkes at once warned him not to meddle, threatening to answer any cartoon by an attack in the *North Briton*. Hogarth ignored the threat, and Wilkes accordingly devoted his paper of the 25th of September to a reply—a reply which had too much truth in it to be relished. Hogarth, said Wilkes, "possessed the rare talent of gibbeting in colours"; he was "a very good moral satirist"; but "the darling passion of Mr. Hogarth is to show the *faulty* and *dark* side of every object. He never gives us in perfection the *fair face of Nature*, but admirably well holds out her deformities to ridicule." This faculty, Wilkes inferred, "has arose in some measure from his head, but much more from his heart", and boldly declared that "when a man of parts dedicates his talents to the service of his country, he deserves the highest rewards; when he makes them subservient to base purposes, he merits execration and punishment". Hogarth never forgave Wilkes, and in due course took his revenge.

The next month Wilkes was accused of bullying Bute's son, a schoolboy at Winchester. The report shocked Wilkes, who had a genuine love of children, as he showed in later life by the interest he took in Christ's Hospital and Lady Daker's Charity School for Girls. He was also pained at the idea of visiting the sins of the father on the child. He therefore took great pains to refute the story, and persuaded Churchill to write up the facts in the *North Briton* of the 23rd of October.

About this same time he laid up in pickle a more thorny rod for himself. At Winchester he invited a captain of the Hampshire Militia to dinner, a plump little man called Edward Gibbon. Wilkes was in his best form and half fascinated, half horrified this student so thoroughly ill at ease in uniform. "I scarcely ever met with a better companion," wrote Gibbon; "he has inexhaustible spirits, infinite wit and humour, and a great deal of knowledge; but a thorough profligate in principle as in practice, his life is stained with every vice, and his conversation full of blasphemy and indecency. These morals he glories in; for shame is a weakness he has long since surmounted. He told us himself, that in this time of public dissension he was resolved to make his fortune." This remark, which seems harmless enough, has been held up ever since as evidence of Wilkes's depravity. Only once in the course of nearly two centuries has this verdict been challenged—by Sir Charles Dilke. Yet, if Gibbon had shown rather less of the confiding militiaman and rather more of the critical historian, he would have seen that, whatever his resolve might be, Wilkes was putting his fortune to a desperate chance; and that if by good luck he succeeded, it would only be by restoring Pitt to power—a consummation devoutly to be wished.

The fact is that Wilkes had never for a moment kept his eye on the main chance. He had yawned through four years of parliamentary life, lounging mutely on the back benches and hurrying away at the first moment to militia duties. He had frankly told his leader that he preferred an active life, and when he had asked for a modest appointment, had to all appearance met with a blank refusal. Shortly afterwards Pitt fell into disgrace, resigned, and was followed by two men alone; he was without a party in the House, in disfavour at Court, losing his popularity, and talking loudly of retirement. There was no inducement here for a fortune-hunter. Now, if ever, was the time for Wilkes to cut his losses and look elsewhere. It was so obvious that even Temple told him again and again, with the bitter conviction of offended pride, that he and Pitt stood alone, outcast and rejected; that the plums were in the other basket, and that Wilkes had better make terms while he could. Instead, Wilkes did his best to follow his leader's example, resigning, not from office—for he held none—but from the prospect of conciliating power, by flaunting his defiance in the face of the world, and raising the standard of opposition, unsupported even by his idol. He was playing a lone hand, and one that became steadily more lonely. All his friends and cronies, with Dashwood at their head, were crowding into the Government ranks and receiving their rewards; even Bute, as a man, inspired Wilkes with no loathing; many years later he told Bute's daughter that he had felt no personal animosity. On the other hand, all his pet aversions remained in opposition— politicians whose minds were high rather than broad, starchy gentlemen full of jealousies, puffed up with their own importance, horrified and querulous at their defeat, but wholly unable of themselves to win their way back to power. These punctilious but by no means forceful gentlemen were half frightened, half delighted, at Wilkes's efforts, but far too high-minded to do more than profit by his work; they would not for the world be openly mixed up in his concerns. Pitt despised most of them, and Wilkes, so far as his natural affability allowed him, shared his feelings. Wilkes had everything to lose and nothing to gain. Yet he never faltered, and the real difficulty is to explain the splendid folly of this very astute man. What urged him on was partly an honest patriotism, the glow of pride in his country's magnificent victories; partly it was admiration of the genius who had conjured glory out of despair; partly it was real friendship for Lord Temple. As for his own fortunes, Wilkes declared in a private letter that he coveted neither money nor power. All he ever asked of friends or life was a competence sufficient for a reasonable standard of comfort, including, let us admit, a certain tincture of vice. He rushed lightheartedly to the fray, certain of his aims and enjoying the bustle. His loyalty would have been wholly quixotic but for his incorrigible humour, which if it gave him no hard cash at least paid a handsome dividend in laughter and excitement.

(5)

Wilkes had taken a line that was definite and unmistakable. The remainder of the Opposition were by no means so decided. They looked to Pitt for their cue, but on being driven from office Pitt adopted a curious attitude of aloofness—an attitude which had been implicit in the whole of his career, and from this point became more pronounced. For whatever reason, he observed a sort of benevolent neutrality towards Bute, playing a languid, puzzling part, though there are hints that he was not entirely blind to personal ambitions, and reason to believe that he was privy to Wilkes's actions.

For the moment, however, he appeared in Walpole's phrase "sullen and silent", while Newcastle was "feeble and impotent". With the Opposition thus weakened, Bute seemed to have a clear run for his policy, and as the summer wore on he spread abroad rumours of peace. With that Wilkes became serious, whatever tone he may have adopted before. "Peace", he agreed,

F

"is the great object of every honest man's wish"; but it must be "a safe and *honourable* peace, adequate to the successes of the war". He had never believed in Bute; now he definitely distrusted him, and still more the instrument he had chosen to discuss the terms with France. This was the Duke of Bedford, who was notoriously inclined to peace at any price, and in the words of Lecky "peculiarly unfit to carry on the negotiations". As the year turned into winter and the preliminaries of peace began to leak out, Wilkes's attacks became stronger and more fiercely argued, keeping popular feeling at white heat. So successful was he that Parliament began to waver and even members of the Government grew restive at the long list of concessions granted to a beaten enemy. Before long it was evident that the peace proposals would have a stormy passage.

Bute hoped to carry the Lords; the real difficulty was the Commons, where he had no leader capable of confronting Pitt, who was almost bound to denounce terms so far behind his own expectations. Bute began anxiously searching for new men and corrupter methods, and discovered his ideal in Fox—a politician of outstanding ability and no scruples. Fox bargained for a peerage. "We must call in bad men to govern bad men", sighed George III, and sealed the bargain with cynical resignation.

Fox diagnosed the situation accurately. "Does not your Lordship", he wrote to Shelburne, "begin to fear that there are but few left of any sort, of our friends even, who are for this peace? I own I do." He measured out the remedy in accordance with the desperate state of the patient, embarking on the most wholesale system of bribery ever yet attempted. He was a past-master in the art, and even outdid Newcastle, snapping up that old intriguer's followers under his very nose. "He has agents everywhere," Newcastle complained peevishly to Charles Yorke; "he knows whom to employ and how to work upon different dispositions and constitutions." He wormed his way in among the soldiers, till the Duke of Cumberland rapped out in exasperation, "that devilish Fox and Calcraft get in everywhere". Nothing abashed him; there was a peerage to be earned and no risks must be run. "He directly attacked", said Walpole, "the separate members of the House of Commons; and with so little decorum on the part of either buyer or seller that a shop was publicly opened at the Pay Office, whither the members flocked and received the wages of their venality in bank-bills, even to so low a sum as two hundred pounds for their votes on the Treaty. Twenty-five thousand pounds, as Martin, Secretary of the Treasury, afterwards owned, were issued in one morning, and in a single fortnight a vast majority was purchased to approve the peace." It was with this golden aura hanging around it—so infinitely superior to Wilkes's scurrilous writings — that Parliament met on the 25th of November, 1762.

The people were as downright as Fox in expressing their wishes, only their methods were less refined. A howling mob surrounded the approaches to Parliament, and when Bute drove up, tore him out of his coach and would have torn him to pieces but for the timely arrival of the Guards. But the wishes of the people and the woes of Bute were nothing where coronets were to be earned. He had bought his majority, and by a mixture of money and threats had muzzled the greater number of writers and cartoonists. The Guards would save his skin. All he feared was the voice of Pitt, which might yet revive drugged consciences and snatch the ermine from his shoulders. So far, however, Pitt had proved himself difficult, affecting, as Walpole said, to be a leader without a party. No one could make head or tail of him; even his friends admitted sadly that he was unduly secretive, and when he was asked to join in forming a plan he lost himself and his hearers in lofty and ambiguous phrases.

When Parliament met, to Fox's relief Pitt was tied to his bed by gout—or so it was alleged. The question was brought up at once, and on the 9th of December the debate began in a languid style with Pitt still absent. Fox was overjoyed, quite forgetting that among other things Pitt was a consummate actor. Suddenly, amidst the dull droning of hirelings, there was heard the sound of distant shouting. It drew nearer and nearer; it swelled louder and louder, until at last the doors were flung open, and, amid a thunder of acclamations, Pitt was carried in on the shoulders of his servants and placed on the floor at the bar of the House, dressed from head to foot in black velvet, his hands muffled in gloves, his legs swathed in bandages. It was tremendously dramatic, and an expectant hush settled on the House, while Pitt, with a white and drawn face, to all seeming more dead than alive, crawled painfully to his seat. He spoke for three and a half hours, but with every sign of bodily distress, asking leave to be seated from time to time, and again struggling to his feet, speaking in a low and broken voice as one who had come to utter a few last gasping words before death carried him away. Then to Fox's unutterable relief he betook himself off without voting. The Ministry were left masters of the field, and Fox earned his peerage by 319 votes to 65.

The King was jubilant and the Princess triumphant. "Now", she exclaimed, "my son *is* King of England." The peace treaty was signed at Paris on the 10th of February, 1763.

There is a tendency nowadays to maintain that the treaty was right and that it would have been a mistake to press France too far. What might have happened in other circumstances is always a matter of idle speculation. What did happen is known; from the moment peace was signed France began preparing for the next war. Probably the best and undoubtedly the wittiest comment was made by Wilkes, who remarked: "It is certainly the peace of God, for it passeth all understanding."

(6)

Having gained the first round, Fox, Bute, and the King acted with prompt vigour. Everyone belonging even remotely to the beaten party was stripped of place, pension, and position.

Newcastle, Rockingham, and Grafton were deprived of their Lord-Lieutenancies, Devonshire and others were struck off the list of Privy Councillors. As for the rank and file, "to-day", wrote Walpole on the 20th of December, "has been execution day. Great havoc is made amongst the Duke of Newcastle's friends, who are turned out down to the lowest offices." No one was small enough to be overlooked—excisemen, porters, charwomen, were engulfed in the common disaster. There was a complete overthrow of Pitt's party.

Wilkes lost nothing because he had nothing to lose; but he gained a new dignity in defeat. "The friends of liberty and the revolution", he declared in the next number of the *North Briton*, "have now no countenance but from the nation." That, however, was no reason for desertion or despair. On the contrary, "an opposition, therefore, to measures evidently calculated, on the one hand, to restore our inveterate enemy, France, to her pristine state of greatness, and, on the other hand, to depress the noble spirit of freedom . . . becomes the duty of every honest man, and every sincere lover of his country. It was under such circumstances, at every period, undoubtedly the *duty* of a good man, now it becomes his *glory*; because he is likely in so noble a cause to be reviled and persecuted."

In this debacle Wilkes alone stood firm. Pitt retired to his chamber and his gout; Newcastle spent his time writing querulous letters; the rank and file took bribes or were kicked into oblivion. Only the *North Briton* kept the flag flying and focused the indignation of the country. Wilkes even went a step farther, and on the 15th of March, 1763, brought out an edition of Ben Jonson's *Fall of Mortimer*, with a Dedication to Lord Bute, written in his best style of irony. Defeat seemed to key Wilkes up to his highest pitch, for never was a public man more mercilessly flayed.

Nor were Wilkes's irrepressible spirits damped. "He has writ", Walpole confided to George Montagu, "a dedication too to an old play, *The Fall of Mortimer*, that is wormwood, and he had the impudence t'other day to ask Dyson if he was going to the Treasury, 'because', said he, 'a friend of mine has dedicated a play to Lord Bute, and it is usual to give dedicators something; I wish you would put his lordship in mind of it.' "

CHAPTER VIII
NO. 45

(1)

BUTE continued his mischievous career till the 8th of April, 1763, when he suddenly resigned for reasons that no one knew. History has given Wilkes the credit, maintaining that he wrote Bute out, just as he wrote the *Briton* and *Auditor* to a standstill in the previous February. But history is pleased to exaggerate. Though the victims were anxious enough to escape the tingling irritation of weekly attacks they disappeared from public life for other and more obvious reasons. The Government papers came to an end when the peace was signed and they were no longer necessary. Bute left for the same reason, merely delaying his departure till he had introduced the Budget and named his successors. George Grenville became First Lord, with Halifax and Egremont as Secretaries of State, all three being the faithful, and as yet inconspicuous, henchmen of Bute.

Wilkes was in France at the time, having crossed over to place Polly in a school, but he returned on the 11th. Whether because he was abroad, or because of Bute's resignation, no *North Briton* had appeared since the 2nd. Wilkes was certainly hoping that Bute's fall would be followed by Pitt's return to power.

Finding his hopes frustrated, he issued an advertisement on the 13th, declaring that as he had opposed "a single, insolent, incapable, despotic Minister", so he was equally ready "to combat the *triple-headed, Cerberean* administration, if the Scot is to assume that motley form". He soon found that it would be necessary to redeem his promise, and on the 23rd of April, 1763, published the forty-fifth and last *North Briton*.

This famous paper was written with no thought of its actual effects. It was one of Wilkes's more sober and serious efforts, restrained and a trifle dull, breathing a profound regard for the King, which was far greater than the King deserved and immensely unlike anything Wilkes felt. The criticisms of the Government in which he indulged came from Pitt and were as legitimate as they were sound. Wilkes had happened to be present while Pitt and Temple were discussing a draft of the Speech, and it was on the basis of this conversation that the offending article was constructed. By way of preface Wilkes laid down in a clear and attractive form the doctrine that Ministers were responsible for the contents of the King's Speech. To Wilkes himself, and indeed to Parliament as a whole, this was a mere commonplace. Pitt had voiced the doctrine in the House as far back as 1742, and Wilkes himself in 1761. It was not, however, a commonplace with the people, and as Wilkes believed, and intended to say, that passages of the Speech were simply untrue, he felt that some such introduction was at once wise and conciliatory. Nothing could have been more correct and decent than his handling of the point. The King was represented, not only as more sinned against than sinning, but as deserving the fullest sympathy of his subjects. It was the Ministers alone who were to blame for putting lies into his mouth, and their blame was enhanced by the King's shining merits.

But however the paper came to be written and whatever it contained, George Grenville decided to take a strong line. The idea of prosecuting the *North Briton* had been mooted before, but had come to nothing. This last paper gave a better opportunity and one not likely to recur. To the nation at large the doctrine of Ministerial responsibility was a complete novelty, and there were many people who were genuinely shocked at what they could only regard as a direct charge of falsehood against the King. Nothing would be easier than to create odium, while the change of administration gave an excuse for a change of policy. Lastly the King, who had been fretting and fuming at the *North Briton* all these months and was very far from allowing his Ministers any responsibility, saw fit to gather the thrust into his own bosom, and loudly demanded action.

(2)

Government proceeded with a proper sense of responsibility. The paper was published on a Saturday, and after sleeping on it for the week-end Halifax asked the Law Officers of the Crown what action could be taken. The Attorney-General, Charles Yorke, and the Solicitor-General, Sir Fletcher Norton, took two days to consider the matter, and then gave an opinion as long-winded as it was long-pondered. The paper, they declared, was "a most infamous and seditious libel, tending to inflame the minds and alienate the affections of the people from His Majesty, and to excite them to traitorous insurrections against the Government, and therefore punishable as a mis-demeanour of the highest nature in due course of law by indictment for information".

Thus fortified, Halifax issued a warrant for the arrest of "the authors, printers, and publishers" of the *North Briton*, and for the seizure of their papers. As the warrant did not name the persons to be arrested, it was commonly known as a General Warrant, but it was in no sense peculiar. Such warrants had been employed for centuries past in similar cases and lay in the Secretary of State's office as printed forms. Yet simple, and indeed routine, as his action seemed to be, Halifax had put his name to a document which was destined to become notorious in the annals of the law—though it was reserved for Wilkes to crown it with immortal ridicule.

Armed with this pregnant warrant, the four "messengers" to whom it was addressed proceeded to the house of a certain Dryden Leach, who was erroneously supposed to be the printer. They entered in the middle of the night and dragged the unfortunate man out of bed, bundled up his papers, and haled him and his employees off to justice. They next rounded up Kearsley, the real publisher, with his workmen and papers, and shortly afterwards Balfe, the real printer, once more with his workmen and papers. By this time forty-eight people were trembling in very literal apprehension, and the pile of documents was growing formidable.

Busily active in the cause of justice, as he conceived it, Halifax examined Kearsley and Balfe on the 29th, and extorted from them an admission that they had received No. 45 from Wilkes. Beyond this they could not go. It was still a matter of conjecture, however small the doubt, if Wilkes had actually penned the words or not. But even if he were proved the author, that fact merely added to the complications of a case sufficiently knotty. Wilkes, as a Member of Parliament, was entitled to his privileges, among them being freedom from arrest except in certain rather ill-defined circumstances. With commendable caution Halifax once more approached the Law Officers to know "whether Wilkes could be arrested".

This was an extremely nice question which the Law Officers were by no means anxious to tackle, and with a finesse that did more credit to their hopes of self-preservation than to their ideas of loyalty, they expressed a verbal opinion alone. Halifax, however, was not to be fooled, and though content to work on this verbal intimation for the moment, insisted on a written answer. It was duly delivered on the morning of the 30th of April, and declared that "the publication of a libel being a breach of the peace, is not a case of privilege". Never was caution more justified, never red tape more happily tied; this written opinion ultimately saved Government, indirectly but decisively. It also cut the throat of the Attorney-General— a terrible penalty for a reluctant error.

Meanwhile, on the evening of the 29th, the messengers were sent out again, armed with the original warrant, to arrest Wilkes. The choleric Egremont ordered them to drag Wilkes out of bed, but Halifax, who was much more fitted to hold a responsible office, told them "to treat him with great civility". As a matter of fact it made no difference what instructions they gave; Wilkes and the messengers had long since reached an understanding.

(3)

The truth is that although Grenville thought he was taking a strong line and the Secretaries imagined they were surprising Wilkes, the three of them were puppets dancing to his strings. If the drama of his arrest is approached only from the angle of Government, its full flavour is lost. Wilkes was no mere libeller, no random pedlar of abusive paragraphs. He had from the very beginning laid a plot for the Ministry, deeply pondered and carefully planned, and he had laid it with a full knowledge of the risk to himself as well as of the end which he had in view. Wilkes's sole object in writing the *North Briton* was to restore Pitt to power, and he proposed to do it, not by "writing the Ministry out", but by tempting them to their own destruction.

The mainspring of his whole plot was that Government should arrest him, and arrest him for political reasons under a General Warrant. It was this requirement which governed the tone of his papers. While they must need be provocative, at all costs they must not be libellous. So from beginning to end Wilkes submitted them to Counsel before publication, and when Churchill was introduced, warned him "to consult Charles Sayer, Esq., No. 1, Inner Temple, King's Bench Walk". Thus he ensured, as far as might be, that the arrest would be political. That Government would act under a General Warrant was probable, and to make it more certain Wilkes steadily preserved his anonymity, though the authorship was an open secret.

But Wilkes was too wary not to face the possibility of the unexpected. If in spite of everything Government acted under some other form of warrant, Wilkes had another line of defence. He would plead parliamentary privilege. What this covered was not altogether clear, but it certainly did not extend to treason, and when in the General Warrant Government described the paper as "seditious and treasonable", they swept that line of defence aside. It so happened, however, that in a subsequent warrant committing him to the Tower they dropped the word "treasonable," substituting "infamous", and Wilkes, who for various reasons had to fall back on privilege, was never tired of pointing to a change so full of significance for himself.

But to guard against mishaps was only secondary. Wilkes's ardent hope was that Government would act according to his plan, when they would be more than hoist with their own petard. Locked away in his desk was a copy of the General Warrant, which he had read and re-read more than once, and his clear and logical mind, trained on the magistrates' bench, had hit upon the overwhelming fact that it was illegal. From the course of subsequent events it appears that he had taken this tremendous discovery to Pratt, Lord Chief Justice of Common Pleas, and the friend of Pitt, who had confirmed him in his opinion. Indeed, it seems clear that Pratt and Pitt and Wilkes had discussed both lines of defence, and while the Lord Chief Justice had promised support on the one, the Great Commoner had promised support on the other.

Wilkes's plot, which had all the simplicity of genius, was based upon his great discovery and these two promises of support. His idea was that immediately on his arrest Temple should apply for a writ of Habeas Corpus addressed to the messengers, and make his application not, as was usual, to the Court of King's Bench, but to the Court of Common Pleas. This would result in the messengers appearing before Pratt, and producing the General Warrant as authority for arresting their prisoner. Pratt would there and then pronounce the warrant illegal and release Wilkes. Such an incident could easily be magnified into an attack on the liberty of the subject, on the strength of which the Government would be discredited and Pitt brought back to power as the people's champion. There was only one risk. Everything would depend upon Temple acting promptly, and it was therefore essential that Wilkes should have notice of his intended arrest a short while before it was actually put into execution. It was to ensure this that Wilkes had made friends with the official messengers.

(4)

By good fortune the Chief Messenger, Carrington, was ill, and Wilkes's particular friend, Blackmore, was in charge. As the "insult" was large enough, Wilkes was well posted with news, and from the moment the General Warrant set out on its omnivorous course was waiting with impatience for his own turn. So anxious was he to get the first intimation that he spent most of his time at Blackmore's house, more particularly the 29th, when he was encouraging Kearsley all the morning and making merry with Leach in the evening. It was whilst he was still there that Blackmore received his orders. As it was then too late to obtain the writ of Habeas Corpus, Wilkes calmly remanded himself till the morning and remained in Blackmore's company, bubbling over with excitement, until midnight, when he returned home.

Appearances, however, had to be kept up, and so, while they were careful not to break in, the messengers posted themselves round Wilkes's house at an early hour next morning. Shortly afterwards, at about 6 a.m., Wilkes appeared, and according to plan chose the route which brought him face to face with Blackmore. The two friends greeted each other pleasantly, and Wilkes passed on his way. All would have been well, but that an unbribed messenger on another route noticed the meeting and, not unnaturally surprised, rushed up to learn the meaning. Blackmore, whose cupidity was greater than his inventive powers, could think of no more plausible story than that "on Mr. Wilkes's telling him he was going to speak to a friend in the Temple and promising to call at Blackmore's house that morning, Blackmore let him go".

Wilkes's business did not take him to the Temple or anywhere near it. He went straight to an alehouse in the Old Bailey, over which was the workshop of Balfe, the printer, taking with him one of Balfe's employees, John Williams by name. The premises had been locked up on Balfe's arrest, but Wilkes, nothing daunted, borrowed a ladder from a neighbouring bricklayer and sent Williams up with orders to break in through the window, and after taking an impression of the *North Briton* No. 46 to bring down both the proof and the type. Wilkes, in the meantime, kicked his heels in "a room upon one pair of stairs". Williams printed off a copy, sent it to Wilkes by the bricklayer, and then laboriously carried the type down the ladder. On arriving at the bottom he found that Wilkes had left, and so carried the type up again. In doing so he accidentally dropped one of the three "forms", which fell to pieces.

It is usually assumed that the object of this rather mysterious visit was to destroy all trace of No. 46, so as to baffle the Government. But the explanation is clearly wrong. Government knew nothing about No. 46, and were no more interested in it than in the first forty-four numbers. Moreover, if that had been his intention, Wilkes would have given definite orders, or more probably would have seen to the work himself. What he was actually doing was to make sure that the paper was preserved, and a few weeks later he printed it in the volume edition of his *North Briton*.

On returning home Wilkes ran into the unbribed messenger, who was still fretting over his apparent escape. It was an unfortunate meeting, but Wilkes was equal to the occasion. He demanded to see the warrant, and then "I told him the warrant did not respect me. I advised him to be very civil, and to use no violence in the street, for if he attempted force, I would put him to death in the instant, but if he would come quietly to my house, I would convince him of the illegality of the warrant." So by a little display of force and argument he got into his own house again with the messenger at his heels.

Here was Wilkes in a pretty pickle. By some means or other he must keep his enemies at bay till the Court of Common Pleas was open and he had sent a message to Temple. How was he to do it with an unbribed messenger in the house, clinging to him like a shadow and making the despatch of a message almost impossible and the prospect of arrest much more imminent? With great difficulty, but imperturbable humour, Wilkes kept up his end, carrying on a bantering conversation with the unwelcome intruder, whilst constables and messengers were passing and repassing in a continual stream between his house and the Secretaries' a few doors away, trying to persuade the wary bird into their net, and considerably puzzled how to do it.

At last the chance appearance of Almon eased a situation that was growing intolerable. Through him Wilkes smuggled the news to Temple, and then after a short interval submitted with a fine show of reluctance to be carried off.

Being wholly confident in the result, Wilkes bore himself at the Secretaries' with a suave insolence and care-free wit. He swaggered into "a great apartment fronting the Park", where he found himself before the two Secretaries and an array of officials sitting at a long table with all the grave appurtenances of inquisition. Nothing abashed, Wilkes fenced contemptuously with Halifax and flashed stinging sarcasms at Egremont, thoroughly enjoying the embarrassment of the one and not at all dismayed by the angry growls of the other. Halifax, always courteous, expressed his great concern at seeing Wilkes in such a position. Wilkes agreed heartily; a set of "ignorant, insolent, and despotic Ministers" had dared to arrest him under an illegal warrant, and he would have the great satisfaction of impeaching them on the first day of Parliament. As for the series of questions which Halifax had carefully prepared, Wilkes swept them on one side. It was obvious, he remarked, that the Secretaries were badly in need of enlightenment, but he declined to assist their darkness—he would not open his lips, not even, he added, turning sharply on Egremont, "could you employ tortures". In despair, Halifax ended a very one-sided examination by offering him his choice of prison, a choice that Wilkes refused on the ground that he never received an obligation from anyone but a friend. His main need at the moment was justice and liberty, both of which he demanded.

The upshot was that Halifax signed a warrant for committing Wilkes to the Tower, while Egremont, exasperated beyond endurance, persuaded the King to cashier him from his colonelcy of the Militia.

(5)

Meanwhile Temple was busy "pursuing the proper measures", but found difficulties in the way. The Court of Common Pleas was not accustomed to the issue of writs of Habeas Corpus, and though Pratt granted the application without demur, the preparation of the document took an unconscionable time. Temple did his best by sending a message to the Secretaries' house that the writ had been granted, but it was not actually served on the messengers till about 8 p.m. By that time Wilkes was out of their custody and safely in the Tower, so that they could not bring him into court.

This impasse produced a quaint *bouleversement*. Carteret Webb, the Solicitor to the Treasury, acutely aware that failure to produce the prisoner could only create prejudice, spent a worried week-end entreating Wilkes and his solicitors to apply for a fresh writ addressed to the Lieutenant of the Tower. If only they would act, he would offer every facility.

But Wilkes's perplexity was as great as Webb's eagerness. He had been committed to the Tower on a new warrant in which he was named, and which was perfectly in order. The Lieutenant would, of course, produce this warrant—and where was Wilkes's plot? So Wilkes and his friends, who had been clamouring for a writ on the Saturday, maintained a stubborn reserve during the week-end; and on the Monday in the Court of Common Pleas Webb, who had shrugged an indifferent shoulder at Temple's message two days before, was urgently assuring Wilkes's Counsel, Sergeant Glynn, that if he would only move for a new writ "Mr. Wilkes should be brought into court in an hour's time". Glynn, wholly at a loss, insisted on another day for preparing his case.

So Wilkes languished in prison till the Tuesday, by no means too certain what would become of him. He had now to rely on his plea of privilege, and his main scheme had apparently vanished. Yet in hopes of snatching something out of the ruins, Wilkes maintained a brave attitude, making the most of the prejudice in his favour, created partly by the failure of the messengers to produce him, and still more by the words of the warrant, which ordered him to be kept a "close prisoner". To Webb's dismay the Lieutenant had taken his orders very literally, refusing admittance to Wilkes's friends and solicitors. This was, of course, a complete mistake, and was put right directly Halifax returned from his week-end, but it aroused great feeling. It is also possible that Wilkes had not fully grasped the blow that had fallen.

However, on the Tuesday he enjoyed a great personal triumph. The court was crowded, and Wilkes delivered a short but very confident speech, in which he complained of his unparalleled grievance, and expressed the hope that "the consequences will teach Ministers of arbitrary principles that the liberty of an English subject is not to be sported away with impunity in this cruel and despotic manner". At the conclusion the crowd cheered boisterously and were gravely rebuked by Pratt.

That was easy. The decision of the case was much more difficult, and Pratt, as puzzled as Glynn, deferred expressing an opinion till the following Friday, when Wilkes scored another personal triumph. He was far from regretting his extra confinement because it afforded Pratt "an opportunity of doing, upon mature reflection and repeated examination, the more signal justice to my country. The liberty of all peers and gentlemen, and (what touches me more sensibly) that of all the middling and inferior sort of people who stand most in need of protection, is in my case this day to be finally decided upon; a question of such importance as to determine at once whether

English liberty be a reality or a shadow." This speech would have been much more to the point if Pratt had been about to deal with the General Warrant. The question whether a Member of Parliament could or could not be arrested for libel was not really a matter that touched "the liberty of all peers and gentlemen", still less "that of all the middling and inferior sort of people".

Pratt delivered judgment very carefully. The warrant of commitment was "not illegal", but Wilkes was covered by his privilege as a Member of Parliament. Such privilege extended to everything but treason, felony, and breach of the peace. Wilkes was accused of writing a libel, but a libel was none of the three, "and consequently could not be sufficient to destroy the privilege of Parliament". This was the unanimous opinion of the court.

Wilkes was discharged amid tremendous enthusiasm. Cheer after cheer broke out, and Wilkes was escorted home in triumph. But the really vital point was that Pratt's verdict cut right across the opinion expressed by Charles Yorke, the Attorney-General, on the strength of which Halifax had issued the General Warrant.

Among the spectators at this famous trial was an old man making a rapid sketch of the prisoner from behind a pillar. Shortly afterwards his sketch appeared as an exceedingly clever and diabolical cartoon. It was Hogarth taking his revenge.

CHAPTER IX

A DEEP-LAID SCHEME

(1)

WITH the release of Wilkes the position was ripe for compromise, but Wilkes at once took steps to make compromise
impossible. While he had been closeted with the Secretaries
his drawers and cupboards had been ransacked and his papers
seized. Directly on his return home he wrote to the Secretaries,
"I find that my house has been robbed, and am informed that
the stolen goods are in the possession of one or both of your
Lordships. I therefore insist that you do forthwith return
them." Such a letter was in no sense conciliatory, and by way
of emphasis Wilkes applied at Bow Street for a warrant to
search the Secretaries' house. When the acting magistrate,
John Spinnage, rather nervously refused, Wilkes sent an
account to the papers with copies of the correspondence.

His object is clear. His mine had been exploded, but by
the mischance of the unbribed messenger and the warrant of
commitment to the Tower, it had not produced the desired
results. The expected cry of the people's liberties had been
whittled down to parliamentary privilege—interesting, but not
all-important. But the incident was not yet over, and it might
still be possible to guide the plot back to its prescribed course.
Hence the provocation; hence the instant closing of the door
on any hope of compromise.

In later life Wilkes agreed that his letter had been unneces-
sarily abrupt and "unbecoming", and explained this lapse of
good manners by the natural jubilation of the moment. But
the language was one thing, the policy another; and while he
half regretted the actual terms, he never regretted the letter
itself. On the contrary, he claimed that "the thought was
undoubtedly just", and stressed the fact that the letter had
been approved by Temple, Cotes, and Glynn. Whatever Temple
and Cotes might have been, Glynn was both an able lawyer

and a temperate man; he must have known that this letter would reopen the whole question and make compromise impossible.

Wilkes's action and Glynn's attitude are important as sign-posts. The plot to which the facts point so clearly was never openly admitted, and because of subsequent events has never yet been recognized. Every hint must be treasured, since none of the actors in the drama had any reason to explain his motives, and some had the best of reasons for hiding them.

(2)

Of all the actors Pitt had the strongest grounds for reserve. At the outset open participation would have ruined the plot; at the end denial was, or seemed to be, imperative. Pitt covered up his tracks well, and the impression he desired to make has persisted to this day. Yet puzzling as his behaviour was, it is not inexplicable.

The *North Briton* began on the 5th of June. Before Wilkes was able to see Temple, Pitt paid a visit to Stowe and "expressed himself very warmly against all kinds of political writing, as productive of great mischief". Temple passed on the protest to Wilkes, who took it very lightly. According to his own account, "Mr. Wilkes observed to Lord Temple that such a declaration was in character from Mr. Pitt, who ought to fear the shadow of a pen, that he was undoubtedly the best speaker and the worst writer of his age, that he would do well to harangue the five hundred deputies of the people in the cause of liberty, and the *North Briton* would endeavour to animate the nation at large." It was a curious remark for him to make. On any interpretation he was writing his paper to vindicate Pitt, who was the hero to Bute's villain, and it is inconceivable that he would have continued if Pitt had maintained his strong objection.

Something happened; though what was never divulged. Its effect, however, was obvious. The Opposition "*soon* warmly espoused the *North Briton*". So apparently did Pitt. At all events in the following October he protested strongly against a proposal put forward by Warburton, Bishop of Gloucester, for a law to prevent the abuses inherent in the liberty of the Press. "Allow me to observe", wrote Pitt, "that the bare supposition of a possibility that the guardians of liberty could ever be induced to pass such a law appears to me big with danger." It would "be breaking the way for an idea that must revolt every friend of liberty". In such vigorous terms did Pitt express his reverence for "the sacred liberty of the Press, unshackled by any general preventive law, in any case possible to suppose", at a time when the *North Briton* was flooding the country.

Had Pitt really disliked these papers, he had an excellent opportunity of giving his views to the world about a month later. The *North Briton* was not the only Opposition paper; there was another of long standing and no particular merit, known as the *Monitor*. Towards the end of November Government suddenly issued a General Warrant for the arrest of the authors and publishers of this paper. Pitt took precisely no steps either to vindicate the liberty of the Press or to crush an abusive periodical. Instead, he gave an interview to Wilkes, who was trying, though without success, to persuade Beardmore, the editor, to fight the General Warrant. Writing to Churchill on the 2nd of December, Wilkes said, "I passed three hours to-day in Pitt's bedchamber at Hayes. He talks as you write —as no other man ever did or could. I am to have Sayer to dine with me." It is incredible to suppose that Wilkes and Pitt during that three hours' conversation never touched upon the *Monitor*, nor the possibility of the *North Briton's* arrest. Any lingering doubt that remains is swept away by the subject-matter of the next *North Briton*, which appeared two days after the interview. This dealt solely with the arrest of the *Monitor*, telling Government that "to drop the prosecution is, in the last instance, a desertion of the public". It went even farther, and by every legitimate means dared Government to take action also against the *North Briton*. By one means or another both Pitt and Wilkes were anxious to get the question into the courts.

The connection between Pitt and No. 45 has already been mentioned. At the very least this series of coincidences suggests that Pitt and Wilkes were in close touch throughout the progress of the paper, and that Pitt was standing behind Wilkes in his endeavours. That he subsequently denied Wilkes is a matter of common history, and the explanation of his puzzling behaviour may easily be found in a study of his character and the vicissitudes of his career.

The long uphill road to power and the blaze of splendour which had there awaited him had left their indelible mark on Pitt. Thenceforward he neither could nor would head a mere Opposition. He was resolved to regain his crown, if he ever did, on a wave of national enthusiasm that with one sweep would overthrow his enemies and replace him in his rightful position. The difficulty was to find that tidal wave. No sign of it appeared in the humdrum schemes of the Opposition, but Wilkes's plot could not fail to produce a great constitutional point, perhaps two—liberty both for the Press and the people, and the sanctity of parliamentary privilege. The temptation was sufficient to overcome Pitt's natural distaste for abusive papers, and the consciousness, deep down and half-smothered, of guilty connivance would amply account for the strange twists of his conduct, and in the end the fiery outburst that came to scorch Wilkes's reputation—Wilkes who was damned, not because he had tried, but because he had failed.

CHAPTER X

A FAMILY INTRIGUE

(1)

WILKES was arrested toward the end of April, and Parliament was not due to meet again till the winter session. There were therefore some six months in which Wilkes and the Opposition could elaborate their plans and Government take such steps as it thought fit.

With Temple to help on the financial side and Glynn on the legal, Wilkes at once engineered a masterly scheme, which should bring the main issue to a head. His idea was that all the forty-nine persons, including himself, who had been arrested under the General Warrant, should begin proceedings before Pratt for wrongful arrest. The legality of the warrant would thus be raised directly, and, as Wilkes knew in advance, forty-nine verdicts would be obtained against the Government. No Ministry could hope to stand against the storm of indignation which would follow, still less a Ministry already unpopular.

The scheme could be made more effective and still more safe by being long drawn out. Dryden Leach and his employees, who had had no hand in the *North Briton*, were obviously the proper persons to open the campaign. Government had no case against them, while they had a twofold case against the Government; as innocent persons they should not have been arrested at all, still less under an illegal warrant. The verdict was a foregone conclusion, and thereafter Wilkes and the others could press forward with complete confidence. Leach's printers were persuaded to bring actions against the messengers, while Wilkes reserved to himself the right of proceeding against the main offenders, the higher officials and the two Secretaries of State.

The printers' action was heard in July, and resulted in a signal victory. Public feeling was running high, and the jury awarded damages commensurate with their feelings rather than the plaintiffs' sufferings. This was all to the good, but more important still was the decision on the legality of the warrant. Government asked that the jury should confine themselves to a special verdict on the facts, leaving the points of law to be decided by the judges. Wilkes had anticipated this move and had distributed handbills explaining the right of juries to give a general verdict if they chose. Pratt, with a sense of the responsibility resting on him and conscious that the legality of the warrant had little bearing on this particular case, was inclined to urge a special verdict, but the jury remained firm. Thereupon Pratt directed them on the points of law, expressing his opinion that the warrant was not legal.

Government at once put in a Bill of Exceptions, which was in effect an appeal on the point of law. They were, of course, amply entitled to do so, but it was unlikely to promote their popularity, and it offered Wilkes a further opportunity. The Bill had the effect of putting off the payment of damages until the printers had taken the Bill into court and obtained a decision on it. Wilkes realized that if the appeal were deferred until all the cases against the Government had been tried, his position would be infinitely stronger. So many more verdicts would have been obtained, so many more juries would have awarded heavy damages, so many more pronouncements would have been made by Pratt. It would be correspondingly more difficult for the judges to overthrow these verdicts; and if they did would create a correspondingly greater prejudice against a Government which sheltered itself behind a technical point against the expressed wishes of the people. So the printers were persuaded to wait, and the other cases against Government pushed on.

Government made one more effort to stop proceedings by an appeal for a fresh hearing on the ground that the damages awarded to the printers were excessive. Pratt dismissed the appeal on the 26th of November, and in doing so once more declared the warrants to be illegal and oppressive.

On the 6th of December Wilkes gained his action against Wood, being awarded £1,000 damages. On this occasion Pratt was more decided than ever, declaring that his opinion was given "upon the maturest consideration", and adding that while the full bench could override him, yet "if these higher jurisdictions should declare my opinion erroneous . . . I must say, I shall always consider it as a rod of iron for the chastisement of the people of Great Britain".

To conclude the purely legal question, the General Warrant was ultimately discussed by the whole bench of judges, who all endorsed Pratt's view.

(2)

Directly his scheme of a series of prosecutions had been launched Wilkes was at a loose end. He could only wait for the trials to come on. Being essentially a man of action, and perhaps over-confident, this pause irked him, and he began to turn once more towards his pen. But in spite of his release and in spite of popular feeling, no printer was prepared to accept his work. Accordingly, in an evil day for himself, for Pitt, and for the Opposition, he decided to erect a private printing-press in his own house.

His first efforts were one or two pamphlets dealing with his own case. Towards the end of May, however, he decided to print off a few copies of the *Essay on Woman*. He had for some time past been contemplating a private edition for the amusement of his friends, and a plate for the frontispiece had already been prepared. It was the idle work of an idle moment, and went to prove the adage of Satan and idle hands. Exactly how much of the piece was set up in type is uncertain and hardly matters. On the 20th of June he suspended this work to bring out an edition of the *North Briton* in book form. It is said that his friends doubted the wisdom of this course; but there was very little reason against it, and one reason in its favour which probably appealed to Wilkes. At the end of the original No. 45 he had advertised a reprint in volume form, and Wilkes always prided himself on keeping his word. He is also reported to have had a bet on the matter. Whatever his motives, the book was brought out and resulted in a heavy loss. It was finished by July 17th.

(3)

Meanwhile Government and the Opposition had not been idle. Government possessed one potential advantage—they were nominally a united body. It is true that Halifax if left to himself might have let the matter drop, but the King was furious and Egremont overbearing, and the two egged each other on. Lastly, Grenville was finding the King difficult and so the more readily accepted Wilkes as a scapegoat. Between them they fell easily into the trap of Wilkes's letter, allowed themselves to be provoked, and definitely ordered a prosecution, though in view of Pratt's decision that the case was covered by privilege they were very vague as to how it could be carried through. They also dallied with an ill-defined hope of getting Wilkes expelled from the House.

Their decision was most unwelcome to the Attorney-General, Charles Yorke, to whom the work would fall, and he hung back reluctant. His attitude had its effect, and as the first outbreak of petulance simmered down Government became thoroughly alarmed at their position.

Meanwhile the prospects of the Opposition were of the rosiest. The suppression of a popular paper gave them the sympathy of the people; the sight of Government exerting its full force against an individual stirred up all the natural British antipathy to bullying; the question of privilege was ready-made to present when Parliament met, and with the least luck before they faced the House Government would have been found guilty of using an illegal warrant. That this over-whelming advantage was not driven home was due to two main factors—Pitt's want of candour and the subtle machinations of Hardwicke.

Hardwicke at this point was an old man, seventy-three years of age. His life had been splendidly successful. Born of humble parents in 1690, he had been called to the Bar in 1715, and four years later had entered Parliament. From that moment he never looked back. At thirty he was Solicitor-General; at thirty-four Attorney-General; a peer at forty-three, and Lord Chancellor four years later. Throughout the Pelham administration he had been the unseen controller of England's destiny, and in 1754 was rewarded with an earldom. When Pitt became Prime Minister he had retired to the background content with his honours and position; but while refusing office he was not allowed to lose his interest in affairs. He had been the lifelong friend and confidant of Newcastle, the brains behind that empty façade, and Newcastle's constant need of advice kept him informed of events. When Pitt fell and Newcastle was driven out, Hardwicke became automatically a member of the Opposition, concerned in their plans and anxious for their restoration. But his position was complicated. On his withdrawal from active life he had tended to live more and more in the ambitions of his children. Of these he was proudest of Charles Yorke, who appeared to be following in his father's footsteps as a brilliant lawyer and great parliamentarian. The appearance was deceptive, Yorke's reputation being the reflex of his father's greatness; but paternal pride blinded the imperious old man's eyes, and paternal love, pouring upon the vacillating, amorphous young man a shower of wisdom, strength, and experience, gave a fictitious vigour to an otherwise backboneless character. Hardwicke regarded the Woolsack as belonging to Yorke by a kind of hereditary right, and this ingrained faith, in which his son eagerly shared, muddied the stream of their political loyalties. Yorke shaped his career half on his father's principles, half on his own knock-kneed opportunism, and Hardwicke struggled manfully to reconcile the two. For years he had watched lovingly over the young man's progress, glowing with pride at his meteoric rise, and employing his keen, piercing intellect to supply

Yorke's deficiencies, to advise and warn, and above all to save from mistakes.

All seemed set on a prosperous course, when on the 30th of April, 1763, Webb visited the old man to discuss the Wilkes affair. In the course of conversation he showed Hardwicke the Attorney's written opinion, and Hardwicke's shrewd eyes at once saw the red light ahead. As a lawyer, fiercely tenacious of the Law's rights, he was prepared to defend General Warrants; after all, justice was justice, and any method of bringing offenders to book was good enough. But privilege was another matter. It was full of snags and difficulties, only too likely to set Parliament and the courts by the ears, and here was his son rashly placing his views on paper. Full of apprehension, Hardwicke sat down to write to Yorke: "I desired Mr. Webb not to produce the opinion; or if he did, to take it back and to manage it properly."

The apprehensions growing in his mind were confirmed when a few days later Pratt's verdict upset Yorke's opinion; they were enhanced by the attitude of the Opposition. From the outset Temple had strained every nerve to whip up party feeling; directly Wilkes was in the Tower he had rounded up the leaders of the Opposition, urging them to visit Wilkes and lend him their support. The more responsible men hesitated, with a natural desire to see how the cat would jump; but the younger men were enthusiastic, while some of the notables were influenced by the forces arrayed against Wilkes. The number who actually went to the Tower was not unimposing, and meanwhile the town was buzzing with excitement, and the people generally in a ferment. Everything pointed to a fierce struggle by which Government could win very little and might lose a great deal. If things went wrong Yorke's opinion would be remembered against him and his reputation blasted for the time at least.

That was bad enough, but it would inevitably lead to worse. In the race for the Great Seal Charles Yorke had only one dangerous rival—Pratt, who, as it happened, was favoured by

Pitt. There had been a time when Pitt and Yorke were on friendly terms. In Pitt's famous administration Yorke had accepted the post of Solicitor-General (to the disgust of Hardwicke, who had hoped he might be Attorney), and a month after Pitt's fall had made a speech in his favour and resigned. But weakly ambitious, he had allowed Bute to tempt him back and had gone over to the enemy in return for the post of Attorney. There he had given his sanction to the Treaty of Peace, and when Bute resigned had continued to hold office under Grenville. It was inevitable that a coolness should grow up between Pitt and himself. Apart from this family matter, Hardwicke had his own cause of irritation with Pitt; it was the old story of two strong, imperious wills clashing. Hardwicke was in the legal world much what Pitt was in Parliament, the high-handed autocrat; and Pitt had displayed at times an impatience of legal views. He had dared before now to flout Hardwicke's opinion; he had dared to lay down "as a maxim that *the lawyers are not to be regarded in questions of liberty*"; and the memory rankled.

There were many reasons, therefore, why Hardwicke should dislike Pitt and fear his return to power. And at this juncture it became painfully evident to the watchful father that if the Wilkes affair led to a parliamentary struggle it was only too likely to restore Pitt, and then the fatal written opinion would become Pratt's passport to the Woolsack and Yorke's certificate of political suicide. At all costs the Wilkes affair must be hushed up; Government must swallow their pride, and the Opposition be warned off. Hardwicke set the whole of his mind, trained in the logic of the law and experienced in the finesse of diplomacy, to achieve this end.

A chance soon presented itself. The affair had hardly begun when three or four of the younger and more ardent members of the Opposition rushed down to Claremont, bubbling over with excitement, to break the news to Newcastle and assure him that "the City and the Suburbs are in the utmost alarm at these proceedings, which they call illegal and oppressive".

This urgent mob of enthusiasm threw the elderly intriguer into a violent agitation, and almost swept him off his dithering legs. But constant to a lifelong habit, before finally throwing in his lot with the fire-eaters, Newcastle wrote to Hardwicke for advice.

If Newcastle had not been so easy to handle, Hardwicke's reply would have been masterly. He appealed to the fussy old gentleman's sense of propriety and played to perfection on his nerves. No gentleman could have written such a libel, which "is certainly not only unjustifiable, but inexcusable"; as for the warrant, there might perhaps be objections, but there were also precedents, "perhaps in your Grace's own time". So one way or another it would be better "not to suffer yourself to be too much possessed and warmed by the discourses of the zealous young gentlemen"; a little prudence, a little caution—"all I mean is that we should not too hastily make *cause commun* with Mr. Wilkes".

So for the moment he left the wriggling doubts to do their work, well knowing that the awful question of precedents would terrify the old humbug and the want of decency affront the punctilious nobleman. He was justified. Newcastle wrote a quaking letter of thanks: "the whole is a very unlucky affair. I always feared that the *North Briton* of Saturday last would bring on some examination and prosecution. To be sure it was wrote with very little consideration, or caution, and in times like these people should be cautious." Hardwicke knew that he would be writing similar letters all round, as indeed he was, admitting with a tremble in his pen that "I fancy Lord Temple and perhaps my Lord Chief Justice Pratt are a little mistaken when they call the warrant *illegal* and *unprecedented*. If I remember right, I have signed many in the same form and words."

Having set fire to the train, he watched the effects, and if his paternal anxiety had not been so keen he might have been cynically amused. He also kept Yorke informed of developments, regardless of the rank treachery of his methods, except

for the reiterated caution "burn this letter as soon as read".
The news he had to pass on was satisfactory. "I could perceive that my last night's conference with the noble Duke
had produced a good effect, for his Grace had seen several
of these gentlemen this morning. The nature of the libel, as
it regards the King personally, as now explained to them,
strikes many of them in a way they did not feel it before";
and again, "their topsail is lowered since Saturday".

(4)

As both Government and the Opposition confided in the
old man there was a touch of farce in his efforts to save his
son. There was also more than a touch of pathos, since these
efforts were to end in his son's suicide. Death spared him that
knowledge, and for the moment, with tireless patience, he
damped the Opposition's ardour and revived Government's
drooping spirits.

But with unerring instinct he realized that Pitt alone really
mattered. Government were only too anxious to escape from
the net; he knew as much from his son, and if he still had
doubts they were swept aside when Egremont came on the
13th of May to make overtures. As for the other Opposition
leaders, they were perfectly easy to bamboozle. Not one of
them had the least idea of constitutional principles; not one
of them cared a pin for the liberty of the Press, and being,
peers they were quite uninterested in parliamentary privilege.
It was simplicity itself to distress them with the enormity of
libelling the King and fuddle their modicum of brains with
subtleties about the General Warrant.

Everything depended on Pitt, and Pitt was pursuing his
usual mysterious methods. Hardwicke set himself to discover
Pitt's intentions and was soon satisfied that Pitt was determined to back Wilkes, was manœuvring to that end, and was
not to be shaken. Only one course therefore remained—to
win over the rest of the Opposition, leaving Pitt high and

dry with no follower but a discredited Wilkes. With this in view he kept up a constant pressure, urgently warning the Opposition against the "mischievous consequences" of the part Pitt proposed to play, and before very long had confounded the magnates. They really did not know what to do. Pitt was their great champion, but after all Hardwicke was a greater legal luminary than Pratt, and where the King was concerned personally they must be sure of their ground.

So successful was Hardwicke that by the beginning of June the Wilkes affair had gained the unique distinction of shaking both Government and Opposition almost to pieces at one and the same time.

It was at this point that Hardwicke's machinations took a new turn. As Government was so obviously tottering Yorke thought of ratting. The magnates, who had an undeservedly high opinion of him, were delighted, imagining that his resignation would be a shattering blow to Government. They fixed up an interview between Pitt and Yorke, confident that Pitt would be talked out of his unfortunate attitude. But Pitt refused to be dazzled; he went as far as he could to meet Yorke, but hinted plainly enough that he must drop his written opinion on Wilkes's case, which Yorke was not willing to do. The negotiations therefore hung fire.

This was the state of affairs when on the 20th of July Wilkes suddenly decamped to France. Nominally he went to visit Polly, but he took care to let the world know that he was leaving in a disgruntled mood. "I know from a good hand", Newcastle wrote the same day, "that Wilkes complains extremely of his friends."

His disappearance naturally had little effect upon the magnates or Government. But it had an extraordinary effect on Pitt, who was well aware that matters had been drifting dangerously far. He at once cut short the negotiations with Yorke and had several stormy interviews with the bewildered Newcastle. Pitt's access of vigour stirred Hardwicke to greater but no less subtle efforts, and he began insinuating more openly that Pitt meant to become "absolute master"—a thought that was bound to rankle.

(5)

While the Opposition were doing their best to drop Wilkes overboard, Government were moving heaven and earth to circumvent him. Hitherto they had found no way, but at this darkest point the whole position was radically altered by a sudden and unexpected discovery. Government got wind of the private edition of Wilkes's *Essay*. With the utmost secrecy and reviving hope they concentrated on this heaven-sent chance.

Although Wilkes had given strict injunctions that only twelve copies were to be printed, his workmen had drawn one or two extra copies for their own amusement. The head workman, Curry, possessed a complete copy, and an underling, Jennings, had a few pages. Jennings, not unduly impressed with his prize, used it for wrapping up his dinner, which he happened to eat in the company of Thomas Farmer, employed on a Government newspaper by William Faden. Farmer read it, and being thoroughly intrigued with the contents, took it away on loan to show to his fellow-workmen. Not unnaturally the news spread, and finally Faden himself saw the paper. Thinking it offered opportunities for a scoop, he discussed a series of letters attacking Wilkes and his *Essay* with Kidgell, Lord March's chaplain and a man whose character did no honour to his cloth. At first Kidgell, who was much in need of cash, played with the idea, but subsequently thought he might get more by informing Government. As he rightly surmised, Government were delighted, and ordered him by any and every means to secure a copy—a task which he entrusted to Faden. As Curry was the only man who possessed a copy, Curry was tempted in every way, but without success. Towards the end of August, however, the prospects were brighter, and Faden wrote to Kidgell on the 23rd, "I believe I shall be able to procure the sheets for good".

Three days before this letter was written Egremont died suddenly in an apoplectic fit. His death precipitated the crisis which had been hanging over Government. The King was prepared to change the Ministry, and Bute, appearing once more upon the scene, urged him to recall Pitt. To all appearance Wilkes's plot had succeeded, and on Saturday, the 27th of August, Pitt attended the King at Buckingham Palace. The interview was *couleur de rose*, and Pitt, confident of his return to power, summoned his friends and allies to Town. Grenville first learnt of this sudden move by arriving at the Palace during Pitt's audience. He waited until Pitt had gone, and then saw the King himself and had a second interview on the Sunday. The result was that when Pitt arrived again on the Monday he found that the promising aspect had vanished in smoke. No satisfactory explanation has ever been given. Pitt himself was quite at a loss, and the various theories put forward were unconvincing. Where all is dark a further theory may be pardoned. It seems not improbable that Wilkes himself was indirectly the cause of all the trouble.

The King may, or may not, have known Pitt's views on the Wilkes affair, but his demand for the inclusion in the Ministry of Temple, who had just been struck from the list of Privy Councillors and dismissed from the Lord-Lieutenancy of Buckinghamshire for supporting Wilkes, was a clear hint. To give up his revenge on his libeller was a hard morsel for the King, and if Grenville had been able to satisfy him on this point it may well have been enough to swing over the balance. By the 27th of August Grenville ought to have seen Faden's letter of the 23rd, and its contents should certainly have been brought to his notice by the 28th. He had therefore an opportunity of assuring the King that Wilkes's downfall was reasonably certain.

This is, of course, conjecture; but it must be remembered that the crushing of Wilkes was a matter of supreme importance in the eyes of George III, and that when Government actually had the *Essay* in their hands their jubilation was as great as it was sudden. It is also worth remembering that when the Wilkes affair was out of the way the King found no difficulty in recalling Pitt or accepting Temple. But be that as it may, the negotiations with Pitt failed and Sandwich was appointed in Egremont's place.

(6)

The negotiations, however, had certain clearly defined results. It had now been published to the world that the Ministry had all but fallen, and as nobody knew or could discover why the King had changed his mind, a number of defections took place, and Yorke wobbled more than ever.

It was also clear that if the Ministry did fall, Pitt would succeed—a fact which inevitably gave Pitt the leadership of the Opposition. As Hardwicke rather bitterly said, "everybody has, in effect, concurred to throw everything into his hands". Pitt was consequently in the best of humours, and the Opposition leaders began writing of their pleasant visits to Hayes. The only drawback was that while Pitt treated them with gracious condescension, he refused to say a word of his plans or intentions, expecting everyone to follow him blindly. Such an attitude of majestic aloofness offered Hardwicke an excellent opportunity for sowing the seeds of doubt. Surely, he urged, it was unreasonable to ask men of standing and importance to give up their wills entirely without even a word of explanation. At first he made little impression against Pitt's popularity, but events suddenly took a new turn.

Wilkes returned from France—presumably as a result of the new position. Nothing could have been more ironical, since his return finally set alight the train which was to blow him up. Curry had not yet handed over the incriminating document. He had been, or thought himself, ill-used by Wilkes's servant, but believed that Wilkes would do him justice, and soon after Wilkes's return presented himself at the door. On being refused admission he handed over the

Essay. Wilkes, of course, had no idea of what was in store. Directly he landed, Sandwich, who was an old friend, renewed the offers which the Ministers had already made in the hopes of buying him over. Wilkes rejected them absolutely, said he was "devoted to the service of the Opposition", and talked of renewing his weekly papers. He was, as George Onslow declared, "in great spirits".

He had not been back four days—just time enough for Curry to hand over the *Essay*—before Government began to adopt a wholly new tone. Newcastle noted "the monstrous behaviour of the Ministers, and particularly of my Lord Sandwich, who talks like a madman". Legge observed "a certain spirit which is reviving in the public papers". Members of foreign embassies told how they had dined with the Secretaries of State and found them in the highest spirits, saying they were "sure of their point", that they "had nothing to fear", that "there would be warm work for the first four or five days" of the session, but that before the 23rd of December "*l'opposition sera reduite au silence*".

This surprising change of tone alarmed the more nervous members of the Opposition but did not impress Pitt, who regarded it as mere bluff. Nor did it much impress Yorke, who was not in the secret. He had been threatening to resign ever since the negotiations of August, and chose this particular moment to interview Pitt again. Not unnaturally he found Pitt's attitude much stiffened. Pitt told him bluntly that "the matter of privilege" was the only question he proposed to touch. As Yorke, in spite of his miserable hesitations, refused to withdraw his opinion, Pitt bowed him out politely, and made up his mind to end the shilly-shally. He recognized that the Opposition in general wanted to barter Wilkes for Yorke, but Pitt rejected the exchange absolutely, well-knowing that Yorke had nothing to offer him which was worth receiving, Wilkes everything. Unfortunately, he followed his usual tortuous methods. Instead of attempting to argue, he wrote sternly to Newcastle: "I could wish I had been told the full state of the

thing sooner, that I might not have proceeded in the vain
dream that some solid union upon real Revolution Principles
and an assertion in earnest of the freedom of the Constitution,
in so sacred an article as Privilege of Parliament, was indeed
practicable."

This roundabout method gave Hardwicke an advantage in
the Homeric contest over Wilkes's body, which the old diplo-
matist used to the full. Why, he asked the perplexed Opposition,
all this bother over a difference of opinion on a trifling point?
Pitt was demanding something that was "unreasonable,
impracticable". Yorke had given an opinion, and was quite
willing to withdraw it "if he should be convinced in his
judgment". But instead of trying to convince him Pitt merely
reversed his previous attitude: "Mr. Pitt, who in his first
conversation treated the affair of Wilkes slightly, and as what
would little affect public affairs, makes it now his principal
point." He does even more, he magnifies it into a constitutional
point and prates about Magna Charta and Revolution doctrines,
"as if the differing in opinion upon a question of privilege of
the House of Commons, never yet determined by that House
itself, and which Mr. Onslow himself [the Speaker] declares
still to be very doubtful, was of the essence of Magna Charta,
and of the Liberty established at the Revolution". Pitt must
really be more reasonable. "Upon my word, great and able as
he is, if he goes on in this way, he will be thought to give
too much countenance to what the King was once reported to
have flung out: 'What do they mean? Do they mean to put
a Tyrant over me, and themselves too?'"

The magnates were shaken. They really did not know the
rights and wrongs of the case and cared less. What was obvious
was the split in their own party and the growing exultation
of Government. If Pitt would not exchange Wilkes for Yorke,
then it would be best to compromise by simply dropping the
affair. Such a solution would bring Yorke over to their side
without necessarily driving out Wilkes. It was ideal. With
fresh hope Newcastle, Devonshire, and Rockingham urged this

view, and the only reply which Pitt vouchsafed was through the devious channel of his solicitor, who passed the message on to Thomas Walpole, who sent it to Newcastle: "Your Grace knows how immovable this man is when his conviction goes with his inclination. He has studied and made himself perfectly master of the subject and is determined to declare his sentiments publicly; in the meanwhile he expresses much dissatisfaction at being left in doubt of the disposition of Your Grace's friends."

As a last effort to force Pitt's hand the magnates asked the Duke of Cumberland to approach him, and in order that he might go with some sort of olive-branch Yorke agreed to resign and to let Cumberland inform Pitt of his intention. But the result of this effort was simply to put Pitt's back up. He refused all co-operation, demanded support upon his point of privilege, and abused Yorke. When Cumberland told him of the intended resignation, to his intense chagrin "Mr. Pitt grew more violent; said he was sorry for it; that by this resignation Mr. Yorke would have more influence in the opposition he would give to his great point of privilege". The Duke pointed out that Wilkes had had the satisfaction of being released, and it was quite unnecessary to reopen the matter; but "all this signified nothing; Mr. Pitt was as tenacious as ever".

Pitt's mixture of disdain and silence finally alienated the magnates. As Newcastle wrote: "The Marquess [i.e. Rockingham] notwithstanding the partiality he has for Mr. Pitt, is now so provoked with him, that he declared clearly and strongly to Mr. Yorke that he thought his behaviour had been so great and so meritorious to us, that we were obliged in honour and gratitude to engage our friends to support him in this point of privilege. . . . I suppose it may finally end so." Hardwicke had apparently won the last round. Honour and gratitude had been diverted from Wilkes, the steadfast friend, to Yorke, the ratting schemer.

CHAPTER XI

FLIGHT

(1)

THOUGH they were deeply and desperately divided on the one point of importance, though they had no vestige of a plan of campaign, though they were dubiously fearful that Pitt would be absent, the Opposition awaited the meeting of Parliament with confidence. It would be hard to say why. It was true that in appearance they had two grounds for optimism—the defection of Yorke and the confusion of Government. But it was obvious that in adopting Yorke they had thrust out Pitt, and they were quite determined to drop Wilkes. Hence they were not even building on sand, but on a vacuum, and the fact that they still hoped was more to the credit of an ostrich-like faith than of any parliamentary acumen. Worse still, they took no steps to find out the intentions of Wilkes or Government, apparently convinced that both alike must obey their wishes, though they never disclosed those wishes even to Wilkes. Providence, one must presume, would look to that. As for Government, they did indeed learn that urgent whips were being sent to the Bishops, which as most of the Bishops had been appointed by Newcastle and were his warm supporters, ought to have roused their suspicions. But they were blinded by a lying spirit of optimism, and Newcastle, chuckling at the thought that "this poor vain man, my Lord Halifax, certainly flatters himself", did his best to make ruin certain by entreating the Bishops to obey the summons.

The meeting of Parliament on the 15th of November disclosed their futility. Wilkes and Grenville both came down to the House determined to raise the same question, and both stood up at the same moment, confronting each other across a sea of eager and expectant faces. Wilkes, quietly insistent, demanded leave to complain of a breach of privilege, Grenville, grimly pertinacious, to deliver a message from the King. By all custom Wilkes had the right to speak first, since the weighty matter of privilege took precedence over everything, especially messages from the King. But Government felt strong enough to resist, and Grenville turned on Wilkes the fury of that smouldering obstinacy which in after days was to sear the ties that bound America to England. A raging debate arose, and Government by weight of numbers alone ensured the reading of the King's message. It did no more than ask the House to take the case into consideration.

The House at once proceeded to discuss No. 45, ignoring the authorship for the moment, and concentrating on the contents. Lord North moved that it was "a false, scandalous, and seditious libel . . . manifestly tending . . . to excite to traitorous insurrections against His Majesty's Government". Wilkes, with more courage than finesse, objected to the word false, but in the temper of the House this was not a point likely to be considered. It was brushed contemptuously aside. What was truth where the King's honour was concerned? What falsehood when the existence of the Ministry was at stake? The battle centred round Pitt's more skilled amendment, to leave out the words "to excite to traitorous insurrections".

Willy-nilly the Opposition were swept into the fight. They might have come prepared; they might have come united; but if that was now past praying for, at least they had a general of consummate abilities to rally them at this eleventh hour. Like one of Homer's heroes, Pitt was omnipresent. Wherever the fight was fiercest, there was Pitt battling like one possessed. Twenty-one times in the course of the evening he was upon his feet, denying, refuting, arguing, pouring scorn on Government and all their machinations, and upholding the liberty of the Press and the sacred right of criticism. On his own amendment alone he fulminated eight times, replying to almost every opponent personally. What if the Government disliked No. 45? He disliked all political pamphlets, but mere personal preferences did not make a libel. He himself "never could learn exactly what is a libel", but he would stoutly maintain the liberty of the Press and "he would die if a day were not appointed for hearing Wilkes".

There can rarely have been a sterner fight, or one more strenuously contested. All that a single man could do, Pitt did; but even genius could not overcome the want of union in the Opposition. Pitt lost his amendment by 111 votes to 273, and Government gleefully ordered the paper to be burnt.

Having thus obliterated No. 45, the House allowed Wilkes in the early hours of the morning to state his complaint before a dwindling group of members, weary and listless after the fight. Wilkes spoke shortly and to the point, merely setting out the facts of his arrest and ending with the words, "if, after this important business has in its full extent been maturely weighed, you shall be of opinion that I am intitled to privilege, I shall then be not only ready, but eagerly desirous to waive that privilege and to put myself upon a jury of my country-men". Utterly indifferent to what Wilkes might say, the House barely heard him to the end before adjourning.

(2)

Meanwhile a much more formidable attack was being launched in the House of Lords. The House was crowded and the Bishops were there in full force. If they had known what was in store for them one must hope that they would have been hurrying to the farthest ends of England. But only one knew—my Lord of Gloucester. He was the Dr. Warburton, celebrated for his edition of Pope's works, whose name had been taken in vain in the *Essay on Woman*. He was also the politically-minded prelate who had proposed the law against abuses of the Press which Pitt had found reason to criticize. Since that time Pitt had fallen foul of Warburton once again over an address from the clergy of Gloucester to the King on the subject of the Peace. Pitt had expressed displeasure, and

Warburton was rash enough to write a letter of defence. Pitt's reply, dated 10th of September of this very year, has only been preserved in part, but that part is enough; Pitt had rarely been more crushing or ironical.

Warburton and Sandwich had concocted the line of debate. The noble peer, notorious for the utter and emphatic profligacy of his life, was to read the *Essay* to the assembled House, and do his best to smother his natural delight in its lewdness under a mask of simulated abhorrence. Warburton was to follow with pious indignation at the slur cast upon his character, and through him on the House of Lords.

If Government were depending on the element of surprise, they certainly attained their object. Sandwich, mouthing the obscenities of the poem with a rich chuckle only half covered by a threadbare suggestion of disgust, was a sight for the gods, and made at least one-half of the hearers gape with unaffected astonishment. Sir Francis Dashwood, now Lord le Despencer, as soon as he could collect his scattered wits, remarked that he had never before heard the devil preach—a sentiment shared by his fellow-peers, who clamoured for more of this enthralling phenomenon.

Warburton followed, as arranged, and made dullness funny by calling God to witness that he had not written the notes with which he was credited. No one but the devil, he asserted, was capable of such a production, and then, for fear that this would exonerate Wilkes, he besought the devil's pardon, "for I do not think even him capable of so infamous a production"—thereby foreshadowing an interesting situation when Wilkes should come face to face with the Prince of Wickedness.

Of course the result was a foregone conclusion. It was impossible for anyone, whatever his private sentiments, to approve publicly of the poem, and Government automatically obtained a resolution condemning the work as "a most scandalous, obscene, and impious libel"—though exactly who was libelled it is hard to say. The effect went much farther. Those who had enjoyed the poem were bound to decry it the loudest, while those who were genuinely shocked had no sort of inducement to shelter the author. Only one man attempted the task —Pitt, who on hearing the news in the lobby exclaimed indignantly: "Why do they not search the Bishop of Gloucester's study for heresy?" The Archbishop of York voiced the opinion of respectable men in a letter which he wrote the next day to Newcastle, a letter full of an honest indignation which completely overwhelmed his political perplexities: "I can very shortly give my opinion; that in this infamous affair of Mr. Wilkes, I will never concur in obstructing or parrying the blow that he so justly deserves. I neither think it for the honour of any person, nor the good of the cause of the Whigs, to espouse such a man and put yourselves so totally in the wrong in the eyes of all the world." Wilkes had undoubtedly put himself out of court, and Government had obtained a crushing victory. With this fact to buoy them up they could endure very lightheartedly the jeers and sneers of the common people, who were not slow to fasten on the degraded methods Government had adopted. It was well known that Sandwich was as black as Wilkes, if not blacker; that the pair of them had been boon companions, roaring out their ribald blasphemies in the same low haunts; that Sandwich had superadded to his private vice the public shame of treachery; and when at the *Beggars' Opera* Macheath—who resembled Wilkes in more respects than one—said "that Jemmy Twitcher should peach me, I own surprised me," the whole house rose to the allusion, and from that moment to the day of his death Sandwich was known as Jemmy Twitcher.

But to return to the House of Lords, the horror, real or pretended, was such that Government could do as it liked. Witnesses were summoned, and Wilkes would have been condemned out of hand had not Mansfield retained enough of his judicial calm to suggest that even criminals taken in the act were entitled to be heard. On this reminder, the Lords adjourned the matter for a couple of days.

(3)

The Houses rose in the early hours of the morning, but their rising did not end the day's events. In the course of the Commons debate, Samuel Martin, ex-Secretary to the Treasury, who had been roughly handled in one of the *North Britons*, made a speech full of personal bitterness and obviously intended to draw Wilkes. Rumour said that he had been assiduously practising with a pistol for months past—a wise precaution, since the main channel of Fox's wholesale bribery could hardly trust to the righteousness of his cause. As he flung out his scarcely veiled challenge, all eyes were turned on Wilkes. But Wilkes maintained a smile of indifference and the affair seemed to have blown over. Appearances, however, were deceptive. He rose early on November 16th and wrote to Martin: "You complained yesterday before five hundred gentlemen, that you had been stabbed in the dark by the *North Briton*. . . . I whisper in your ear that every passage in the *North Briton*, in which you have been named, or even alluded to, was written by your humble servant."

Martin replied at once: "I desire that you may meet me in Hyde Park immediately, with a brace of pistols each, to determine our difference." It was not Martin's right but Wilkes's privilege to choose the weapons, and the rumour of Martin's practice might have suggested swords; but perhaps Wilkes did not care, or perhaps he was growing weary of privilege; at all events he hastened to the spot without a protest. Martin, for all his practice, missed with the first shot, while Wilkes's pistol flashed in the pan. The second effort was more successful. Martin's bullet struck a button on Wilkes's coat and glanced off into his groin. So honour was appeased, and as often happens left Martin at a loss what to do next. Wilkes, practical even on his back and honourable in spite of his *Essay*, told Martin to escape as fast as he could and promised to keep his own mouth shut.

The wound was very painful, but two days later he was

able to write to his daughter, "both physician and surgeon
declare me out of danger, and I hope in a fortnight to go
abroad. You may depend on seeing me at Paris before
Christmas, if I am tolerably well."

It was not, however, his daughter that drew him out of
England, nor the wound that drove him. It was the *Essay*.
Its production had dashed his hopes; he was ashamed; he
was perturbed, and he ran to hide his face. Probably he had
hoped his duel would give an excuse. Should Martin fall,
Wilkes must fly; if he fell himself, either his troubles
would be over or as a convalescent he could expect a little
latitude.

Whatever hesitations he may have had were swept away
when Parliament resumed the debate on November 23rd.
Government, intent on pressing their advantage to the full,
decided to brush aside the privilege which stood in their way.
The terms of their resolution were "that the privilege of
Parliament does not extend to the case of writing and publishing seditious libels". By moving it in this particular form
they were behaving in a manner at once rude and tyrannical
—the manner of a bully sure of his point. To say baldly that
privilege did not cover a point which Pratt, as Lord Chief
Justice, had said it did, was to give Pratt the lie direct. It
was also of doubtful legality, for while the Commons were
entitled to give up their own privileges they were not entitled
to interpret the law of the land. The occasion made it tyrannical,
since their only reason was the crushing of an individual.

The question of privilege raised so directly was one which
neither Yorke nor Pitt could decently avoid. It was the rock
on which they had split. So to it they went, hammer and
tongs. This open duel between the Opposition's doughtiest
warrior and their latest recruit delighted the Government, who
extolled Yorke's speech as "in every respect the greatest per-
formance that could be made". To the Opposition benches
it sounded more flat, and they waited with impatience for
Pitt's reply.

That reply is famous enough. Pitt was a consummate actor, and on this occasion had a part to play worthy of his abilities —a difficult part which should avoid the odium of the *Essay*, while extracting the fullest advantage from Wilkes's actions. The first effect of the *Essay* had been to dash him. He realized as fully as Wilkes or Government the tremendous effect of its production, and had shown himself subdued and quiet in the House. On the 16th Grenville had noted with pleasure that "his manner was extremely temperate and very parliamentary". Others also had seen the alteration, and even went so far as to suggest that he was "endeavouring to pare away the asperity of yesterday's speeches". Since then he had had time to reconsider his position, and the course on which he decided—reluctantly, one must hope—was to throw Wilkes overboard, differentiating between the man and the points which he had raised.

To create the right atmosphere he came to the House in his most theatrical manner, hobbling on a crutch and swathed in flannel. Everyone should know that he had risen from a bed of sickness and come at the peril of his life to proclaim his views. This voice from the edge of the grave declared the surrender of privilege to be highly dangerous to the freedom of Parliament and an infringement of the people's rights—a view which has hardly been endorsed by subsequent history. From these grandiloquent sentiments it passed to a fierce denunciation of Wilkes and all his works. "He condemned the whole series of *North Britons*; he called them illiberal, unmanly, and detestable. He abhorred all national reflections. The King's subjects were one people. Whoever divided them was guilty of sedition. His Majesty's complaint was well-founded, it was just, it was necessary. The author did not deserve to be ranked among the human species—he was the blasphemer of his God and the libeller of his King. He had no connection with him." Not that Pitt was truly happy—it would be injustice to him to suppose it possible—and having made his speech he left the House and retired to Hayes to "think as seldom as I can of the surrender of both Houses, and of those doctrines and assertions by which a large stride indeed towards arbitrary power is made".

Yorke, whose written opinion had now been vindicated, was more self-satisfied. He observed that Pitt had been remarkably civil towards him, more so, he believed, than he had ever been towards an opponent. With a smirk of complaisance he attributed the change to his own eloquence, boasting that Pitt "seemed very short, or defective, in his answer and much embarrassed". Newcastle, with more sense than manners, ventured to doubt the effect of Yorke's oratory; he hoped that perhaps Pitt was holding out an olive-branch. But Pitt was swayed by no eloquence except his own, and had no desire to be reconciled to Yorke. It is equally probable and more honourable to him to suppose that a troubled conscience stemmed the flow of his words and a haunting spectre embarrassed his imagery. Yet, spoken trippingly or the reverse, it is easy to see how the speech came to be made, when the facts are set out and the dates called to mind. The *Essay on Woman* had abashed Wilkes; it infuriated Pitt, who found his ambitions thwarted by an idle poem—truly a "strange phenomenon", an "unaccountable story", a mean and dastardly trick of fortune, made none the sweeter by the memory of former smiles at those very parodies.

But the fury of frustration is no excuse for a gross betrayal and Wilkes was justified in feeling resentment. "I shall demand", wrote Horace Walpole to Lord Hertford, "a satire on Mr. Pitt from Wilkes, and I do not believe I shall be balked, for Wilkes has already expressed his resentment on being given up by Pitt; who, says Wilkes, ought to be expelled for an imposter." From that moment, in spite of one or two hesitating approaches and in spite of support given to each other in Parliament, there was always a strained feeling between the two.

Whatever disgust Wilkes may have felt at his desertion he was not the man to cry over spilt milk. "I will make use", he told Cotes on one occasion, "of the understanding God has given me." He made use of it now, and decided that flight was necessary. But his coolness did not desert him. Though he was lying in bed disabled; though he was surrounded by spies; though his letters were opened and read; though the two Houses of Parliament were waiting, like spiders, to pounce upon him; though Mansfield was licking his lips over the sentence he would pronounce when, no longer covered by privilege, he had to stand his trial; though Pitt had denounced him and he was friendless and oppressed, he never faltered for a moment, keeping a brave face to his enemies and quietly preparing his plans.

His own prosecutions against the emissaries of Government were pushed forward, and on the 6th of December he gained the first, against Wood, the Under-Secretary. The verdict was hailed with delight by the common people, who, as so often, had a deeper, if blinder, grasp of the issues, and realized that Wilkes stood for a freedom denied by King and Parliament alike. A vast crowd rushed from the court to cheer for "Wilkes and Liberty" beneath his bedroom window, and then passed on to hoot and groan at Halifax and Grenville. They had already shown their feelings when the public hangman tried to carry out his orders to burn No. 45. The scene outside the Royal Exchange had been exciting enough. The crowd had snatched the torch out of the hangman's hand and thrust it in his face. When the Peace Officers interfered they were roughly handled, and the High Sheriff, Harley, who was present to see the order executed, had his coach broken to pieces.

Parliament, regardless of juries and mob and only too eager to avenge their dignity, grew impatient of delay. Wilkes must appear before their offended majesty as soon as possible, and for fear that he might be malingering two doctors were ordered to visit him. Wilkes, game to the end, wrote to the two doctors in a strain at once complimentary to themselves and delightfully ironical. He was "duly sensible of the kind care and concern of the House of Commons, not only for his health, but for his speedy recovery", but he was perfectly satisfied with his own doctor; at present he was not well enough to see visitors, but when he was, he hoped they would come and eat his mutton. To his own doctor he wrote a still more delicious letter, in which he expressed the opinion that Parliament should have referred the matter first "to the Committee of Ways and Means, to contrive how the State physician and surgeon can get into my house. Secondly, to the Committee of Supply, to vote the fees due to the gentlemen for their attendance; but I have public economy so much at heart (though I make no parade of it) that I will save the nation that expence."

Meanwhile he summoned his friends, Cotes, Churchill, Sayer, and possibly Temple, to his bedside, to concoct a new plan to meet the new circumstances. Whilst he was abroad, Sayer was to approach the Government to see if a compromise could be reached. Though deserted by the Opposition he had still something to offer. His prosecutions against Webb and the two Secretaries of State were outstanding, and the victory he had already gained over Wood was an omen of success. Government was most anxious to avoid the stigma of an adverse verdict and the payment of heavy damages, and Halifax, as a matter of fact, was keeping out of court by a series of despicable chicanes. Wilkes was willing to drop these prosecutions and even plead guilty to the *Essay*, provided that his sin could be expiated by a few days in the Tower and that the constitutional issue was assured in the House. In a word, he would sacrifice all personal triumph provided the public points were gained.

Having made his plans, he proceeded to outwit his opponents once more. He bamboozled his doctors into giving him spare dressings for the wound, gave out that he was going to spend a few days with Cotes at Byfleet, and at 8 a.m. on Christmas Eve set out on the Dover road. The next day he was in France.

I

Kidgell, about this time, found his creditors too pressing, and followed Wilkes abroad. This double elopement was too tempting an opportunity for satirical pens:

> When faction was loud, and when party ran high,
> Religion and Liberty joined in the cry;
> But, O grief of griefs! in the midst of the fray,
> Religion and Liberty both ran away.

CHAPTER XII

EXILE AND OUTLAW

(1)

HAD Wilkes been Fate he would have enjoyed his own fall, since it brought on the Opposition the lot of all incompetents. The moment his affair exploded, the moment he and Pitt, each in his own way, had washed their hands of it, the Whig magnates awoke to its merits, and halloed eagerly after its disappearing tail. Government began to talk of Wilkes's expulsion, and Newcastle, bubbling with indignation at the proposal, hoped that Pitt would "vigorously oppose it"; Rockingham, with an air of mild discovery, was convinced that everyone should "take the imprimatur from Mr. Pitt". They formed themselves into a solid rank behind the redoubtable Pitt, and were more than amazed to find him gone.

Yet after disowning Wilkes, what else could he possibly do? To the utter confusion of the magnates he snapped the heads off their proposals and left them to muddle along as best they might. They entreated, they argued, but all in vain. Pitt was immovable; constitutional points—those vague generalities which terrified the Whigs—he was ready to defend, but concrete things like Wilkes or the wickedness of Ministers left him utterly cold. The magnates wrote to each other in the depths of gloom. The absconding of Wilkes just after they had taken him up was the final straw. Even Temple drooped, and those who had any right to approach the absentee urged his return. But Wilkes was determined to rest his decision on the results of Sayer's negotiations. Before he heard the outcome of these negotiations, Government moved his expulsion, and though a dwindling band of stalwarts fought his case, Government, with the aid of Yorke and in the absence of Pitt, gained an easy victory.

Once he was out of the way, Government was in a stronger position to meet the real question—the question of the General Warrants—which was bound to be raised sooner or later and actually came before the House in February 1764. It is proof of the hopeless folly of the Opposition leaders that although Pitt was willing to take part in this discussion as being a point of principle, it was left to private members to engineer the campaign. All through the early days of February these members were pressing for copies of the warrants in Wilkes's case to be laid on the table of the House. Nothing could have been more reasonable, and Government might easily have suffered a defeat if the leaders had been blessed with a modicum of courage. But their merits stopped short at the recognition of lost opportunities. Like the Duke of Plaza-Toro, they led their regiment from behind, and celebrated from afar what they heard of their followers' doings.

On the fatal day, 13th of February, the Opposition were still at loggerheads, and tried to settle their own differences during the course of the debate, while the Government yawned. The first point of a series which came up for discussion was Wilkes's complaint of breach of privilege. The debate raged all that day and all the next, when the Government majority sank to ten.

Elated with this moral victory, the Opposition pressed eagerly forward, and on the 15th moved that "a General Warrant for apprehending and seizing the Author, Printer, and Publishers of a seditious libel, together with their papers, is not warranted by law". The wordy battle continued for two more days. Government with some skill proposed a series of amendments which aggravated the differences among their opponents. Thus the sting was largely taken out of the attack, and the motion was essentially softened by the addition of words to the effect that such warrants were in accordance with usage and had never been questioned in the Court of King's Bench.

The preliminaries safely passed, Pitt in his eagerness went very near eating his own words. "All which Ministers had wished", he said, "was accomplished in the conviction and expulsion of Mr. Wilkes; it was now the duty of the House to do justice to the Nation, to the Constitution, and to the Law" —an admission, if ever one were made, that Wilkes had been unjustly convicted and expelled. He also whittled down his attack on the *North Briton*. General Warrants, he argued, were always illegal, but might be justified in urgent or extraordinary cases, but in Wilkes's case "the plea of necessity could not be urged; there was no pretence for it. The nation was in perfect tranquillity. The safety of the State was in no danger. The charge was the writing and publishing a libel. What was there in this crime so heinous and terrible as to require this formidable instrument? . . . The extraordinary and wanton exercise of an illegal power in this case admits of no justification, nor even palliation. It was the indulgence of a personal resentment against a particular person."

When Pitt could speak in this strain it was evident that the whole debate concerned Wilkes and Wilkes alone. To pursue it in his absence was like playing *Hamlet* without the Prince. Government carried the day by fourteen votes alone, and it is at least arguable that had Wilkes been present in person, and had there been unanimity in the Opposition ranks, Government would have suffered defeat. Wilkes was overthrown partly by the *Essay* and partly by Yorke—a youthful indiscretion and a family intrigue. No wonder Pitt spoke in after days of his strange fatality.

As a commentary and as evidence that Wilkes had been the life and soul of the Opposition, two days later Newcastle was writing "our friends are every day calling out for *a point*. The great difficulty is to find a good one." Pitt had experienced the same difficulty until Wilkes came to his aid. Now that Wilkes was gone the Opposition hovered for a moment on the verge of success, but, unable to press their advantage home, sank back into impotence. The next real point was to come four years later, and it was brought by Wilkes.

(2)

From the parliamentary point of view this was the end of the Wilkes affair, and it may be well to sum up the position.

It is generally assumed that Wilkes was made by the folly of Government, and that the Whig magnates were embarrassed by Wilkes, but stoutly defended the constitutional points when they were freed from his presence. Neither is a fact.

Government's methods were both correct and skilful. It is true that General Warrants were illegal, but they can be pardoned for their failure to realize this; otherwise they made few mistakes. They were entitled to ask Parliament to give up its privileges, and since they had not taken the case into court, they were entitled to ask Parliament's opinion of No. 45. When that opinion proved unfavourable, they were entitled to ask for Wilkes's expulsion. All this was quite straightforward and, more to their purpose, successful. It cannot be argued for a moment that their line of action made Wilkes, or even that he was made at all, since in fact he was exiled and ruined. His only opportunity he made for himself by being the first to realize the illegality of General Warrants. He gained no single advantage out of any other step Government took.

It was the Opposition themselves who were to blame for his failure. Their action was both feeble and reprehensible. They fought and squabbled among themselves until it was too late, and that not over Wilkes's character, but over the constitutional point they are supposed to have supported but never understood. When in February 1764, after the flight and expulsion of Wilkes, they really came to grips, their action was wholly wrong. The line they took, Pitt included, was to argue that General Warrants were illegal. Now this was a question of law, which was not only one the House of Commons were incompetent to decide, but one that was definitely before the courts. Parliament's opinion would do no good if it coincided with the judges' verdict, and could only lead to trouble if it differed. The Opposition had no business to introduce the matter, and Government's argument was unanswerable. The fact that even so they only won by fourteen votes is an indication of the wholesale rout they would have endured had the plot gone as at first intended.

What foiled the plot was the sudden production of the *Essay on Woman*. The Ministers had rightly gauged its effect, and by its means snatched victory in the moment of defeat. Whatever may be thought of their sense of decency and fair play, their action was a master-stroke. If it brought a torrent of abuse upon their heads, they had not been popular before, and skins as thick as theirs need something harder than words.

(3)

Meanwhile Wilkes was in France, and no one knew whether he meant to return and face the Commons or was really running away. Without for the moment discussing his intentions it is certain that he did not return, and that tactically his absence was a profound mistake. It dashed the leaders of the Opposition, perplexed his supporters, destroyed his own chances of a triumph, gave point to the charges against him, and left the Government with a free hand to manipulate the proceedings and gain an emphatic victory. His friends were fully alive to the drawbacks and summoned him urgently. They pointed out in letter after letter that Government could do very little; their case for his expulsion and prosecution was weak, and even if they succeeded Wilkes would have plenty of time to make good his escape. To return meant little risk and the probability of a still greater triumph; the popular disgust with the Ministers was overwhelming, the legal position safe, honour demanded his presence, and common sense supported it. If he stayed abroad the case against him would go by default, and he was bound to be outlawed, a ruined and disgraced pauper.

Wilkes was painfully aware of the facts. This and his well-known courage have led to the conclusion that he was prevented by ill-health, which was the explanation that Wilkes himself gave. But it can hardly be sustained. Wilkes refused to return unless Sayer had first succeeded in his negotiations. Until he had definite news of those negotiations he played a part, and played it skilfully. On his arrival in Paris he behaved with the utmost decorum, leaving his card on the Ambassador and attending the English chapel. At the same time he wrote home letters which alternately declared his longing to return and harped on the state of his wound. The question of his expulsion was to come before the House on the 19th of January, and at the last moment, as he had received no news from Sayer, he made a hurried effort to gain time, writing to the Speaker that he was too ill to travel, and enclosing a medical certificate. How he obtained the certificate he explained subsequently in a confidential letter to Cotes: "I wrote to the Speaker on the 11th of January, and enclosed to him a certificate of a King's Physician and a Surgeon of eminence here, who are really gentlemen, and from friendship to Goy gave me the certificate in the handsomest manner. I have, to keep up appearances, been in my room sick and complaining ever since." The House brushed this certificate aside on the ground that it was not authenticated, an omission Wilkes at once rectified. His action, however, was much the same as the action of the House— merely technical. Before sending the proofs of authenticity on the 5th of February he had already made up his mind.

It was on the fatal 19th of January itself that Wilkes finally learnt the failure of Sayer's attempt, and from that moment he gave up hope. "Now give me leave to take a peep into futurity", he wrote to Cotes on the 20th: "I argue upon the supposition that I was expelled this Friday morning at one or two o'clock after a warm debate. I am then no longer a Member of Parliament; of consequence a political man not in the House is of no importance, and never can be well enough, nor minutely enough, informed to be of any great service. What, then, am I to do in England? If I return soon, it is possible (I only put the possibility) that I may be found guilty of a publication, etc., of No. 45 or of the *Essay on Woman*. I must then go off to France, for no man in his senses would stand Mansfield's sentence. . . . Am I then to run the risk of this? . . . I have in my own case experienced the fickleness of the people. I was almost adored one week—the next neglected, abused, despised. . . . I will serve them to the last moment of my life, but I will make use of the understanding God has given me, and will neither trust my security nor indemnity to them." He then went very methodically through the various reasons for staying abroad. He could not trust the Government; he owed nothing to the Opposition; there was no call of honour; the Court hated him; his stand for liberty had been vindicated by Pratt's two verdicts. If he returned he could only expect "persecution from my enemies, coldness and neglect from friends". He was driven back on the Micawber philosophy: "Perhaps", he remarked, "in the womb of fate some important public or private event is to turn up." And so, as he admitted in another letter, "I think myself an exile for life, and I flatter myself, my dear Cotes, with no foolish hopes, not even on the restoration of Mr. Pitt and the Whigs." "Nature", he added, rather forlornly, "has given me some philosophy, and the necessity of the case perfects it."

By the 20th of January he was probably right in deciding to stay where he was. But how did it come about that Wilkes fled in the first case and then failed to grasp the truth of his friends' entreaties? Was it his courage or his wisdom that was at fault? The fact is that the publication of the *Essay* completely unnerved him. Perhaps he had never before fully realized the nature of his parodies—publicity has a wonderful knack of enlightening consciences. At all events, he felt unable to look the public in the face, and simply turned tail. But there was one inducement to take his courage in both hands which struggled at the back of his mind. Wilkes's claim to be the champion of liberty was an honest claim, though his conception of liberty had not yet reached its final form. He still wanted ardently to finish the work he had begun, and with that in view had initiated his compromise with Government. When once he was abroad the perturbation grew calmer, and under happier circumstances he would probably have returned. But there was a further difficulty which must have grown in emphasis as the original shame died down. From the first he had relied upon the support of Pitt and the Opposition, and trusting to them had provoked Government beyond endurance. Pitt had supported him steadily, but from beginning to end the Opposition had been at best half-hearted. Now they seemed to be veering round, but Pitt had more than swung in the opposite direction, denouncing Wilkes in the most scathing terms. Could he reasonably trust the waverers? Could he possibly hope for Pitt's aid? Pitt and the others did, in fact, join in fighting the question of General Warrants; but Wilkes had no guarantee whatever. On the contrary the whole history of the past few months was damningly against the Opposition, and Pitt had not only denounced him publicly, but had stirred no finger to prevent his expulsion. His own views are summed up in that pregnant phrase, "persecution from my enemies, coldness and neglect from my friends". One or the other might be endured, but it was asking too much of a man, shamed by the publication of the *Essay*, sore over the desertion of his allies, to face King and Government, Judges and Parliament, with no backing but his integrity and the noisy violence of the people. The *Essay* and Yorke combined had ruined Wilkes as effectively as they had foiled Pitt.

(4)

Having secured his expulsion from the House of Commons, Government decided to prosecute Wilkes for reprinting No. 45 at his private press and for publishing the *Essay*—with the help of Sandwich! It was a clever move, since it avoided the awkwardness which would have arisen had the courts found No. 45 an innocent paper. They hurried on the trial, packed the jury by the simple expedient of cancelling the notices to jurors likely to befriend him, and to make doubly sure brought the case into the court where Mansfield presided. By the terms of their charge they had avoided the real point, which was whether Wilkes was guilty of libel. But they had no hesitation in going beyond the strict charge when it suited them.

Prosecuting Counsel tried to prove that Wilkes was the author as well as the publisher. When Glynn protested that this was wholly irrelevant, Mansfield replied blandly that, on the contrary, if proved, it would aggravate the crime of printing. So this farcical trial came to an end. Wilkes was found guilty, but sentence was postponed, and a writ issued for Wilkes's arrest. It was not until November 1st that, owing to his failure to appear, he was pronounced an outlaw.

CHAPTER XIII

A FLAMING EPISODE

(1)

IN the first bitterness of defeat Wilkes buoyed himself up with two thoughts. In Paris he could live cheaply and attend himself to the education of Polly. There would be financial straits for the moment, but sooner or later Polly would inherit more than enough for two from Mrs. Mead and her uncle Sherbrooke. That was a prospect not without its merits. Polly, as he told Cotes, was a "solid comfort", and his genuine love for her was a true consolation. With that he combined a natural hope of revenge. "I will not be forgot in England," he cried in a fit of anger, "for I will feed the papers from time to time with gall and vinegar. . . . I can do infinite harm where I am." Yet even as he wrote the words an inkling of their futility crossed his mind. "Many important incidents," he added, "of which I am ignorant, must have happened." He made one or two half-hearted attempts, putting an article about Webb into the *French Gazette* and printing his letter to the Speaker. He even drew up proposals for a continuation of the *North Briton*, but it was borne in upon him more and more that he could not possibly write pamphlets at a distance from the scene of action. This conviction drove him to think of "a solid useful book", in which he "would examine our ideas of political liberty at large; then the nature of the English Constitution and government, and afterwards tell my own story". There were to be some slight fruits from this seed, but not for the moment.

Meanwhile the question of finance grew to a head. As an outlaw, Wilkes's estate would be forfeit, and he was therefore keenly anxious to know the result of his trial so that he might put in train the device which with his usual thoroughness he had already prepared. His lawyer, Philipps, was slow in sending news, being in truth annoyed with Wilkes for failing to return. When he did write, he gave no details, "which", he observed, "I daresay you have been acquainted with from oral relations". Wilkes, who rarely if ever moved without being quite sure of his ground, grew intensely irritated and not a little suspicious. "You suppose", he replied in a tone of severe disapproval, chequered, as ever, with a touch of wit, "I am acquainted with the whole from oral tradition. I am not yet enough of a Catholic to trust to it, and that fine phrase for Chit Chat never gives all particulars, but is almost always lost in generals." However, as soon as definite information arrived, he wrote to Cotes, "I signed, while I was in England, a conveyance drawn up by Mr. Life, of everything I had, to Miss Wilkes, or rather to you in trust for her. If Sayer thinks it proper, I wish it to stand, and you have only to execute the counterpart."

Cotes was a true friend, but hardly the best man for disentangling Wilkes's affairs. By profession he was a wine merchant, by inclination a political intriguer. Not that he possessed the slightest ability or the first rudiments of talent. He united a naturally kind heart to a head that was by no means hard, and the combination brought him in 1767 to the bankruptcy court. Though worried with his own concerns, he did struggle with the insoluble and ever-shifting list of Wilkes's creditors, but there is good reason to believe that his head was not too soft to borrow some of Wilkes's money, no doubt with the intention of paying it back, but also with a full appreciation of its present help to Cotes.

Wilkes had his usual private reasons for needing cash and drew lightheartedly on Cotes, thereby adding to the general confusion. In August the crash came. Cotes, almost brokenhearted at the "cruel necessity", had to refuse acceptance of an order for £375 on himself, and explained (incorrectly as it proved) that when mortgages, bills, and what not had been met, Wilkes would have less than £50 a year. Truly his position seemed desperate, and even Wilkes's irrepressible optimism faltered. "Oh, Cassius," he wrote, "I am sick of many griefs, yet I may truly add with Brutus, no man bears sorrow better. . . . I will struggle as well as I can thro' all my private diffi- culties. . . . My fortitude will ever remain to me." Wilkes was the least resentful of men, and if he hit hard, hit without rancour. But this last blow brought a touch of bitterness to the top—a touch proving by its slightness the essential charity of his heart. Wilkes's troubles were in part due to his own extravagance, but the money spent on his light-o'-loves accounted for little of his position. The crushing weight had been politics; the mad profusion had been for elections (and those not always his own); the reckless squandering had been political pamphlets, written for another. True, he had been helped with money by Temple, but he had given far more than he had received, and now his outlawry and expenses had reduced him to beggary. He showed no bitterness, however, till Cotes suggested that perhaps his friends might come to his aid. "As to my friends", he replied, "serving me *effectually*, I have to be sure much to be very, very grateful for. It is to be sure a proud list, that of my friends. After yourself, a truly noble peer, and the first poet in the world, who are they? I have been too honest and too disinterested to have even the *half friends* you mention. The nation and posterity I trust to. As to the Post Office opening my letters, I grow very indifferent about that. They will see a faithful picture of the mind of a man very ill-used, both by friends and enemies, yet submit- ting with some philosophy, his few virtues entirely forgot, except by one or two, and all his failings aggravated with bitterness."

However, the blow had to be faced. There was one method of getting money to tide over the present, and that was to push on with his prosecution of Halifax. He realized that Government could foil this scheme by hurrying forward the sentence of outlawry, and he therefore dallied with the idea of returning to London and facing the music. Though he reminded Cotes that the cause against Halifax was the one in which the General Warrant would be formally condemned, and declared that he would bear his own punishment with fortitude and dignity "if the cause of liberty can be essentially served", it is likely that his own pressing needs had at least something to do with his determination. Wilkes and the whole world knew that whatever Government might do to save its face, General Warrants were dead and buried; Wilkes knew that a formal condemnation at this late date was merely a matter of epitaphs on a grass-covered grave. But if there was a touch of eyewash there was also an element of truth, and in any case he can hardly be blamed for clutching at the benefit of the doubt.

His friends, however, though few and not influential, were more devoted than he thought. They dissuaded him from any notion of return, and held out hopes of his earning a reasonable income. On the 23rd of October, 1764, Almon, the publisher, sent him a letter of admirable delicacy, suggesting that Wilkes should write an account of his own case. "Do not be affronted", he went on, "if I say the profits of the sale ought to be yours; for no man has so well deserved of the public." He hinted further at contributions to a weekly political paper, which would be highly to Wilkes's advantage, and would ruin the adminis-tration, since Wilkes was the one man "capable of writing out the administration".

It was in connection with these schemes that Cotes and Churchill paid a flying visit to Wilkes at Boulogne. Wilkes arrived tuned to fresh endeavour. He had just written *A Letter to the Worthy Electors of the Borough of Aylesbury*, in which he defended himself with skill and attacked his enemies with vigour. He had no difficulty in defending himself so far as No. 45 was concerned; indeed, the defence was almost too easy. It was another matter to explain away the *Essay on Woman*, and he contented himself with attacking the means used to procure a copy.

At Boulogne Wilkes agreed to write, not only political papers, but also a history of England. In the midst of the negotiations Churchill became ill, and died early in November, leaving Wilkes his literary executor. Wilkes therefore added to his good intentions the editing of his friend's works with full notes. A month or so later he set out for Italy to cope in quiet with the works, which were to be "for my fame and for my purse too".

(2)

Wilkes did not intend to go alone. For some time past he and Churchill had been contemplating a tour in southern France and Italy with their respective mistresses, and Churchill's death merely reduced the party from four to two. Cotes, fearful that Wilkes would put pleasure before work and return from his tour poorer rather than richer, sent many remonstrances. But all to no effect. "I will not be chaste I hope this many a good year," Wilkes replied with direct truthfulness, adding with less probability, "but I will be in everything very prudent, and my eye is fixed, *not straitly, but steadily*, on my two great works, Churchill's edition and the History." Wilkes was nearer the truth than Cotes, though in the results Cotes was justified. Wilkes did not produce either his edition of Churchill or his History; but his failure was not due to his charmer. It was impossible for any man to carry facts and figures in his head sufficient for the task. Wilkes was too far removed from all sources of information; he had already found obscurities in Churchill's poems, and what was dark in Paris was not likely to be lighter at Naples. Nor were the Neapolitan archives likely to throw much light on England's past history. Added to these obvious difficulties, Wilkes was putting too great a strain upon his powers. He was not by nature, upbringing, or talent an author. He was a journalist, as is well illustrated by the fact that while he was dallying with the idea of a book all the early months of his exile, he was at the same time indefatigably sending Almon interesting titbits from the Continent. Now, at a moment's notice and with all the dice loaded against him, he proposed to throw off the habits of a lifetime and turn paragraphs into chapters. It was impossible, with or without a charmer.

(3)

Wilkes's companion was a lady of the name of Corradini. She was not the first and she was not to be the last; she had no particular influence on him, neither developing nor retarding his political views. In the normal course she would not have been worth mentioning, but, as it happens, later in life Wilkes began an autobiography, and true to his journalistic instincts soon forsook the orderly sequence of events to plunge into a flaming episode—the episode of this very liaison—set down too frankly for public print.

Corradini's attraction was utterly and wholly physical. Wilkes felt not a spark of love, not an atom of respect—and no one was more aware of the fact than himself. The girl was a native of Bologna and had drifted to Venice, where at sixteen she failed as a dancer, but became the mistress of the British Consul. On the bankruptcy of her lover she wandered to Paris, and there, when not yet nineteen years of age, met Wilkes in the spring of 1764. It required no effort to see to the bottom of her shallow merits, and Wilkes has laid bare her poor pennyworth of soul, but his treatment of the fretful little chit and his account of their relations are both characteristic. He paints her physical perfection with obvious enjoyment in the recollection, but has only a sneer—perhaps levelled in part at his own infatuation—for her other acquirements. "Impartial heaven", he remarks, "had not bestowed on her a common share of understanding or wit", and then adds with that touch of dry, judgmatic pity peculiar to himself, "of consequence her whole life had been sacrificed to the interest of others".

But if "in conversation she was childish and weak", if she enjoyed no other education than that "fit for a courtesan, born with little or no wit, the art of adorning gracefully her person", she was something more and something worse than a mere statue. The void left by intellect was filled with gusty humours —a jealousy that was now outraged vanity and now unfounded

K

fears, but never the child of love; gales of passion shook her delicate body and peevish whims made her almost unbearable. Beyond her outward form her sole recommendation was "the divine gift of lewdness", curiously chequered by a rank superstition. Wilkes records his hopeless efforts to soothe her jealousies, and laughs goodnaturedly at the quaint morality which made Corradini draw a curtain over a picture of the Virgin before yielding herself to her lover—"the more amusing", he comments, "because there were no curtains either to the bed or to the windows".

It was, of course, her beauty that most appealed to Wilkes, but ranking not far behind this obvious lure came "an air of modesty, diffidence, and timidity", a true, if rather squalid, family life, coyness, and a sense of religion—curious bait for a worthless libertine! One half begins to wonder if the tenderness for Polly were not something more than a mistletoe growth upon the tough and hardened oak; whether, in fact, somewhere among the tares of Wilkes's soul there was not a seed which might have grown in happier circumstances to a fair flower.

He was not without an ideal, but it was compounded in equal parts of spirit and the senses. In his wife he had found neither—she was too languid to be sensual, too dull to be spiritual; and he had shrugged his shoulders and gone his way, too indifferent to make the best of a bad job. In the early days of his connection with Corradini he thought his exile had been well rewarded by the discovery of his ideal—not in a single woman, but in two, each representing one side of his dual demand. Polly was passing into adolescence, unfolding a fresh young nature of great delicacy and charm. Wilkes watched the expanding of the bud with a depth of tender enjoyment, and in this innocent and pure delight found satisfaction for the higher cravings of his nature. So he passed his days, and in the evenings revelled in the fiercer pleasures presented by Corradini. "Nothing", he declared, "could be more luxurious."

But his ideal was soon marred. Corradini fell ill, and want of health brought to the surface all the flaws in her character—angry jealousy, peevish claims, resentment, and suspicion. Hard upon the heels of this disappointment came financial worries. Wilkes had placed his lady in a magnificent home overlooking the gardens of the Palais Royal. He had undertaken to provide not only for Corradini, but also for her mother, and surrounded them both with luxuries and servants. At the same time he was sparing no money on Polly's education. The double expense would have pressed hard upon his income in any case; it began to be overwhelming when under Cotes's management the remnants of his fortune disappeared. To add to his troubles, Corradini began to pine for southern skies, and badgered him to break up his little paradise and follow her to Italy. He was averse to change in any case, and was really unable to gratify her whim, at least until he had settled his affairs. So they parted in October, Corradini setting out for Bologna and Wilkes preparing for his interview with Cotes and Churchill.

He had intended after that meeting to follow his charmer in the company of Churchill and his mistress, when all plans were upset by Churchill's death. Wilkes was overwhelmed by something approaching despair. Truly his lot was hard—exiled and ruined for the benefit of others; ostentatiously denied by the great man for whom he had worked; bereaved of his dearest friend. "No event", he declared, "had ever struck Mr. Wilkes so deep to the heart. He had never before suffered the loss of any friend to whom he had been greatly attached. He was long in the deepest melancholy. On his return to Paris he passed the day and night alone in tears and agonies of despair. At last the three great remedies mentioned by Cicero came to his aid, *necessitas ipsa, dies longa, et satietas doloris*. Several friends concurred in forcing him again into the world. A variety of company by degrees engaged his attention, and his grief at length mellowed into pleasing reflections on the numberless virtues and wondrous abilities of the manly genius he had so much admired in life. The thought he had always entertained began to return upon him with new force, that we ought to endeavour the rendering our own being as happy to all around us, and to ourselves, as it is in our power"—a philosophy of life that is not without its merits.

With returning hope he despatched Polly to England, and on Christmas Day left Paris for Italy. At Bologna he rejoined Corradini, threw off dull care, and began a second honeymoon. They journeyed in leisurely fashion towards Naples, where he had decided to begin his literary labours, making short stays at Florence and Rome. It was all very pleasant, and in the rejuvenation of his spirits Wilkes was able to indulge the poetry of his nature. In his attitude towards the sights and sounds of the country, Wilkes was ahead of his age, which regarded the country as a sad fraud because it was not an everlasting pastoral of Corydons and Chloes. His autobiography abounds with pleasant descriptions of the roads along which they drove, the mountains, the scenery, the beauty of the orange-trees, and the fairy enchantment of the fireflies.

Not that the journey was without its tempests. Corradini diversified her kinder moments with demands for money, invitations to innumerable ragged relations, and outbursts of furious temper. But it had its compensations. At Rome the strange *ménage* made the acquaintance of Abbé Winckelman, Secretary to the Vatican and superintendent of the antiquities of Rome. He found an appreciative but fitful audience in Wilkes, and a less appreciative and more fitful audience in his charmer. The lady, bored to death, used to escape out of the room whenever she could, and, as Wilkes invariably followed her, the Abbé was too often left to pass the interval "very ill with the mother of Corradini, who had as little conversation as beauty".

At Naples they set up house, and Wilkes, with unnecessary self-condemnation, admits that "so sweet a situation and so beautiful a woman engrossed the mind of a man naturally too susceptible of pleasure, and tho' his faculties were not ener-vated, yet his schemes of ambition and public life were as much neglected as his own private concerns". The truth is that "public life" was impossible, and the "schemes of ambition" went no farther than literary projects which were almost equally impossible. In any case, the Italian episode lasted less than six months.

The end came quite dramatically. Throughout the early months of 1765 Grenville's administration had been hastening to a collapse. By May their fall was in sight, and Wilkes's friends at once wrote urging his return nearer to England. It was now that the influence of Corradini might have proved a bane, but Corradini, knowing nothing of events, chose this moment to decamp. She was, or claimed to be, pregnant, and demanded to be taken to Bologna. When Wilkes refused, she seized the opportunity of his temporary absence to pack up his valuables and depart. Friends notified Wilkes of her intentions, but he was always the punctilious gentleman in his amours, and on this occasion also half inclined to be glad. So he replied gallantly that she was incapable of stealing anything but hearts, and was free to come and go as she pleased. Her letters first ordered him to follow, but when they hinted that she would return, he sent her £200 and escaped himself. Fearful of his own resolution, he did not travel by land, since that would have meant passing her very door. Instead, he embarked on a small French trading vessel for Marseilles, where he drowned Corradini's memory in fresher faces. Thence he travelled quietly to Geneva, and passed some weeks with Voltaire, whose laugh, he tells us, "banished all the serious ideas the Englishman nourished of love and the fair Italian". Thence he returned to Paris.

One other event of his Italian tour deserves mention. At Naples he renewed his acquaintance with James Boswell, and flattered that ridiculous baby of a genius to his heart's content. Boswell, who was very young at the time, and as fond of the ladies as Wilkes himself, was revelling in that pose of melancholy dear to the hearts of youth. No doubt his affectation made him the better able to appreciate Wilkes's genial society;

at all events, he found in him "cheerfulness, knowledge, wit, and generosity".

A year later Boswell had better reason for sadness and hurried to Wilkes for consolation. Wilkes proved himself as sympathetic in trouble as he was bantering in prosperity. Boswell wrote gratefully: "I shall never forget your humane and kind behaviour to me at Paris, when I received the melancholy news of my mother's death."

CHAPTER XIV

"WE ARE ALL DELUDED THUS"

(1)

GRENVILLE's Ministry, which had begun with the turmoil of
the Wilkes affair, was neither long nor brilliant. Grenville himself was a man of the same mould as his Sovereign—narrow,
meticulous, and unyielding. In quieter times he would have
lived and died in decent obscurity, but the welter of public life
resulting from the King's intrigues and Pitt's pride pushed
him to the top, where his smouldering passions and diseased
obstinacy made confusion worse confounded. Having thrown
England into an uproar over the Wilkes affair, he began hector-
ing the King into sullen anger. "When he has wearied me for
two hours", the unfortunate monarch complained, "he looks
at his watch to see if he may not tire one for an hour more."
Then he turned his meddling mind to the taxation of America.
The Stamp Act, which was to be the fount of such unnumbered
woes, was passed in February 1765. It was followed by the
first of the King's illnesses, which gave rise to that strange
piece of legislation dubbed by Burke "the vertigo of the
Regency Bill". Hard upon its heels came a proposal to tax
foreign silks, which the Lords rejected. This rejection led to
a ferment among the weavers of Spitalfields, who, believing
the Duke of Bedford to be responsible, laid a regular siege
to his house, and began pulling down his courtyard walls and
invading the garden till the Riot Act was read and the Guards
summoned.

With the country in this state of chaos the King felt strong
enough to attempt a change of Ministers, and ordered his uncle,
the Duke of Cumberland, to negotiate with Pitt, who would
have returned to power but for a new and wholly unforeseen
impediment. Temple had for some time been growing impatient of the hesitations and manœuvres of the Opposition.
As early as February of this year he was reported to have said

that the struggle was only for places, and so far as places were concerned he was very well satisfied to see his brother, George Grenville, at the head of affairs. So the path had been opened for a family reconciliation, which by a beautiful stroke of irony was completed just in time to scotch Pitt's negotiations. Temple declined to co-operate with Pitt, and Pitt refused to act without him. Three weeks later the negotiations were renewed. Again Temple refused, whereupon Pitt bade farewell to his hopes with a sad quotation from Virgil: *"Extinxti me, teque, soror, populumque, patresque Sidonios, urbemque tuam,"* and retired to Somerset to brood over "a fatality I did not expect".

The King by this time was desperate, and gave the Treasury to Rockingham, who formed an administration as best he could. But truly it was a poor army with Pitt, like Achilles, lurking in his tent, and Wilkes, like Odysseus, chained to the island of Calypso. "It is a mere lute-string administration," sneered Charles Townshend; "it is pretty summer wear, but it will never stand the winter."

(2)

Rockingham's position was, indeed, far from enviable. In the last five years there had been a terrible fall from the glowing optimism of Pitt's administration. The country, which had then been united and invincible, was now seething with discontent —divided, perplexed, and impotent. Riots were breaking out among the lower classes; trade was stagnant, and the merchants at their wits' end. Abroad the prospect was no brighter. Prussia was haughty and annoyed. France and Spain had not been crushed, and from the moment of signing the Treaty had been nursing the thought of revenge. The Stamp Act had agitated the American colonies to the verge of rebellion.

It required a strong man with a strong backing to face such a position, and both requisites were lacking. Rockingham himself was a high-minded man with that type of negative virtue which wealth and position make easy. In the midst of a corrupt generation he was too rich to accept a bribe and too unimaginative to offer one. In the midst of a loose people he preserved an admirably starchy disposition. Undoubtedly he had principles, but they received too little support from his other qualities. He could neither speak nor write with ease, and was handicapped by inexperience, boils, and a passion for Newmarket. The best that can be said for him is that he was more blameless than brilliant, and consequently more fully aware of the existing evils than of their remedy.

If the leader was feeble, the backing was the reverse of strong. Rockingham had to face a House which had supported his rivals for the last four years. They had just passed a series of laws and resolutions for hard cash, which Rockingham now asked them to repeal for love. It was a desperate hope. Nor did he receive the slightest help from the King, who was not enamoured of Rockingham and disliked his policy. He had chosen him simply as less intolerable than Grenville, and from the first incited the "King's friends" to thwart and harass him.

Rockingham was early aware of his delicate position. He also recognized in a vague way that the one hope of improvement lay in a transfer of power from the shifting sands of the King's fancies to the broad foundation of popular favour. For this purpose, as well as out of genuine conviction, he made overtures to both Pitt and Wilkes. The former could be approached without disguise, but the latter needed more circumspection.

By way of placating Pitt he raised Pratt to the peerage as Lord Camden, and then time and again asked Pitt for his support. But Pitt was more than a trifle sore at his own failure, and haughtily suspicious of Rockingham's mediocrity. He told the world in icy fashion that he neither approved nor disapproved of the Ministry, and was sure of only one thing— that they were not in power at his advice. Six months later, in January 1766, having either conquered his aversion or formed a better opinion of the Ministry, he offered to join them—but only as their head. It was unfortunate, but not altogether surprising, that Rockingham had by then convinced himself that he was more fitted to lead than to follow the Great Commoner, and therefore listened in shocked silence to Pitt's frank demand for a "transposition of offices". Pitt's offer was rejected, and the breach between the two became complete. Meanwhile there was Wilkes.

(3)

It was in these circumstances that Wilkes returned to Paris. He did not know the names of the new Ministers, but he had been given to understand that many were friendly to him, and none definitely hostile. At an early date he was receiving letters of encouragement, and it was not long before proffers of aid and friendship came from the Ministry itself through his relations—proffers as welcome as they were unsolicited. Indeed, so unsolicited that Wilkes felt some suspicion. "I had a letter from Heaton," he wrote to Cotes on the 18th of August. "Heaton asks me several questions; I know not by what authority, nor on what foundation. If I am to give my opinion, Constantinople is by far the most eligible. Perhaps he is only amusing himself and me."

But Heaton was doing nothing of the sort. The Ministers were anxious for Wilkes's support; they were also convinced that he "had been extremely useful and ill-used". If they could get him back they would benefit themselves and also salve their uneasy consciences. There was, however, one real difficulty: the King's utter aversion to Wilkes was notorious, and made it far from easy for a weak Ministry to suggest his pardon and recall.

Rockingham hoped that time and some preliminary success in settling America might solve this as well as other problems. He therefore pushed ahead with the repeal of the Stamp Act, and in the meantime offered Wilkes an income with honest, if rather vague, hints of future action. Where he betrayed his limitations was in failing to explain the true facts of the situation.

Being quite in the dark and unable to get information, Wilkes was alternately hopeful, suspicious, and angry. Very naturally he asked why his friends had been sounded if nothing was to be done. Looking at the matter purely from his own point of view, he recognized that there might be difficulties, and by way of meeting them suggested the Embassy at Constantinople. It was vacant, it was the type of work he could do; it was far removed from England, and would not obtrude his presence on the King; no Turk could be offended at his ancient parodies. "Nothing", he declared, "can so effectually heal all breaches of every kind." Possibly his predilection for a foreign embassy came as something of a disappointment to the Ministers, who would much rather have had his active help in England. At all events, nothing happened except a strange offer of £1,000 a year, to be paid by the Ministers out of their own pockets. Not that money was a matter of no importance. Wilkes had received not a penny from Cotes during the whole of 1765; he had treated his ladies profusely, running up bills in Paris, and had not the vaguest notion how he was to pay his way. An income of £1,000 a year would suit him very nicely, and no doubt in the circumstances was rather more than a temptation—almost a necessity. Yet he fought shy of it. That he had earned his keep he was far from denying. "I should myself look upon it as paying very poorly all the costs of suit due to me, Wood's fine, what a Jury would condemn Halifax to, now General Warrants are exploded even by Mansfield, etc., etc."; but it was too secretive, looked like a pension or a bribe, and anyhow was uncertain. If they wanted to bribe him, they might at least do it openly upon some sure basis. To muzzle him with an income which might be stopped at a moment's notice was an insult to his intelligence. In his words, it "does not captivate my imagination".

Concurrently with this offer came all manner of rumours— stories of a break between Pitt and Temple, the usual hints that Bute was at the back of the Ministry, suggestions that they were not in earnest about liberty. Wilkes grew more and more suspicious, looked more closely at the letters he had received, and noted their vagueness. One was "too obscure", another was "couched in general expressions", and meanwhile "all private intelligence is very disadvantageous to the present powers". He began to think that they were playing with him merely to keep him quiet while they pursued their own policy, and in disgust turned over in his mind plans for attacking them: "If we are not good friends on public grounds, I am their determined, implacable enemy, ready to give the stab where it will hurt the most." His doubts were confirmed by letters from friends, such a letter as he received from John Horne, a parson with whom he now became acquainted for the first time, and who was to play a considerable part later on. This parson wrote in January 1766 expressing his fear that "by furnishing you with the means of pleasure, they [the Ministry] intend to consign you over to dissipation; and the grand points of national liberty and your glory to oblivion." Horne's opinion is of no value in itself; he was young and foolish, intent at the moment on kicking up his heels and proclaiming his own importance, but it represented an obvious view which several of Wilkes's friends took, and which Wilkes himself was inclined to believe.

He began to think his best chance lay in forcing the hands of Government, and sounded his friends on the idea of his returning to England in person. Though he was vague as to the exact advantage to be secured, he felt clearly that his presence would bring the issue to a head. Government would not dare to flout the popular feeling by taking a strong line against him, and at the same time would have to do something. With these ideas in his mind, he wrote peremptorily, rejecting the offered bribe as "clandestine, eleemosinary, and precarious", and demanding a full pardon—nothing more.

Unfortunately for Wilkes the time was not well chosen.

His letter arrived in the middle of December 1765, just as
Parliament was about to meet. The air was electric with the
news of tumults in America, and all thoughts were taken up
with the Stamp Act. The Ministry itself was trembling on the
verge of defeat, and as Macleane, one of the negotiators, told
Wilkes, "your warmest friends are afraid of broaching this
subject". The main result of Wilkes's letter was to annoy
Rockingham, who with the courage of despair rapped out that
though he loved Wilkes as a friend he did not dread him as
an enemy. It did, however, stir the Ministers to explain their
position a little more fully. They were genuinely anxious to
make full reparation, but could not do it all at once. More than
politics were involved; there were personal animosities to be
overcome, and the Ministry were not in a position to force
matters. Since they were in earnest, the so-called bribe
was not meant to be more than temporary; hence the objection that it was precarious had no weight. As to clandestine,
the Ministers were prepared to publish the fact to all the
world, since they thoroughly supported Wilkes's political
views.

This train of reasoning put forward by both Macleane and
Fitzherbert and backed up by Burke was sufficient to keep
Wilkes quiet for the moment. It also changed his attitude
towards the grant, and might have convinced him fully had
he known all the facts and been better served by his friends
at home. But his confidant, Cotes, was a man of little penetra-
tion, and his political leaders, Temple and Pitt, were not only
at loggerheads, but playing ridiculous parts. Cotes wrote letter
after letter full of absurd suspicions and still more dangerous
assumptions. The Ministers, he declared, having got into places
of power and profit, were unmindful of the steps which had
helped them to climb, while Temple (who refrained most
carefully from giving an opinion) was represented as urging
Wilkes's return.

If Wilkes was quiet, he was also chafing. "I am never disposed to be peevish," he told Cotes on the 15th of February,

1766, "yet I cannot but more and more lament the cruel situation in which I am, entirely ignorant of what is most necessary for me to know, and scarcely one friendly star left to point out my way." The foundations of his political world seemed to be crumbling, and he was in the dark. "I hear", he said plaintively in the same letter, "from every quarter that Lord Temple and Mr. Pitt are entirely separated. . . . I hear that Bedford, Sandwich, Halifax, etc., are united with Lord Temple and George Grenville. . . . Judge of my impatience to hear the truth of these strange reports from you. I am told a resolution was formed that Mansfield would confine me for life on account of the *Essay on Woman*, besides a pillory." It was the same in the succeeding month: "I am here in as entire ignorance of what concerns the public, as well as my private affairs." Meanwhile he read in the papers ridiculous stories of the enormous pensions granted to himself, though in fact little, if any, money was coming his way.

At last a ray of hope appeared. In the first few months of 1766 the Ministry had succeeded in repealing the Stamp Act. With that behind them, and some sort of order restored in America, they turned gingerly towards the Wilkes affair. As being a mere Treasury matter, they paid over to Cotes the £1,000 damages awarded two years earlier against Wood— though incidentally Wilkes never received the money owing to Cotes's bankruptcy—and in April moved a resolution condemning General Warrants.

Wilkes hailed the news, hoping that pardon would follow. "I am very happy to hear that the affair of General Warrants will come on in the House of Commons before the end of this session. I hope to have every reason to rejoice both on a public and a private account. I have been the great sufferer by them, and the question itself grew out of my case. The opportunity of the House going into this important question seems the most natural for my friends in power to propose my pardon and return. If so fair an occasion is suffered to pass unimproved, I can have no reason to believe that there is any serious design of doing me justice this session, and therefore I shall be necessitated to endeavour to bring about by means very disagreeable no less to myself than to others, what I wish to owe to favour and goodwill, for such I should consider what I have really a right to claim."

The opportunity came and went, possibly because of the topsy-turvy nature of the proceedings. The Ministry moved their resolution; whereupon George Grenville, of all persons, suggested that a Bill should be brought in to abolish General Warrants entirely. Pitt seconded, and this strange alliance perturbed and annoyed the touchy Rockingham so that the matter dropped.

The result was that Wilkes, true to his resolution, returned to England. He made no attempt at concealment, openly declaring his intention and ordering post-horses in his own name. He landed at Dover on the 11th of May, 1766, and was welcomed with a peal of bells. Thence he passed in triumph to London.

But now his lack of knowledge proved his bane. With praiseworthy loyalty he at once told the Ministry that he would do nothing "offensive or in the least disobliging to Lord Temple". Nothing could have been more fatal. Temple was at the moment hand in glove with George Grenville, the leader of the Opposition, and the most virulent of the Government's enemies. It was not an auspicious beginning, and the fact that the Ministry, in spite of this attitude, condescended to negotiate is proof of their real intentions in his favour. Not that they were happy. The Bishop of Carlisle was probably not far from the mark when he remarked, "The Ministers are embarrassed to the last degree how to act with regard to Wilkes. It seems they are afraid to press the King for his pardon, as that is a subject His Majesty will not easily hear the least mention of; and they are apprehensive, if he has it not, that the mob of London will rise in his favour, which God forbid." Temple, meanwhile, graciously sent his blessing to the outlaw, and by way of adding to the trouble, moved for the Bill on the

Seizure of Papers to be read. Otherwise he kept carefully clear of events.

On the 31st of May Wilkes retired baffled, taking his daughter with him. Two points are worth noting. In the first place Wilkes made no attempt to foment the popular unrest, preferring to negotiate quietly with the Government. Secondly, his visit did not in any way antagonize the Ministers. A week after his return to France, Macleane wrote: "I have seen our common, I mean our uncommon, friend Burke. He says the handsomest things possible of you, and bids me assure you of his entire regard. He thinks your matters will be made very easy in a few days. Let not your spirits droop; your character in England, great as it was before, is much bettered by your manner of carrying yourself this last trip." The Ministers continued to subscribe towards his pension, and all went on as before. Only the Rockingham Ministry was upon its last legs. Early in July it was dismissed. Possibly Wilkes was in part the cause; for a fortnight earlier two of the Ministry had been bold enough to apply for his pardon.

(4)

The downfall of Rockingham left the way clear for Pitt. The King sent for him, and at last England seemed to be getting the genius who could heal her wounds. But alas! Pitt was no ordinary man. As in Opposition he had been dogged by a "strange fatality", so now in office he was to be the victim of "infelicities", which appeared to him "incurable", while they "fermented and soured" the Ministry. Shelburne in later days declared that there was a large streak of madness in Pitt's family, and the light cloud of eccentricities which hovered continually over Pitt's head chose this crucial moment to thicken into a pall, which blotted out hope. It may have been a diseased mind, or overstrained nerves, or merely the effect of a body racked with gout, but whatever the cause the genius which had exalted England ten years before now sank into a gloomy abyss. Pitt had for some time been "cold and mysterious", withdrawing himself from the gaze of the world. Haughtiness and impracticability jostled in his mind with splendid gleams of visionary glory; flashes of genius dazzled the man's own mind, and by contrast plunged into deeper obscurity the common sense of life. It was this turbulent wreck of majesty that was entering office, and it brought infelicities in its train from the first moment. Pitt's friends were summoned to the Queen's House (now known as Buckingham Palace) on the 28th of July. Grafton arrived to find Northington, the Lord President elect, and Camden, the Lord Chancellor elect, twittering with agitation in the ante-chamber. Pitt, they told him in scared whispers, had entered the Closet to demand a peerage—a peerage of all extraordinary things when the two pegs on which his whole administration hung were his popularity as the Great Commoner and his ability to lash and blast the Lower House into obedience. Grafton shivered in his shoes, and the same tremor passed over all who heard. To friends and enemies alike it meant the end of the Ministry before it had begun.

Yet this ill-starred peerage brought benefit to one man—Wilkes. Hitherto the people had groaned and laboured under the ill-effects of a tyrannous rule in which they had no share. In their helpless discontent they had found two champions—Pitt and Wilkes—and if they had acquiesced in the rout of the one, it was because the other was still at hand. Now, to their indignation, Pitt had sold them. With the Great Commoner a renegade and the Apostle of Liberty an exile, they were friendless indeed, and hurling bitter execrations at Pitt they gave a double share of confidence to the martyr of their cause.

> As to Wilkes, my old friend, he remains where he was;
>   And as to his friends—why, plague rat 'em:
> But poor squire Pitt (all flesh is but grass)
>   Lies decently buried in Chatham.

Other infelicities followed hot and fast on the heels of this first egregious blunder. Pitt was on the rampage, regardless of

L

everything. Opposition was to be ended by taking odd members of all the jarring groups and dumping them into office. Pitt drew up his list without consultation, and curtly ordered his prospective colleagues to kiss hands, and with equal curtness sent packing whom he would. All attempts at negotiation, the slightest hint of preferences, put him into a rage and led to an abrupt break. He could hardly be civil to the King, if there was any prospect of being thwarted. "Permit me, Sir, most humbly to add that if Lord Rockingham's being *quiet*, as Mr. C. Townshend informs Your Majesty, depends on no other motive than Mr. Dowdeswell continuing Chancellor of the Exchequer, I most humbly beg to advise that a resolution be finally taken that Mr. Dowdeswell be immediately acquainted by Your Majesty's command that he is not to remain in that office."

The effect of this high-handed behaviour was that soon everyone was alienated—Temple, Grenville, the Bedfords, Rockinghams, and Newcastles—and Chatham was reduced to a few faithful, but bewildered, friends, and a jumbled mess of discordant individuals. Burke, with his glowing imagination, likened the Ministry to a mosaic, which lacked the necessary cement. It was more of a shifting kaleidoscope.

That was not all. By a curious lapse in his sense of time, Chatham determined to mount the horse from which he had been thrown five years before. His first move was to propound a northern alliance of England, Russia, and Prussia against the menace of the Bourbon family. The effort was a dismal failure.

His next trouble arose from the scarcity of corn, which was provoking riots throughout the country. Chatham passed an Order in Council forbidding the export of corn, which went some way towards allaying the unrest. No one could reasonably object, as the matter was urgent and Parliament up. But the rightness of his action was spoilt by his attitude in the House. Instead of admitting the Order to be illegal and asking for a Bill of Indemnity, Government rode the high horse. Even

Camden was betrayed into the fatuous remark that "if it was a tyranny, it was only a tyranny of forty days".

Meanwhile, after sketching out the major points to be tackled, Chatham disappeared to Bath, leaving the doubting Conway and the vacillating Grafton to carry on, and when he came back in November refused to take notice of the obvious strength of the Opposition. "Unions," he remarked airily, "with whomsoever it be, give me no terrors: I know my ground, and I leave them to indulge their own *Dreams*. . . . To sum up all in two words: *faction will not shake the Closet, nor gain the publick*." Having made this remark, he went back again to Bath, where he remained till March 1767. By this time his Ministry was wobbling to the verge of falling, but Chatham, still on the rampage, assured the King that "the preposterous Unions of Clashing Factions will not, Till Things change their Nature, outweigh and Finally Overbear the honest Sense of the Nation". With that he fell ill, mysteriously and horribly, so that in August the King had to comment that "the seeing a man that has appeared in so very great a light fall into such a situation is an abasement of human nature". It was the end of the Chatham Ministry, in fact though not in form. Left without guidance, amid a rising flood of opposition and mistakes, Grafton and the King both pleaded piteously with Chatham for one word of advice, but none was forthcoming. In sheer despair Grafton finally made terms with the Bedfords, and thereafter, he could hardly say how, came to stand for everything that Chatham abhorred.

(5)

On his return to France Wilkes gave up hope of storming England, and turned his attention to bread and butter. He meant to write in earnest. "Neither of us mean any more indiscretions," he wrote to Cotes; "we will be prudent and laugh at all our enemies." He had hardly penned the letter when rumours came that Pitt and Temple had been summoned to the King's Closet and were on the point of kissing hands. Wilkes's mercurial spirits rose at once; gone were the resolutions to be prudent and up sprang the old hopes. "I am sure I shall now have justice done to myself as well as to the great cause, in which I have been so deeply embarked. . . . I hope a full and free pardon will immediately be granted me, and I should have leave to return to England by the first post." Yet even now he wanted to avoid hurting sensibilities, and recurred to the idea of an appointment abroad. "I wish'd to have gone to Constantinople; I wou'd go to Quebec, and perhaps I might be found in no mean way useful there."

Disappointment and hope followed each other fast in those last few days of July 1766. Conflicting stories came tumbling over each other, and Wilkes was wholly at a loss. Yet some points were sure. Chatham had many obligations to him, and should at least stand neutral; Grafton had once supported him, and according to his brother, Colonel Fitzroy, was still a real friend; Camden could hardly deny him, and had actually told Fitzherbert that "the Ministry ought to do something for you"; Conway had long been sympathetic. Why not put fortune to the test? He sounded his friends, who agreed reluctantly, and on the 28th of October, 1766, he landed again at Dover.

On reaching London he at once wrote to Grafton asking him to obtain pardon from the King. The letter asked for nothing but permission "to continue in the land and among the friends of liberty". Grafton showed it to the King, who read it through without offering a single comment. Chatham remarked that it was an awkward business, in which it was difficult to meddle. His advice was to take no notice for the moment. Government were sympathetic, and Wilkes might have remained in England unmolested; but not unnaturally he wanted some more specific assurance. His friends urged Grafton to do something, but Parliament had just met and the Ministry were already engaged with their first blunder—the Bill of Indemnity. Grafton, anxious and undecided, replied that he was not equal to the business, which Chatham alone could effect.

Wilkes neither could nor would bring himself to petition Chatham, a course which, he informed Temple, "was irreconcilable to every sentiment of honour, both public or private". On hearing Grafton's decision he at once returned to Paris.

CHAPTER XV

THE WANDERER RETURNS

(1)

THIS prompt return to Paris was not the outcome of panic, still less of despair. It was a sudden resolution which marked the end of one period and the beginning of another—a definite change of outlook and method, which had been growing in Wilkes's mind and corresponded to a ripening of his character.

Hitherto Wilkes had been in all respects a follower. He had entered politics to please his friends, and there devoted himself to Pitt's service. When the outcome had proved unfortunate, he relied, as followers will, upon the efforts of his friends and leaders, expecting that as he had helped them to the best of his abilities they would do their best for him. It was Pitt's denunciation that first opened his eyes, and it was then for the first time that he began to grow suspicious. Yet the lesson was not complete. He still pinned his faith to friends—only to be fooled. Pitt failed him first, then Rockingham, and now Grafton. The conviction had been growing that self-help was necessary and had resulted in two visits to London—not so much to act for himself as to stir up his sluggish friends: "nothing would alarm the present Ministers so much as the idea of my coming to London".

The third rebuff, at the hands of Grafton, put an end to this rather pathetic trust in others. Henceforward Wilkes would rely on no one but himself. If he wanted pardon, he must extort it; if he wanted a competency, he must earn it. Obviously his past services were forgotten, and he must cut his losses, beginning anew.

(2)

It was clear to him now that he must settle the date of his return by reference to facts and not to Ministers. To live in England on sufferance with the fear of arrest continually before his eyes was impossible. Therefore he must face the worst that the law could do, and arrange his return so as to reduce the dangers to a minimum. A General Election was due in March 1768, and he decided that his best course was to obtain election and meet his troubles with the prestige and protection attaching to a Member of Parliament. In the meantime he must live as best he could, and prepare the way for his candidature.

With his mind made up, Wilkes grew happy and calm, and found work comparatively easy. There is a different atmosphere about his letters. Within a few days of his return to Paris he could write to Cotes: "I have, as well as you, struggled through many difficulties, and I hope we shall both ride at last triumphant." Changes in the Ministry no longer excited him. When Almon told him that there were possibilities, he merely replied, "I will write to Mr. Fitzherbert as soon as I find the arrangements you mention take place." What he really thought was betrayed in another letter, where he said bluntly: "You never can trust any Ministers in our country. The Whigs in power turn Tories; though, alas! the Tories do not turn Whigs."

Meanwhile there were two pressing needs—to get some sort of income and to keep his name prominently before the public. To a large extent he combined the two, becoming an assiduous contributor to Almon's political papers. He even got down in earnest to the *History of England*. Not that he wrote much; but the Introduction was duly completed and published. He also produced his second great Philippic—the *Letter to the Duke of Grafton*. It was finished by the 12th of December, 1766, but not published until the end of the next April. The delay was intentional. Wilkes was courting publicity, and had to continue the process for some sixteen months. He did not wish the benefits of the letter to be frittered away too soon.

The two main points of interest in the *Letter* were a scathing attack on Chatham and a full account of Wilkes's arrest in 1763. In the former part Wilkes poured out all his bottled resentment, painting in trenchant style the coldness of Pitt's character and the inconsistencies of his conduct; and yet Wilkes's truthfulness compelled him also to record the glories of his administration. If Wilkes was sometimes wide of the mark, in one point, at least, he showed a profound insight. "The Constitution of our country", he remarked, "has no obligations to him. He has left it with all its beauties, and all its blemishes."

The account of his arrest was singularly opportune. The people had never known the full facts, and their publication swung popular sentiment over in a flood; from that moment Wilkes became a hero, and an oppressed hero at that.

Other papers followed in a stream, sometimes with amusing results. Among them was Wilkes's account of his duel with Talbot. That peppery peer, as touchy as ever, at once accused Temple, who denied the charge hotly; words followed, and a duel was averted only by the combined efforts of the Lords Gower and Harcourt. Talbot retired angry and unappeased, while Temple stamped off declaring that he was ready to fight Talbot at any time or place.

So much for his efforts to keep himself in the public eye. The matter of income was rather more complicated. The Rockingham pension had never been very regular, and became less so when the Ministry fell. But by dint of repeated applications, Heaton and Fitzherbert collected minor sums from time to time. That and the proceeds of his pen went some way towards Wilkes's support. But as it was only a matter of months, Wilkes ventured to stretch all possibilities to the utmost, applying to his friends for further help. So one way or another the months passed, and the time drew nearer for his *coup d'état*.

Towards the middle of 1767 he unfolded his plan to a few friends, not so much for advice as for promises of support. His friends were brutally frank, assuring him that his scheme was "moonshine", "chimerical", "absolutely impossible", etc. Wilkes met these well-intentioned remonstrances by inserting in the papers notices of his determination to contest the City of London. Most people, the Government included, regarded these letters as nonsense, and were ultimately taken by surprise. Those of his friends who did believe them wrote entreating him at least to choose some less pretentious constituency but without avail.

(3)

Wilkes left Paris on the 22nd of November, paid a flying visit to London to make his final arrangements, and then went for a short tour on the Continent. He returned to England finally about the 6th of February, 1768.

England had altered during his exile. He had left shortly after the Peace of Paris, and the country had ever since been suffering from the inevitable aftermath of war. The transition from war to peace is never easy and demands an able Ministry. Unfortunately all the three Governments which had held power had been well below the average, and Chatham's Ministry was in addition divided against itself.

Though no one realized it, England was passing through an economic crisis. The whole of the eighteenth century was a slow, uneasy approach to the industrial revolution, and the riots and discontents arose as much from economic pressure as from Ministerial bungling. The war was certainly not the only factor creating difficulties. India was beginning to pour her wealth into the country, a fact which tended to upset values and at the same time introduced a new element into politics. The "nabobs" evoked the same dislike as war profiteers; they were frankly distasteful to the King and objects of suspicion to the old nobility. Side by side with this influx of wealth and ostentation there came the disorganization of the American trade due to the attempts to tax the colonists, with the result that the old merchants and traders found their fortunes melting away. Meanwhile foreign affairs were menacing; the Peace had done no more than whet the French appetite for revenge, and England was kept on tenterhooks by such incidents as the French annexation of Corsica. Lastly, soaring prices, a series of bad harvests and extremely severe winters, led to something approaching desperation among the people. The whole country was in a ferment. It was quite common for the poor to rise *en masse* and seize food from the flour-mills and warehouses, sometimes selling it in an orderly fashion at moderate prices, the money being handed over to the owners, and at other times simply treating it as loot. During the winters people were frozen to death in the streets, and in 1767 the London Common Council felt obliged to open a subscription for the destitute. It is recorded of January 1768, the month before Wilkes returned, that "the river below bridge bore all the appearance of a general wreck; ships, boats, and small craft lying in a very confused manner, some on shore and others sunk or overset by the ice. A fishing boat was discovered near Deptford Creek, jammed in by ice, and all the people in it frozen to death."

The position was growing steadily more serious. There were no trade unions and no employers' federations, and consequently the workers looked to Government for redress of grievances which were real but not understood. They were demanding higher wages with growing insistence; they were demanding protection; they were furious with the multiplication of machinery which might have helped them. When with the good sense and moderation characteristic of English workmen they attempted to explain their troubles, Government in a panic read the Riot Act and called out the military. The ignorance and cowardice of Ministers clothed their peaceful petitions with the panoply of revolt.

(4)

In the midst of the ferment Wilkes appeared. As the country had changed, so had he. The man who had left was a light-hearted subaltern, relying mainly on his friends and leaders. The man who returned was in his forty-first year, standing at the threshold of middle age, with his vigour unimpaired and his judgment ripened. The wit, the courage, the resourcefulness were still there. Only the wildly exuberant spirits had gone, and their place had been taken by tenacity of purpose.

As for his views, his outlook was more penetrating, if less superficially wide, and he recognized the importance of bread and butter. To a man who had been stripped of fortune and driven into exile by means that were at once illegal and oppressive, the big words of Liberty and Freedom meant something concrete—a great deal more than they had meant when a joke had been turned into an affair of State. The Wilkes who returned to England was far more of a patriot though far less of an idealist; liberty had become less dazzling but more weighty. If he played pranks upon the Government in the future, it would be at least for some definite end and with a limited liability; he would no longer draw a bow at a venture.

(5)

The outstanding feature of the early days of his return was his extreme moderation. For the best part of a month he lay hid, taking a preliminary look round. It is true that he employed the time in drafting a skit on Sir John Cust, the Speaker, and perhaps other political paragraphs, but he refrained from publishing them till later, and in any case they were mainly good-humoured. He began his campaign proper on the 4th of March by writing a personal letter to the King asking for pardon. The letter was delivered at the Queen's House by his own footman, and remained unanswered. It is usual to regard this letter as a piece of stupid impertinence, but it was nothing of the sort. Wilkes had made several efforts to obtain a pardon through the ordinary channels without success. The method he now adopted was the outcome of his new and independent attitude, while the letter itself was a plain hint to the King of his intentions. Wilkes was not returning to be a thorn in anyone's side; he wanted to live peaceably and carve out a career in the

City. Had the King accepted the letter in the spirit in which it was sent, Wilkes would almost certainly have disappeared from the political arena, or at most have taken his seat in the House as a dumb and indifferent member.

It was, however, too much to expect the King to understand. The Royal obstinacy had increased with the years. To the Royal mind, Wilkes was a villain, and whatever he did was open to suspicion; he was a "wicked and disappointed man", indulging in an "outrageous licentiousness"; his actions were *ipso facto* "strange", "lawless", "indecent", or "unjustifiable". The two were poles apart, and Wilkes had reason for complaining that "through his whole reign almost it has been the King versus Wilkes". None the less Wilkes did not intend to shut the door. Though his letter had been ignored, he studiously avoided all violence, so that at any point George III might have an opportunity of relenting.

A week later, receiving no answer, he announced his candidature for the City of London. Both his printed manifesto and his speech on the hustings were in keeping with his new attitude. He rested his claim to favour on past performances, not on future promises. "The two important questions of public liberty, respecting General Warrants and the seizure of papers, may perhaps place me among those who have deserved well of mankind", he wrote in his manifesto, and ended with nothing more inflammatory than, "if I am honoured with so near a relation to you, it will be my ambition to be useful, to dedicate myself to your service, and to discharge, with spirit and assiduity, the various and important duties of the distinguished station in which I may be placed". He could hardly have offered less. On the hustings he held much the same language, but with an even more direct denial of revolutionary feelings. His merits were his past efforts, and they were finished and done. As for the future, "I stand here a private man, unconnected with the great, and unsupported by any party. I have no support but you; I wish no other support." If elected, his object would be to promote to the utmost of his abilities "the trade and commerce of this great metropolis", and to pay "the greatest deference" to the sentiments of his constituents.

What he declared in public he maintained also in private. Horne, who was an active assistant, some years later in a fit of jealousy wrote a series of attacks on Wilkes, in the course of which he described this election. "You thought it proper", he wrote, "to adopt the language of a penitent. To the one you talked of 'Saul transformed into St. Paul'; to another you were more poetical, and told him that 'hitherto your life must be considered as only bearing the blossoms, and that the public might now expect from you the fruits'; and you talked of the follies of your youth." Horne was, of course, charging him with insincerity, but the words which Horne puts into his mouth are of a piece with the rest of his conduct. All his words, deeds, and writings at this time were those of a well-meaning, moderate man, inclined to reform, but the whole world away from riot and disturbance.

Though springing himself on the electorate at the last moment, he won a considerable measure of support. The Joiners' Company presented him with the Freedom of the City; a dinner was given in his honour and funds raised to pay his election expenses. In spite of his efforts, however, he was last on the poll, receiving 1,247 votes as against 3,729 obtained by the first on the list. This was Thomas Harley, who, as Sheriff, had superintended the vain effort to burn No. 45 in 1763. He was now Lord Mayor and the Court candidate; as such, and also, perhaps, because of past recollections, he was at all times the implacable enemy of Wilkes.

In no way daunted by the result, Wilkes made a short speech of thanks to his supporters, pointing out the obvious disadvantages under which he had laboured, and ending with a wonderfully adroit bombshell. "And now, gentlemen, permit me to address you as friends to liberty, and freeholders of the County of Middlesex, declaring my intention of appearing as candidate to represent you in Parliament; and still hoping by your means to have the honour of being useful to you in the British Senate. I recommend it to you, in the strongest manner, to exert yourselves to preserve the peace and quiet of this great city."

So began the famous Middlesex election, the final ripple of which ended in 1928 with the latest Franchise Act.

CHAPTER XVI

THE MIDDLESEX ELECTION

(1)

THIS election was big with fate in a way Wilkes never dreamed. Yet as though foreseeing the need for caution, he lost no chance of urging peace and quietness. His first public pronouncement ended on that note, and as he began so he continued. Elections in those days had more than a touch of Eatanswill, and Wilkes was painfully aware how easily a riot might begin.

The time was short; but short as it was Wilkes performed wonders. He had an able, if wayward, lieutenant in John Horne, the parson of Brentford, and with his aid scampered round the constituency, forming committees, hiring rooms, arranging processions, organizing meetings, and registering his supporters. Meanwhile he set the printing presses to work and distributed thousands of handbills urging his friends "that all possible measures might be used to preserve peace and good order through the whole of the election for the County of Middlesex, to convince the world that liberty was not joined with licentiousness". Wilkes, in short, was giving a striking display of organizing genius.

With all arrangements complete, Wilkes went quietly to Brentford the evening before the poll. He was determined to be on the hustings at the appointed time. Actually he was two hours early, arriving there at eight in the morning. The Sheriffs came by nine, but the two other candidates did not put in an appearance till one o'clock, which annoyed the voters and added to Wilkes's popularity. They were not to blame for their lateness. At an early hour in the morning a crowd of weavers from Spitalfields had occupied Piccadilly and all the roads and turnpikes leading to Brentford. They had nothing to do with the election, but they had adopted Wilkes as their champion and allowed no one to pass who was not provided with a blue cockade or a placard supporting Wilkes. The other two candidates, Sir William Beauchamp Proctor and Mr. Cooke—or rather Mr. Cooke's representative, as he himself was ill—found themselves in the midst of the crowd, and only struggled through with the greatest difficulty.

This zeal of self-appointed advocates was a real problem with which Wilkes was increasingly faced. The many bodies of discontented men in the country had nothing to do with him, and on his first appearance some of them, the sailors in particular, disowned connection. But the refusal of the Government to grant redress soon drove them to hail Wilkes as a champion and thrust themselves upon him as the "Wilkites", of whom he declared that he was not one. His statement was perfectly true, and one of his great difficulties was to cool their disruptive ardour.

But to return to the election. Apart from these self-appointed supporters, Wilkes's followers behaved soberly in the face of provocation. There was some scuffling when his opponents flaunted banners with the device "No blasphemer", but otherwise the voting was a model of decorum—much more so than in the generality of elections.

By the evening of the first day Wilkes had obtained a long lead, and the crowd surged back to London in the highest spirits. When the next day Wilkes was elected by a large majority there was a regular "boat-race" night. "No. 45" was scrawled up everywhere; coaches were stopped until their occupants had cheered for Wilkes and Liberty; every house was ordered to illuminate its windows. Compliance found the crowd good-humoured, but resistance led to trouble. Refractory coaches were pelted with mud, and darkened houses had their windows broken. But the uproar had much more of high spirits than of high treason. If that perfect gentleman, the Austrian Ambassador, complained that he had been taken out of his coach and held upside down while the magic number was chalked on the soles of his boots, it added more to the gaiety of nations than it took from his dignity. If that quaint genius, Alexander Cruden, felt it necessary to patrol the streets with a sponge obliterating the offensive number, it kept him in health for the completion of his great Concordance. If the Duke and Duchess of Northumberland had to broach a cask of their own beer and drink Wilkes's health with the crowd—well, beer is a good tipple and the better for being drunk. As Walpole remarked, "It has ended like other election riots, and with not a quarter of the mischief that has been done in some other towns." The Ministers were nervous enough, but Grafton, accustomed to the crowd at Newmarket, for once showed his common sense. He was opposed to the idea of issuing a proclamation, which, he told the King, "would only appear as finding fault only with the people for their joy too riotously testified".

Wilkes was once more a Member of Parliament—that was the outstanding fact. "Mr. Wilkes's success", wrote the Duke of Richmond to the Duke of Newcastle, "is an event which I think must produce something. I should be glad to know your Grace's sentiments upon it." "Wilkes's merit", Newcastle replied, "is being a friend to liberty, and he has suffered for it; and therefore it is not an ill symptom that it should appear that that is a merit with the nation." Wilkes stood rather high amid the strawberry-leaves. Not only Richmond and Newcastle, but Portland as well, were chuckling over the result. Amongst the lesser nobility, Rockingham and Shelburne were feeling happy, while Chatham apparently was not displeased.

(2)

Wilkes was naturally jubilant; he had consolidated his position, obtained the protection attaching to a Member of Parliament, and shown that he had a numerous following. But he wanted something more: he wanted pardon. With that in view he had already told Government that he would surrender at the Court of King's Bench on the first day of term, and had done his best to show his moderation. In his manifesto after the election he continued the good work. Though he did allow himself a slight dig at "the sons of venality", his main concern was to emphasize his reasonableness. He told the free-holders of Middlesex that his only object was to maintain the civil and religious rights of Englishmen and to promote "the dignity, advantage, and prosperity of the County of Middlesex".

Meanwhile he exerted all his influence to stop even the slight rowdyism that had occurred, and then went quietly to Bath. His appearance there was awaited with much trepidation, and the decency of his behaviour when he arrived affected different people differently. Camden, who had once been deeply in league with him, was at Bath during the visit, and wrote two letters to Grafton, one just before Wilkes came and the other shortly after he had left. The difference of tone is striking. In the earlier letter Camden was full of apprehension. Rumour had been busy magnifying the Brentford riots, and Camden inveighed against "a criminal flying his country to escape justice—a convict and an outlaw". Exactly seventeen days later Camden was in quite another mood. He was now convinced that "till judgment is finally pronounced against Mr. W. by the court, no man has a right to pronounce him guilty". It was extraordinary the difference his opponents found between the Wilkes of flesh and blood and the Wilkes of rumour. Even George III was to experience the same surprise when at long last he was forced to see his libeller face to face.

As for others of the *beau monde* at Bath, when they had recovered from their first fright, they thought fit to indulge in offensive personalities. Wilkes was not so easily to be put down, and his persecutors were silenced, often by a look.

(3)

Government were at their wits' end. What was to be done with Wilkes? The King had no sort of doubt. Wilkes in his eyes was not only an unspeakable outsider, but a very dangerous fellow. He was much too presumptuous, most disrespectful to his betters, and full of these new-fangled and outrageous doctrines. If he were not muzzled, his seditious views would spread, and that would be the end of all order and decency. Much better set the law on his track and have done with him once and for all.

The King's attitude was natural and almost pathetic. It would be a mistake to regard him merely as an obstinate old fool. The trouble lay in his incredible lack of imagination, which could see nothing wrong in himself and nothing right in Wilkes. He did most genuinely believe that all Wilkes did was tainted with inherent rottenness and punishable by law. No one tried to enlighten him till Wilkes himself took the matter in hand. They did tell him that the law was not quite so helpful as they could wish, but they said it rather apologetically, and his comment was much the same as Mr. Bumble's.

The truth is that the Cabinet was divided. The Bedfords to a man supported the King's view; they could neither forgive nor forget the attacks of the *North Briton*. But the Bedfords were not as yet supreme, and a large element of the Cabinet held more moderate views. They would willingly have taken no action, but the King's anger and Wilkes's determination made this impossible. Rather helplessly they left themselves in the hands of Mansfield, who as Lord Chief Justice would have to deal with Wilkes when he appeared in court on the 20th of April. Mansfield turned the whole of his powerful mind to the despicable task of avoiding responsibility, and hit upon a solution about a week before the fatal day. He had been harassed and worried before, but having found the solution he "seemed very cheerful", as Rockingham said, though very mysterious about Wilkes and what he intended to do.

(4)

The 20th of April came at last; Mansfield took his seat on the bench, and Wilkes, true to his promise, appeared. There was no fuss, no riot; Wilkes had seen to that by issuing a special appeal. He at once read a carefully prepared speech. He had come, he said, to submit himself in everything to the laws of his country. He had been found guilty on two counts—the re-publication of No. 45 and the publication of a ludicrous poem. As for the first, he could not yet see that there was the smallest degree of guilt. As for the second, the poem had given just offence, and Wilkes blushed again at the recollection that it had been at any time and in any way brought to the public eye. But he could not hold himself to blame. "The nation", he remarked, "was justly offended, but not with me, for it was evident that I had not been guilty of the least offence to the public." The poem had been carefully concealed, and had not yet been published, "if any precise meaning can be affixed to any word in our language". He ended with a reiteration of his pacific intentions. "I have stood forth, my lords, in support of the laws against the arbitrary acts of Ministers. This court of justice, in a solemn appeal respecting General Warrants, showed their sense of my conduct. I shall continue to reverence the wise and mild system of English laws, and this excellent Constitution. I have been much misrepresented; but under every species of persecution, I will remain firm and friendly to the monarchy, dutiful and affectionate to the illustrious Prince who wears the crown, and to the whole Brunswick line."

If words meant anything, and words, moreover, backed by deeds, Wilkes had done everything in his power to declare his loyalty and law-abiding wishes. On the worst possible con-struction he had some six years before accused the King of a lie and written an obscene poem. He had denied the con-struction put on his words, and apologized again and again for everything, and in any case had paid heavily for both offences. On several occasions he had besought a pardon in the most dutiful terms, and since his return had done nothing in the least blameworthy. Here, if ever, was a man who might be pardoned. But he was guilty of one unpardonable crime—he was popular with the common herd.

The idea of pardon entered no one's head, much less the idea of justice. The most that Mansfield could do was to avoid the responsibility of pronouncing the penalty. His answer to Wilkes was a pronouncement that as Wilkes was an outlaw he was unable to deliver himself up; he simply did not exist in the eyes of the law, and the court could take no notice of him until some person who did exist arrested this non-existent person and brought him up in a regular manner.

The quibble may or may not have been right in law, but in everything else it was pure farce. The common people (with much more respect for law than law deserves, if Mansfield was right) came to the obvious conclusion that Wilkes was now free, and Mansfield suddenly found himself for a short moment popular—almost embarrassingly so. The Attorney-General, on the other hand, found himself obliged to take the step which he thought Wilkes had saved him. He had now to fill up the proper forms, tangle himself in the appropriate red tape, and earn a double share of infamy by arresting Wilkes.

He did not relish the job, and no doubt hoped that Wilkes would help him by doing something outrageous. Wilkes did nothing of the sort, and a breathless, expectant week passed. "The Lord Mayor", wrote Walpole on the 23rd of April, "has turned out some of the Sheriff's officers for not apprehending Wilkes. In short, some are afraid; more want to shift the unpopularity from their own shoulders to those of others; Wilkes does not resist, but rather shifts his quarters, not being impatient to have his cause tried when he is on the wrong side of a prison. The people are disposed to be angry, but do not know wherefore, and the court had rather provocation was given than give it; and so it is a kind of defensive war."

Only the King remained fixed in his opinion, and when Grafton told him of "the desire of His Majesty's principal servants jointly expressed that Mr. Wilkes should not be allowed to sit in Parliament if it could be avoided by any means justifiable by law and the Constitution and conformable to the proceedings of Parliament", the King replied briefly:

"The expulsion of Mr. Wilkes appears to be very desirable, and must be effected." Why it appeared to be so essential, and what method was to be employed, His Majesty wisely refrained from explaining.

This bald command had to be met somehow, but the Government, greatly daring, hit on an expedient for delay. Their one hope now was to gain time. Accordingly, though Wilkes had to be arrested and brought in proper form before Mansfield on the 27th of April, that astute judge had no intention of coming to an immediate decision. If the matter could only be postponed for a few weeks, and Wilkes were meanwhile kept in prison, Parliament would have met and finished its short spring session, and would not be meeting again till the winter. There would be a breathing-space of several months, and luck might provide a solution.

The 27th, therefore, was occupied with mere preliminaries. The non-existent Wilkes materialized at the magic of a writ; and Mansfield, with an impiety that Wilkes would have scorned, shifted the responsibility to the Almighty with the prayer, "God forbid that the defendant should not be allowed the benefit of every advantage he is entitled to by law", before peremptorily refusing bail.

Wilkes was handed over to the Marshal of the King's Bench prison; but the common people, natural repositories of common sense, argued that whatever the law might lay down and whatever Mansfield might pray, a man who had been allowed freedom without bail for two and a half months might very well be allowed it with bail for a few days longer. A huge crowd gathered on Westminster Bridge, took out the horses of the Marshal's coach, turned it round, and dragged Wilkes and his gaolers up the Strand and through the City to the Three Tuns Tavern in Spitalfields, where they tumbled out the Marshal and his men and chivvied them away.

The weavers were once more on the warpath, and as usual filling Wilkes with embarrassment. He was far from pleased at this turn of events. Brave as he was, he had no occasion to

be desperate, and had no desire to become a species of bandit
chieftain. With admirable presence of mind he harangued his
deliverers, persuaded the majority to go home quietly, and
then slipped away in disguise to hand himself over to the
prison authorities. For this he obtained a certain amount of
credit among the more moderate men. But it was the fate of
Wilkes to be eternally misunderstood; his enemies forgot his
action, remembering only the fact of rescue and the ridicule
it had brought upon themselves. Like Pharaoh of old they
hardened their hearts and laid the foundations of fresh trouble
by meditating the employment of soldiers and sending out
whips to their supporters in Parliament. They managed to
alarm themselves still more by assuring each other that Wilkes
meant to corrupt the Army by moving for an increase of pay,
and when they had assured each other of this often enough,
thought they had found further evidence of his desperate
villainy.

(5)

Wilkes was obviously disappointed. No one could pretend that
to refuse bail at this point was meeting him half-way. To all
appearance Government meant to declare war, and Wilkes
would have to accept the challenge.

In his new attitude of self-reliance he was taking much greater
pains to prepare for all eventualities. From his prison he issued
another address, still breathing submission and resignation; he
found consolation in the consciousness of innocence, and could
endure far greater sufferings cheerfully since his countrymen
reaped the happy fruits of his persecution. Yet the die was
being cast, and the probability of a clash was in his mind when
he wrote the concluding words: "Under all the oppression which
Ministerial rage and revenge can invent, my steady purpose is
to concert with you and other true friends of this country the
most probable means of rooting out the remains of arbitrary
power, the Star-Chamber inquisition, and of improving as well
as securing the generous plans of freedom which were the boast

of our ancestors." This is the first hint of active reform, and it came as an answer to his imprisonment.

As he was fully determined that if all doors were to be shut Government should do the shutting, he may have been only half conscious of this new twist to his mind, or he may have been deliberately giving a veiled hint. In either case, he was not anxious to renew the war. Why should he be? His own prospects were much poorer than before. In 1763 he had been free, he had been a member of a strong party, and above all had relied on the genius of Pitt and the magic of his name. Now he was in prison; Pitt was lost in Chatham; the Opposition was distracted and feeble; and though the people were angry, they could do nothing but riot—a game that Wilkes disliked. He had every inducement to make his peace.

Hence, while he may have been collecting ammunition, he kept his stores carefully hidden. He already possessed a copy of a letter which he afterwards published with great effect—a letter written by Lord Weymouth urging Justices of the Peace to call out the troops if necessary against the mob. He held it back, though fully aware of the storm its publication would arouse, because it was not yet open war, but only the preliminary state of tension.

(6)

His trial took place on the 7th of May. Wilkes himself was not brought into court, and when Glynn demanded his presence he was told cynically that the Marshal and all his officers were busy and could not be spared. So the question of outlawry was argued in his absence. The arguments over, Mansfield blandly declared that the case was so knotty that it must be argued all over again the next term, and maintained his decision in spite of everything that Glynn could do. As the next term would begin after Parliament had risen, the immediate problem was thus solved—but at a serious price. Private letters from all quarters testified that the delay was causing great dissatisfaction, that there was a sullen discontent throughout the kingdom, and that, in short, affairs wore an ugly look. Government, half pleased at their own ingenuity, and more than half terrified at its results, placed guards of soldiers round Wilkes's prison.

CHAPTER XVII

THE MASSACRE OF ST. GEORGE'S FIELDS

(1)

GOVERNMENT had only themselves to thank for what followed. Anyone can understand vigour or leniency; most people can appreciate compromise. It is vacillation that leads to disaster. The people had been definite enough; they had elected Wilkes Member for Middlesex, and on every opportunity testified their devotion. Government, on the other hand, had first ignored him, then clapped him into prison—no one knew why—and finally failed to come to a decision.

Such a position could not go on for ever. Either Wilkes was guilty or he was not; and if not, then clearly he must be allowed to take his seat when Parliament met on the 10th of May. There were generally crowds round his prison, and Government, with an uneasy feeling that the crowds would be larger than ever on the 10th of May, increased the military guard and waited helplessly on events.

They did not have to wait long. The crowds duly assembled day after day, and the prison authorities, in their anxiety, entreated Wilkes to calm them. Always obliging, he appeared at the window, and did all that was asked of him. But on the 10th of May the authorities themselves gave the provocation. Some doggerel verses in praise of Wilkes were stuck on the prison walls by the mob and promptly torn down by an officious justice of the peace. The verses did no harm, but their destruction did. Thoroughly roused, the mob yelled for the paper, and when it was not restored began throwing stones. The Riot Act was read in a hurry and a volley from a detachment of Scots Guards killed six spectators and wounded others. Worse still, a party of soldiers pursued a man who appeared to be a ringleader into a cowshed, and there managed to shoot an entirely innocent man of the name of Allen.

The events which followed were typical of both sides. The next day Lord Barrington, Secretary for War, issued a letter thanking the troops for their action and promising that "in case any disagreeable circumstances should happen in the execution of their duty, they should have every defence and protection that the law can authorize and this office can give". Under the law as it then stood the letter was in a sense necessary. The wretched troops were liable to be shot if they disobeyed orders and liable to be hanged if in the execution of their orders they killed any civilians. But the occasion was unfortunate and the language indiscreet. Wilkes obtained a copy and published it "with the hope of promoting a parliamentary inquiry into that bloody transaction".

Meanwhile the coroner's juries returned verdicts of accidental death in the case of the six spectators, and of wilful murder in the case of Allen. Three soldiers were arrested on a coroner's warrant, but two were at once released on bail by Mansfield. No doubt he was right, but the people were bound to contrast the difference in treatment between the soldiers accused of murder and Wilkes accused of nothing in particular, and the difference was emphasized by the fact that Wilkes again applied unsuccessfully for bail on the same day that the two soldiers were released.

The incident came to be known as the massacre of St. George's Fields, and played a considerable part in Wilkes's subsequent history. The immediate effect was to cause further ill-feeling and alarm. An angry crowd surged round the House of Lords shouting "Wilkes and Liberty and no Boot", while the Lords inside complained haughtily of the mob's insulting behaviour, and much more humanly endorsed Grafton's exasperated decision to patrol the streets with troops. To make matters worse Lord Suffolk proposed a mark of favour to the Lord Mayor, Harley, for his activity against Wilkes, which Grafton readily promised.

(2)

On the 8th of June the question of Wilkes's outlawry was once more argued in court. Mansfield delivered judgment in a speech which is usually admitted to have been a fine example of judicial eloquence. But the admission is very little to the credit of legal proceedings. Wilkes's original outlawry was declared invalid on the most trumpery of technical points, and the whole speech, as Wilkes very truly remarked and as most of the hearers thought, would have been far more appropriate to condemnation than release. However, technical and absurd or the opposite, the verdict of outlawry had been reversed, and Wilkes had wrung another victory out of Government. It would have been far wiser if they had either continued their career of illegality or given way graciously.

The reversal of the outlawry at once revived the two outstanding verdicts against Wilkes—for republishing No. 45 and for publishing the *Essay on Woman*—since it was for failing to appear for judgment that Wilkes had been outlawed. Although these verdicts were four years old, the court needed another ten days to consider the sentence. On the 18th Mansfield very wisely absented himself, and the duty of pronouncing sentence fell on Justice Yates, who informed the prisoner that the court condemned him to twelve months' imprisonment— ten of them still to run—and a fine of £500 for republishing No. 45, and a further twelve months' imprisonment and another fine of £500 for the *Essay*. Then he was smuggled back to prison.

The sentence appeared to be a stroke of genius. Wilkes would be confined for the best part of two years, by which time, with luck, he would be forgotten; and in any case he was hopelessly bankrupt and could never pay the fine.

But, clever or not, it decided Wilkes. Government had flouted all his hints and offers, and he would take up the challenge. Directly sentence had been passed he played his counter-stroke. If his outlawry had suspended his own punishment, it had also suspended his action against Halifax, and if Government demanded their pound of flesh, so would he.

That very evening a handbill was issued in which Wilkes set out his case and his intentions. Truly his case was overwhelming. "In the whole progress of Ministerial vengeance against me for several years", he remarked, "I have shown to the conviction of all mankind that my enemies have trampled on the laws, and been actuated by the spirit of tyranny and arbitrary power." General Warrants had been adjudged illegal; the seizure of papers had been condemned judicially, and now the outlawry had been declared contrary to law. "It still remains", he continued, "in this public cause, that the justice of the nation should have place against the first and great criminal, the late Secretary of State, Lord Halifax, not so much for the punishment he has merited, as for the example of terror to any present or future Minister." He pledged himself to carry the business through, and to make assurance double sure added: "I am determined to remain entirely independent, uncorrupted, even unbiased in an improper manner, and never to accept from the Crown either place, pension, gratuity, or emolument of any kind."

The manifesto sold by the thousand, and by eight o'clock in the evening copies were fetching half a crown. The feeling of unrest grew and the riots continued. Well might Walpole write in a fit of despondency: "No Government, no police, London and Middlesex distracted, the Colonies in rebellion, Ireland ready to be so, and France arrogant to the point of being hostile! Lord Bute accused of all and dying of a panic; George Grenville wanting to make rage desperate; Lord Rockingham, the Duke of Portland, and the Cavendishes thinking we have no enemies but Lord Bute and Dyson, and that four mutes and an epigram can set everything to rights; the Duke of Grafton, like an apprentice, thinking the world should be postponed to a whore or a horserace; and the Bedfords not caring what disgraces we undergo, while each of them has £3,000 a year and 3,000 bottles of claret and champagne."

As though determined to plumb the depths of folly, Government applied for an attachment against the printer of Wilkes's manifesto on the ground that it would prejudice the jury who tried Halifax. The Court of Common Pleas dismissed the application with contempt.

(3)

A pause followed until the meeting of Parliament in the winter. For Wilkes it was a pleasant pause, crammed with evidence of his popularity. For Government it was full of uneasiness. Their attention would have been sufficiently distracted with the alarming reports that came from America; but they had almost more distractions at home—all of a harassing kind. Parliament and the people were at daggers drawn, and, while Parliament generally had the advantage, there was one sphere where the people were supreme. It was from the people that juries were formed. Trials could not be avoided, and if the juries were not so flagrantly partial as Ministers, there was no doubt of their bias. In July a grand jury returned a true bill of indictment for murder against the magistrate who had ordered the firing of St. George's Fields, and Government had an anxious time securing his acquittal. In August they had a similar scare over the soldiers who had shot Allen. Finally, there was the Halifax case, where Wilkes would certainly be awarded extravagant damages—and Halifax had long since taken the precaution of extracting a promise of indemnity from Government.

If they were unhappy in their relations with the people, they were not much happier in their relations with the King. He was as violent as ever for Wilkes's expulsion from Parliament, and the Cabinet's division on the question gave him an excuse for intriguing against the Ministers distasteful to himself. As a beginning he decided that Shelburne must go. That, and a slur cast on Sir Jeffrey Amherst, had a surprising result. Ministers had by this time almost forgotten the wounded lion in whose name they were acting. It came, therefore, as a shock to receive a letter from Chatham asking to be allowed to resign, and more than half suggesting as the reason that he could not "enough lament the removal of Sir Jeffrey Amherst and that of Lord Shelburne". As a matter of fact Shelburne was still a Minister when the letter arrived. It required little imagination to see the advantage of Shelburne following Chatham into retirement rather than Chatham resigning in anger because Shelburne had been dismissed. Accordingly Grafton and the King held the axe suspended over Shelburne's head until they had half cajoled, half bullied Chatham into sending another letter of resignation with no reference to either of his friends. With that the Chatham Ministry ended—not altogether to Grafton's joy, and certainly not to his ultimate good. Chatham had lost much of his popularity, but his name was still one to conjure with, and in any case his disappearance led to much searching of heart among his friends in the Cabinet—men such as Camden, who were not easily to be replaced. The upshot was that the Ministry lost prestige and power at the very moment they most desperately needed both.

(4)

Parliament was due to meet on November 8th, and Wilkes took care to get in the first blow. Exactly a week earlier he published anonymously *A Letter on the Public Conduct of Mr. Wilkes*, in which he outlined the course of events since 1763, and defended himself against the prejudice which was being assiduously promoted. "He is said to have spurned at all law and government, to have raised and fomented the riots and tumults, so frequent of late years in this kingdom." Wilkes's answer was complete: "the whole of his conduct demonstrates the injustice and malice of this charge." The country was certainly in a state of unrest and riots broke out from time to time; but the fact remains that the unrest preceded Wilkes and wherever Wilkes was able to exert his influence the riots died down. In his *Letter* Wilkes declared that "he has only sought the legal redress", adding with irresistible truth "the laws have fully justified the appeal". So he summed up his own conduct, "after the sharpest provocation, the conduct of Mr. Wilkes has been cool, temperate, and prudent".

Two days later he issued a manifesto over his own name, in which he outlined his immediate plans. "I mean", he said, "to petition the House of Commons, as the grand inquest of the nation, in the full hope of a redress of all my grievances." He reminded the people that he had already lodged an appeal against his sentence with the House of Lords, and added that he proposed to raise the whole question of legal proceedings. He hoped that "grand juries may through my efforts recover the power and right given them by the first principles of the Constitution, which are at present entirely lost in the mode of proceeding by information". The meeting of Parliament would suspend the case against Halifax, but Wilkes would be none the less unwearied in his endeavours to destroy "all the remains of despotic power among our free-born countrymen".

As a method of producing riots the manifesto can only be called feeble. As a popular appeal it was not very exciting with its insistence on parliamentary action and legal arguments. But as a home-thrust directed against the Government it was admirable. It reintroduced the Wilkes affair into both Houses, and by attacking the doctrine of judicial prerogative, as laid down by Mansfield, opened up a prospect of dispute between Parliament and the Courts of Law. Yet it was constitutional to the last degree. Nobody could say it was stirring up sedition, and unless Government had a guilty conscience nobody could object to his case being ventilated in Parliament.

Government were dismayed. They had hoped that Wilkes would be forgotten; they had compromised by leaving his problems suspended in the air. Now he was forcing them to make a decision—the very last thing they desired. In something of a panic Grafton began overtures. At his desire Fitzherbert told Almon on the 10th of November that if Wilkes refrained from presenting his petition, "no attempt should be made in Parliament against him". Almon carried the message to Wilkes, who sent no answer. The result was that three days later Fitzherbert crept like a conspirator to the King's Bench prison in the dusk of the evening and tried hard to seal the bargain. Wilkes told him bluntly that the offer came too late; he had pledged his word to his constituents, and in the circumstances the offer ought never to have been made.

(5)

The very next day Sir Joseph Mawbey, Member for Southwark, presented Wilkes's petition, which so far from proving flamboyant was a mild request for "an effectual and speedy redress of all his grievances".

In presenting the petition Mawbey declared that he did so on the instructions of his constituents. This was taken at the time as an indication that Mawbey thought very little of the matter, and of course it inspired the House generally with supercilious contempt. But from another point of view it was of tremendous significance, marking a real stage in the birth of democracy. Whatever might be said at elections, in the House no one pretended that he was representing the views of the people, still less voicing the wishes of his constituents. It is true that Pitt had appealed to popular feeling; but Pitt would have been mortified to the last degree if it had been suggested that his dazzling dreams were the property of anyone but himself. He merely used his popularity as a weapon of offence, with a profound contempt for the ladder by which he rose. Wilkes might have adopted the same attitude, but for the disconcerting logic of his nature. Perhaps he was too honest, perhaps he was merely narrow-minded, but whatever the reason he was quite clear that the duty of a representative

N

was to represent. As far back as Berwick in 1754 he had hoped to be "your faithful representative . . . delivering your sentiments". Since his return to England he had constantly asked his constituents to make their wishes known to him. This reiteration was beginning to make an impression, opening the eyes of the constituents to new possibilities. Before long they were holding meetings and issuing their instructions, and so the people were made a real factor in politics. With this new awakening among the voters there was bound to be an agitation for reform, partly to sweep away the rotten boroughs, partly to enlarge the franchise, and partly to ensure that the House responded to the wishes of the electors. In short, just as the trouble in 1763 had sprung out of Wilkes's clear perception that a General Warrant meant a warrant against the whole nation, so now the whole scheme of reform, including the publication of parliamentary debates, sprang out of his equally clear perception that representation meant exactly what it said. Such is the genius of true sanity.

(6)

Handicapped as he was, Wilkes possessed two enormous advantages—his own clear conscience and the accusing conscience of his adversaries. He had merely to take the obvious steps one after the other, and each of them threw Government into a fresh panic and a deeper quagmire.

A week after his petition he asked to be heard on it in person. Even such a simple request involved a full-dress debate. But a much more terrifying request was to follow. On November 28th Mawbey demanded that Lord Temple should be summoned as a witness. The House agreed with a shrug of the shoulders, upon which Mawbey added the names of Sandwich and March. The Government at once took fright, though their alarm was nothing to the terror of the two Lords. In view of the promise that Temple should be sent for, it was hardly decent to refuse Sandwich and March, but it was very unlikely that those two delinquents would readily agree, and there was every prospect of a first-class wrangle between the two Houses. The Ministry were put to their usual shifts, and only just scraped out of the difficulty. Eventually Temple asked to be excused on the plea that he could not decently give evidence in a case that concerned his brother, and the other two were persuaded reluctantly to acquiesce.

As a further shock Government were asked to publish an account of all the moneys issued recently for prosecutions. They refused, as indeed they had to if they were to cover up their tracks, but obviously it did them no good.

After these preliminaries Wilkes let off another bombshell. During November there appeared in the *St. James's Chronicle* a copy of Lord Weymouth's letter to the Justices written in the preceding April and urging them to use the military in case of disturbances. It was headed by a short preface: "I send you the following authentic State paper, the date of which, prior by more than three weeks to the fatal 10th of May, 1768, shows how long the horrid massacre in St. George's Fields had been planned and determined upon before it was carried into execution, and how long a hellish project can be brooded over by some infernal spirits without one moment's remorse."

The Lords were up in arms at what they regarded as an insult to themselves and a breach of their privileges, and Grafton insisted on being allowed himself to lodge a complaint before the House. The outraged peers eagerly agreed to summon the printer to the bar, but their courage oozed away when the printer, one Swan by name, informed them that Wilkes had given him the document and had told him to admit as much. Now Wilkes, whatever his defects, was a Member of Parliament. Dare the Lords summon a Member of the Lower House to their bar? And if not, what were they to do? Grafton adopted the usual course—procrastination.

But they had to deal with a determined man whom they had shockingly abused. Wilkes was not content with this state of suspended animation. The Lords had complained publicly, and he clamoured to be heard in justification. When they showed reluctance he issued a manifesto admitting responsibility not only for printing Weymouth's letter, but also Barrington's letter of thanks to the troops. "My hand trembled", he wrote, "while I copied what I blushed to read, and I gave it to the public in the only way my present situation could admit, with the hope of promoting a parliamentary inquiry into that bloody transaction, which I trust this second publication will now accomplish, and because I think this free nation has a right to be fully informed of the conduct of administration in so important a concern as the loss of the lives of so many subjects."

Though the language may have been high-flown, the sentiment was right. A popular tumult in a civilized country which results in the death of six or seven persons demands something more than a mere coroner's inquest; and if the root cause is the complete alienation of Government and governed, an inquiry is all the more necessary. Wilkes summed up the matter in the fewest words. "Administration", he wrote, "complains of me for having published the letter of the Secretary of State. I complain to the nation that such a letter has been written." At bedrock bottom it was the publication of the letter, not Wilkes's comments, that touched the Government upon the raw.

The Lords held a conference with the Commons by way of discovering what could be done. Strange but true, the Commons were inclined to take more interest in Weymouth's letter than in Wilkes's comments. One of them, Macleane, was even bold enough to declare that "if Mr. Wilkes's preface to the letter was conceived in gall, the letter itself was written in blood". There were other opprobrious remarks, and even George Grenville insisted that evidence must be heard before Wilkes was condemned. The Commons finally decided to hear both evidence and Wilkes, and the Ministers were left more than ever undecided as to the policy they should pursue.

(7)

Wilkes's affairs were becoming very complicated. He had lodged an appeal with the House of Lords against his sentence of imprisonment and fine; and had laid a petition before the Commons, which not only outlined his fortunes, but brought two specific charges in connection with his trial in 1764—one against Mansfield on a technical point and one against Webb for bribing the witnesses. On the other side the Lords had complained of his publication of Weymouth's letter, which the Commons had agreed to consider; and the Ministers were pondering the wisdom or otherwise of moving for his expulsion.

All these questions came up separately, and all were interwoven with, or led to, further complications.

One such complication arose at once. During the recess Cooke, the second Member for Middlesex, died, and Government were faced with the ticklish prospect of another Middlesex election. It took place on the 8th of December. The two candidates were Sir William Beauchamp Proctor, whom Wilkes had defeated in the previous March, and Sergeant Glynn, who was Wilkes's Counsel. Everything went smoothly at the outset, but about two o'clock in the afternoon, when it was clear that Glynn would be elected, a sudden riot arose, orderly voters were knocked down, the hustings were invaded, the books seized, and the sheriffs driven away. In the course of the tumult an inoffensive man, one George Clarke, was bludgeoned to death. At the inquest a verdict of wilful murder against some person or persons unknown was returned, and the general belief was that the Court candidate had engineered the proceeding. The election was renewed on the 14th, when Glynn was returned by a substantial majority. Illuminations took place in the City and down the Strand, but at the urgent entreaty of Wilkes none of his admirers appeared in the streets, so that the evening passed off quietly.

Here was another triumph, and it was driven home by the events that followed. Two men, Edward Macquirk and

Laurence Balfe, were arrested for the murder of Clarke. They were tried at the Old Bailey on the 16th of January, 1769, when the evidence was conclusive that Proctor had engaged a notorious boxer, Broughton by name, to hire a band of Irish desperadoes and take them down to the election. At a given signal they had created the disturbance in Proctor's favour, and Clarke had been their victim. The cause of Clarke's death was obvious and was confirmed by medical evidence, and the jury found both the prisoners guilty. They were sentenced to death, and in pronouncing sentence the Recorder did not scruple to add that the instigators were equally guilty with the accomplices. The result of this hint was that a few weeks later a Grand Jury found a true bill against Proctor, though Government managed to squash the proceedings.

The common people were delighted with the verdict, and actually cheered in court. Their feelings can be understood; it really was shocking that the moderation of the popular party should be continually met, not only by force, but by murder—first Allen and now Clarke. However, the blame clearly lay with the ringleaders, not the unfortunate instruments, and reprieves were suggested in the Commons by members of the Opposition. Even so, the Ministers appeared to be unable to act a straightforward part. They waited for two and a half months, and then wrote to Surgeons' Hall informing them that there were doubts as to the cause of Clarke's death, and asking for their opinion. The Master, Wardens, and Examiners met the same evening and without more ado expressed the unanimous opinion that "the blow was not the cause of death", on which the culprits were pardoned. A mere piece of chicanery—not likely to reflect credit on anyone.

(8)

To return to Wilkes. The first of his numerous cases to be heard was the appeal to the House of Lords against his sentence. It was hardly likely that he would get justice, but the

Lords went out of their way to proclaim the fact. The 21st of December was fixed for the hearing, and Wilkes asked that he might be allowed to appear in person, mentioning a precedent. Camden, as Lord Chancellor, pointed out that the particular precedent was not good, but proposed to search the journals before coming to a decision. The Lords, however, were going to run no risk; they pooh-poohed Camden's suggestion, and returned a blank refusal to Wilkes.

When the 21st arrived, Glynn happened to be ill, and Wilkes accordingly asked that his case might be postponed. With incredible levity one of the Lords proposed to name counsel for him and hear the case forthwith; but Camden put his foot down and quite shocked his fellow-peers by commending Glynn for his defence of Wilkes "since his misfortunes". The hearing was put off till January 15th, when, as everyone expected, Wilkes's sentence was confirmed "without one lord saying a syllable in his defence".

CHAPTER XVIII

EXPULSION, ELECTION; ELECTION, EXPULSION

(1)

On the 27th of January, 1769, the Commons reached Wilkes's petition. In accordance with his request he was brought from prison to the House, and was followed by a large and enthusiastic crowd. Once more he showed his moderation. So far from wanting a revolution, he did not even desire the moral support of a mob. He persuaded his admirers to disperse quietly, and entered the precincts alone, to kick his heels for several hours.

The Ministers were anxious to limit the proceedings, and at all costs wanted to avoid reviving the old dispute over General Warrants. Barrington, therefore, moved that Wilkes should be confined solely to his two allegations—the technical complaint against Mansfield and the subornation of witnesses. At 10 p.m., after a long debate, Government carried their point.

Wilkes was then called in, and though to their intense surprise his behaviour was exemplary, his opening speech knocked endways all their plans. In a very few words he reminded the House that he had been elected for the County of Middlesex, and submitted that he ought at once to take his seat. This possibility had never occurred to the House, whose lack of imagination was phenomenal. It threw them into consternation, and involved another debate of two hours or so, when the request was refused. By this time it was too late for further action and the House adjourned.

On January 31st they came to the question again; but once more Wilkes plunged them into confusion. Immediately on appearing he complained that the House had libelled him. "I find", he protested, "it is asserted three times in the Votes of last November that there is a record of blasphemy against me. I am sure that no such record ever existed. The assertion is entirely void of truth." Such a complaint could hardly be ignored, and the bewildered members had to submit to the evidence. It appeared that some time in November, Lord Clare, by way of blackening Wilkes's character, had demanded that the rolls of his various convictions should be laid on the table of the House. They were duly laid, but in keeping with the general slackness then prevailing were found to have no endorsement. The Clerk was ordered to rectify the omission, and hit upon the titles "seditious libel" and "blasphemy" —titles which were forthwith copied into the Votes. A long debate now took place as to whether Wilkes had been convicted of blasphemy or not, and as it was perfectly clear that he had not, Government did their best to show that he ought to have been. But at last they had to give way. Here was another rebuff for them and another victory for Wilkes.

That disposed of, the House settled down to the main points. Wilkes brought in Curry as a witness, and had no trouble whatever in proving that he had been paid for stealing the *Essay on Woman*. Sandwich and March were then summoned, but as his case was already so clear, Wilkes hardly asked them any questions.

The next day Webb's Counsel was heard, and Certainly if revenge had been Wilkes's main object, he had already secured it. Webb was blind, and as his Counsel urged, "decayed in understanding"; he sat through the debates, patiently and silently, listening to the recital of his old misdeeds—truly an object for pity. Government moved that the charge against Webb had not been proved, and was frivolous and groundless —a motion that Wilkes's supporters offered to accept out of compassion, if the last part were omitted, and so the point was settled. The charge against Mansfield was debated much more hotly. Government pressed hard for a decision that Wilkes's complaint was frivolous and trifling, but the sense of the House was against them, and they had to be content with a compromise—to the effect that as the action complained of was not unprecedented, the charge against Mansfield should be declared groundless.

It was a victory for the Ministers, but a poor one, based half on pity and half on compromise.

(2)

The next day the House turned to the more pleasurable task of baiting Wilkes on the subject of Weymouth's letter. Here again they had misunderstood their man. If they imagined that he was to be intimidated, they were soon undeceived. His reply to the charge is worth transcribing: "Mr. Speaker, I acknowledge that I transmitted to the Press the letter of the Secretary of State, and that I wrote and published the prefatory remarks to it; and, Sir, whenever a Secretary of State shall dare to write so bloody a scroll I will through life dare to write such prefatory remarks, as well as to make my appeal to the nation on the occasion. I ask pardon, Sir, that I made use of too mild and gentle expressions, when I mentioned so wicked, so inhuman, so cowardly a massacre, as that in St. George's Fields on the 10th of May. I pledge myself to the House, that whenever a day shall be appointed to make this important enquiry, I will bring evidence here to prove the truth of every word I have asserted. I hope the House, Sir, will send for Mr. Proctor, and examine him whether he did or did not receive that letter from the Secretary of State. If he answers in the affirmative, I am sure from the virtue of this House that they will immediately order an impeachment against the Secretary to be carried up to the bar of the House of Peers."

Horrified at his boldness, Government moved in a hurry that the preface was "an insolent, scandalous, and seditious libel, tending to inflame and stir up the minds of His Majesty's subjects to sedition, and to a total subversion of all good order and legal government". This was straining the loyalty of their followers and a fierce, long-drawn-out debate ensued.

But as Walpole had written to Mann a few days earlier: "he [Wilkes] goes again to the House, but whatever steps he takes there, or however long debates he may occasion, you may look upon his fate as decided in that place". So it proved, and although even Ministerial supporters argued that questions of libel ought to be tried by the Law Courts rather than the House of Commons, at 2 a.m. the preface was declared to be a libel.

Lord North hastened to inform the King, who replied with unconscious sarcasm: "nothing could be more honourable for Government than the conclusion of the Debate this morning, and promises a very proper end of this irksome affair this day".

The proper end to which the King was looking forward was the expulsion of Wilkes. He had been labouring hard to achieve it, brazenly extracting promises of votes, and Government pushed ahead with the motion on the 3rd of February. The debate lasted all day and most of the night, ending at 3 a.m., when Government got their way. But they succeeded by means that were felt to be despicable. Wilkes was not expelled solely for his so-called libel of Weymouth. That was recited, but the charge then went on to include his conviction for No. 45, his conviction for publishing the *Essay on Woman*, and the fact that he was undergoing imprisonment.

The opponents of the motion had no difficulty in displaying the unfairness of the method. Indeed, the case was self-evident. The first charge of libelling had been decided by the House's *ipse dixit*; as for No. 45 and the *Essay*, whatever one might think of them, Wilkes had already been punished, not only by the law, but by expulsion from a previous Parliament, and this, therefore, was the third official punishment, without counting his unofficial disasters; the last charge—that of undergoing imprisonment—if it were a crime, was involuntary and unwilling. But the conglomeration of counts had its use; some members were swayed by one, some by another; some were angry with No. 45, some were shocked at the

Essay. So one way or another a majority was collected for expulsion.

Amongst the speakers who argued on the other side was George Grenville. He was influenced partly by a recent family reconciliation between Temple, Chatham, and himself, partly by the fact that he was in opposition, and partly, one may hope, by the scandal of the proceedings; but certainly not by sympathy with Wilkes or his aims. On the contrary, he harped as much upon the worthlessness of Wilkes as upon the meanness of Government. Later in the year his speech was published, though it is only fair to add without his sanction. Wilkes replied forthwith in a pamphlet entitled *A Letter to the Rt. Hon. George Grenville*, etc., in which he dealt very faithfully with his opponent. It was not difficult to be "severe" as Wilkes called it, because Grenville had laid himself gapingly open. His arguments in 1769 were confronted time and again by the precedents he had himself created in 1763. Wilkes's *Letter* was essentially a tract for the times, and as such has largely lost its interest. It did, however, contain a description of his plan of reform. "The nation", he declared, "wishes an effectual Place and Pension Bill, which would only leave in either House of Parliament the *few necessary* servants of the Crown in the revenue, in the public offices, in the Army and Navy; Bills to restore triennial Parliaments, to destroy the mode of proceeding by *information*, to establish a fair and equal representation of the people in the Lower House, to give the public the revenue of all sinecures, or to sink the places themselves, etc.; but above all at this critical period to establish a Committee for taking and stating the public accounts, not to be appointed by the House of Commons only, and consequently to end with the session, but to be erected by Act of Parliament, to be composed of the most able and honest men in the nation, as well as in the two Houses, with full powers and to continue sitting till the great work was finished. . . . These things would soon restore both the public confidence and the public credit." If such a plan of reform, aiming at purer domestic politics, better finance, and more impartial justice, betokens a demagogue, it is a sad fact that most of England's statesmen have been demagogues from that day onwards.

(3)

The expulsion of Wilkes was a trifle in itself, being no more than the spiteful revenge of the King. Wilkes himself gave it no greater importance at first; but the sequence of events expanded it into a tremendous constitutional issue, the implications of which Wilkes was easily the first to grasp.

The day after expulsion he offered himself for re-election in a manifesto which clearly showed that he regarded the struggle as one between himself and the Government, his main preoccupation being to make the freeholders of Middlesex a party to the quarrel. Government, he told them, had "robbed a very respectable part of this kingdom of their noblest inheritance, of their share in the legislative power"; and he warned them that if they allowed Ministers to say whom they *should not* elect, they would soon find Ministers dictating whom they *should* elect. They must bestir themselves to safeguard their own rights.

The new election took place on the 16th of February. Wilkes was returned unanimously, which he regarded as proof that his constituents had identified themselves with him. But he knew that Government would make "fresh efforts to crush and destroy me", and wanted to enlarge his following. So in his letter of thanks he hoped that "our steadiness will draw to us the firm and generous support of the numerous, sensible, and magnanimous friends whom Liberty has ready at her call throughout this island".

Government's one chance was to confine the quarrel strictly to themselves and Wilkes, for which purpose they should have stressed his deficiencies rather than their rights. They were entitled to expel him with or without reason, but the feebler their excuse, the greater the sympathy he would attract.

Walpole had already told Mann that "as worthless a fellow as Wilkes is, the rigours exercised towards him have raised a spirit that will require still wiser heads to allay. Men have again turned seriously to the study of those controversies that agitated this country a hundred years ago." It was certainly true; directly the expulsion was a fact, the freeholders of Middlesex resolved not only to re-elect Wilkes, but to support him entirely at their own expense. Men who are ready to back their opinion with their money are obviously in earnest.

In spite of this warning Government merely moved that as Wilkes had been expelled, "he was and is incapable of sitting in the present Parliament". Lord North went even beyond this, and when Townshend threatened that the freeholders would in a body petition the King to dissolve Parliament, declared that "every individual who shall be guilty of it, will commit a breach of privilege, the most culpable, the most punishable, that the annals of the country can produce". Nothing could have set in a clearer light, not only the cleavage between members and their constituents, but the outrageous powers which Parliament arrogated to itself. So far from agreeing with Wilkes's view that representatives should represent, Lord North denied the right of the electorate even to criticize.

This peremptory attitude was beginning to rouse the people. The City of London made their feelings abundantly clear. So did Westminster, Southwark, and Middlesex. Still more ominous, the provinces began to stir, and Bath sent positive instructions to their members to support Wilkes.

Government's only reply was to look round for a candidate who would oppose him. The best they could find was one Dingley, an ex-private of the Guards and the proprietor of a saw mill at Lime House. This misguided individual, by way of preparation, attempted to procure a loyal address in the City. A meeting was held at the King's Arms Tavern in Cornhill, where a hot debate took place. Dingley was rash enough to hit an opponent, who forthwith knocked him down, drove out his supporters, and generally cleared the room. After this inauspicious beginning it was not surprising that when Dingley appeared on the hustings not a soul would even nominate him. Wilkes was returned for the third time on the 16th of March.

His attitude towards this third election shows a marked progress in his ideas. His manifestos took on a much more serious tone. He not only told the electors that he would offer himself as often as he was expelled, but went much more deeply into the constitutional point. The privilege of electing their own representatives was "the first principle of the Constitution", and "the essence of that power which the people have reserved to themselves". It was something that could not be taken from them, certainly not by the House of Commons, which was at most a third part of the legislature. Confident in this inalienable right of the people, Wilkes declared that he would very deliberately pursue the way of truth and honour, and would, if possible, expose and bring to justice "those exalted offenders" who were betraying their sacred trust.

In returning thanks for his re-election he definitely claimed that the point was now of national importance, and more openly announced his views of Government. They were "a corrupt administration", guilty of low cunning and weak malice; while the freeholders of Middlesex were resting on the Great Charter and Bill of Rights, and were bearing their testimony to the " just claims of every freeholder, and the best rights of our inheritance".

Having gone so far, Government had little option beyond going a step farther. Wilkes was not even expelled; but instead the election was declared null and void and a new one appointed for the 13th of April. By this time Wilkes had clarified his ideas and crystallized them. The matter had progressed far beyond a personal issue, beyond the rights of Middlesex. It was no longer even a question affecting men of good will. It had become universal and dealt with "the fundamental rights of the subject". The people, he asserted, "have an inherent right to be represented in Parliament by the man of their free choice, not disqualified by law". This right is "coeval with our Constitution . . . it began at the very first faint dawn of liberty in our island, and will survive to the last convulsive pang of expiring freedom. It is a part of the original compact between the sovereign of this nation and the subject, expressly stated in the Bill of Rights." It is "no less clear by reason than by the positive statute . . . a representative without, or against the consent of the parties is an insult to common sense, an absurdity scarcely to be paralleled, an injustice and insolence not to be forgiven." And so "this contest is now becoming of the most interesting nature. It is between the present administration and all the electors of Great Britain. There is nothing personal in it. The cause is national and of the first magnitude."

Government made up their mind to end the struggle at all costs. Their method was simple in itself, but difficult of realization; if they could only find some other candidate capable of obtaining a few votes, they proposed to declare him elected. With this in view, they approached one man after another, without success. At last they discovered a tool in Colonel Luttrell. Their choice could hardly have been worse; Luttrell was already a Member of Parliament, and in order to qualify had to be given a minor post which involved re-election. Still more unfortunate, his character was so bad that even the Wilkes of romance appears a white sheep beside him. He was the son of Lord Irnham, and both father and son were desperadoes of the deepest dye; both were drunken ruffians; both kept and openly paraded a regular harem of mistresses; both were tyrants and bullies; both were for ever squabbling in public, and Luttrell had once signalized his intelligence and filial piety alike by refusing his father's challenge to a duel, on the ground that Lord Irnham was not a gentleman. The only point in his favour was a reputation for courage which this election largely destroyed. Otherwise

JOHN WILKES

After a painting by R. E. Pine in the Guildhall Library

he was not to be compared with Wilkes, who resembled him only in the coarseness of his language and the number of his mistresses.

On hearing that Luttrell was to oppose him, Wilkes issued a further manifesto, which is remarkable partly for the tone of quiet confidence pervading it and even more for the last sentence: "May we be the happy instruments of perpetuating the blessings of a free Constitution to the latest inhabitants of the whole British Empire." With these words Wilkes had extended his case to its farthest limits.

(4)

The course of this fourth Middlesex election emphasized the glaring fact that Parliament and people were at variance, and emphasized it in the most alarming fashion. Parliament, though utterly corrupt, stood upon its gentility. The mere fact that the King was bidding against the Whig magnates never for a moment changed the firm belief of everyone concerned that power belonged by right to Society. It is hard to say who despised the "mob" most—King or Parliament. Both disliked Wilkes because he was not a gentleman, and both were inclined to hate him because of his popularity. Any movement from below was incipient revolution, and this ridiculous, and wholly indefensible, attitude would have led to revolution in good earnest but for Wilkes himself.

By way of greasing the path to revolution, Luttrell issued an advertisement calling for "*gentlemen* to accompany and defend him, and not to suffer the mob to govern". Here was direct provocation. Throughout these hectic days Wilkes had kept the mob in hand, so that however high the excitement had run, the elections had been models of propriety. The suggestion that Luttrell needed defence was in common parlance "asking for it"; the appeal to "*gentlemen*" a plain summons to class warfare.

Very few "*gentlemen*" were willing to sacrifice themselves,

o

but a party of about twenty met at Lord Irnham's house on the 13th, and in terror of the mob assembled at the front-door, broke down the garden wall and scampered towards Brentford by back ways. Even so they encountered the enemy at Hyde Park Corner, where the redoubtable Colonel was forced to ride over a man in order to escape and left his hat behind as spoils of war. The party breathed more happily at Brentford, where they were protected by the strict discipline of their opponents. In contradistinction to this undignified scuttle, the freeholders formed themselves into bands, and marched in orderly fashion from all quarters of the county, with music and banners before them and ribbons and cockades in their hats, their favourite mottoes being "Magna Charta" and the "Bill of Rights". Nothing marred the tranquillity of the election beyond the mirth occasioned by two further candidates offering themselves at the last moment—Serjeant Whitaker, a legal light who swore by Rockingham, and one Roach, an Irish captain who swore for the most part blasphemously. The result was an overwhelming victory for Wilkes, who polled 1,143 votes to Luttrell's 296 and Whitaker's 5. Roach brought up the rear with a well-deserved nought.

Quite automatically Wilkes was rejected by the House, but when it was proposed to declare Luttrell elected, an uneasy feeling ran through the benches. Yet, so blind were the Government and their supporters, that the motion passed— with a somewhat reduced majority, but without serious trouble. It only occasioned a sitting till 2 a.m., the normal time whenever Wilkes was concerned. About a fortnight later the Commons rejected a petition against Luttrell presented by the freeholders of Middlesex, and thereafter were prorogued.

Strangely enough, the expected riots did not follow. There was a calm which wiser men might have thought ominous; but the King was satisfied that the spirited action of the Commons "must greatly tend to destroy that outrageous licentiousness that has been so successfully raised by wicked and disappointed men"; and Walpole could write towards the end of May, "everything here is perfectly calm; Wilkes so much forgotten that he seems to have forgotten himself".

The fact was that Wilkes's case had now in good truth taken hold of all England; the froth and flurry on the top was being merged in the volume of a great wave.

CHAPTER XIX

THE CITY OF LONDON

(1)

DURING the last few months Wilkes had entered on a new phase in his career. In January 1769 the death of Sir Francis Gosling, Alderman of Farringdon Ward Without, created a vacancy among the Aldermen of London. Two candidates offered themselves, John Wilkes and a paper-hanger named Bromwich. On the 3rd of January Wilkes was elected, and thenceforward the story of his life is a slow transition from parliamentary to civic affairs.

The probabilities are that from the moment of his return, and indeed earlier, Wilkes had contemplated this move. From his birth onward he had been connected with the City; here, if anywhere, was his spiritual home, and it was the place to which he would naturally bring his wounds when his pretensions to the status of gentleman had been sufficiently bludgeoned. He had always understood the City and been on good terms with it. So far back as Aylesbury days he was toasting it and carrying messages from the Lord Mayor to Temple, and when his first dispute with Government was at its height in 1763 he found the merchants "firm in the cause of liberty" and "warmly my friend". During his exile the intimacy seems to have flagged, but directly he had made up his mind to return he was continually asking Heaton how his reputation stood, not in the West End, but on Exchange. Side by side with this homing instinct flourished a natural repugnance to the House, which had only been confirmed by his experience. It is true that on his return he stood for election, but he stood for the City, though his friends assured him his chances were better at Westminster; and it is clear that his object was not to push a political campaign, but to secure such protection as membership of the House would give. His next step was to become an alderman as soon as might

be and thereafter to drop gradually out of politics. He has
been blamed for this as a great error of judgment. Perhaps
he called to mind how in 1756 Pitt had declared that "he
should be prouder to be an alderman than a peer". Only, as
it happened, Wilkes became the alderman, Pitt the peer.

(2)

It is striking evidence of Wilkes's magnetism that his entrance
into City affairs at once raised the City's importance. London
has played a great part in English history, but generally in a
rather shy and anonymous manner. From the moment Wilkes
became connected with it, London and her officers began to
write the country's annals in larger letters. Her Lord Mayors,
Sheriffs, and Aldermen, even her Recorders and Town Clerks,
become living men. They share the pages of history with the
lords and politicians of Westminster, and indeed largely oust
them. In these next few breathless years the City Fathers
appear continually in impressive cavalcades, coming in their
chariots and robes of office through Temple Bar to St. James's,
to strike consternation among the pretty courtiers and to
embarrass the King himself. Sheriffs snub the pert officious-
ness of Court Chamberlains; Lord Mayors gravely rebuke
the King; and Aldermen effectively quash illegal warrants,
ignoring the Privy Council and rebuffing Parliament. It was
romance in those days to be a Lord Mayor, and the Mansion
House was more exciting than St. Stephens.

Not that the great men stood alone. Wilkes was too good a
democrat not to give the people their share, and as he brought
the electors to the front, so he brought the Livery in Common
Hall. In his addresses to the "worthy inhabitants of the Ward
of Farringdon Without", Wilkes held the same language as to
the freeholders of Middlesex; he wanted to know their sentiments, he entreated "a full and early communication" of
whatever they thought important; he wanted, in short, to be
their representative.

The City was by no means free from politics and in general the position was similar to that at Westminster. While the Livery were democratic, the Court of Aldermen had a strong leaning towards prerogative. As soon as Wilkes was elected, the King and Government began actively stirring up the Loyalists to oppose and quash him. It was one more sign that he was to have no peace or justice.

As a first petty prick the Court of Aldermen objected to his election on a purely technical point. Before the poll it had been agreed that the books should remain open for a certain length of time; they had, in fact, been closed directly Bromwich withdrew. On the strength of this Wilkes was forced to stand again, when he was re-elected without opposition. Even so the aldermen tried to contend that he was ineligible—a point which they never dared to press to a decision. The only result of this pinpricking was that Wilkes became more popular. When he had been elected, someone gave him his alderman's gown, which cost £40, and other good souls provided sufficient food and drinks to furnish a celebration dinner.

The City as well as Middlesex were thus interested in his expulsion from Parliament, and on February 20th a meeting was convened at the London Tavern to open a subscription for his private needs. Those present decided that "whereas John Wilkes, Esq., has suffered very greatly in his private fortune from the severe and repeated prosecutions he has undergone on behalf of the public, and as it seems reasonable to us that the man who suffers for the public good should be supported by the public, we", etc., etc., and what was more to the point, they at once subscribed £3,340. Five days later this entirely spontaneous effort was organized in a Society known as the Supporters of the Bill of Rights, whose intentions were "to support Mr. Wilkes and his cause, as far as it is a public cause".

Meanwhile the whole question of reform took on a new complexion. The Livery drew up instructions, commanding their representatives, among other things, to be particularly careful of the Habeas Corpus Act; to preserve inviolate the privileges of Parliament and the rights of electors; to prevent bribery at elections; to reform the judiciary; to appoint a standing committee to examine public accounts; to limit the number of placemen in the House, and to press for shorter parliaments. They sent this admirable manifesto to all their representatives, one of whom was Harley! Southwark followed suit.

Government worked hard to check this constitutional move. Some deluded individuals drew up an address complaining of licentiousness and profaneness, and their abhorrence of the attempts made to spread sedition. The first attempt to get signatures cost Dingley his teeth, but later on a few names were obtained, and on the 22nd of March a procession set off to present it. Their progress was infinitely comic. The people lined the streets and groaned heartily. Bow Bells welcomed them with a dumb peal, and when they arrived at Temple Bar the gates were shut in their faces. Attempts to open it led to rougher treatment; the procession was broken up and the addressers had to run in all directions for shelter. Mr. Boehm, who was carrying the precious document, left it in his coach and skedaddled into Nando's coffee-house, while his coachman took the shortest way home. At last the remains of the intrepid band escaped up Chancery Lane, re-formed in Holborn, and worked their way down to the Strand. By this time the people were more annoyed and mud began to fly as well as groans. At Exeter Street they were joined by a counter-procession, the main feature of which was a hearse with a picture of the murder of Allen on one side and the murder of Clarke on the other. In this motley form the Loyalists arrived at the Palace—to discover that the address was lost. A messenger was despatched post-haste to look for it, while the wretched remnant began hastily signing a copy. St. James's began to be sorry for itself. The King, Ministers, and Ambassadors were waiting nervously in the Throne Room, hoping the Grenadiers they had thoughtfully posted at the gates would be sufficient. Finally the Riot Act was read, and Talbot appeared on the scene to try the effect of his Steward's wand. It was forthwith broken, and before long he was glad enough to retire. A very sorry crew it was—bedaubed with mud, hatless, and dishevelled—by no means fit to set before a King, who finally presented the address so curiously expressive of the City's views!

On the seating of Luttrell, the popular party in the City held a meeting to consider their next step, which took the form of a petition to the King. Great efforts were made to see that everything was done decently and in order. Special persons were appointed to present the petition, and Townshend particularly pleaded that all others should keep away lest "it might give a pretence to administration to misrepresent to His Majesty an act of their innocent curiosity as tumult, insurrection, and open rebellion".

The petition was couched in the humble style which Kings expected, but it made no bones about setting out grievances. "We have waited", it went on, "patiently expecting a constitutional remedy by means of our own representatives"; but this expectation had been rudely shocked by the Luttrell affair, and now they were "left without hopes or means of redress but from Your Majesty or God".

The Livery, anxious to follow this example, asked the Lord Mayor to summon a Common Hall, at which they also might consider a petition. This was an innovation, but not unreasonable. However, the intrigues of the Court had stiffened the Loyalist Party and the Council turned down the proposal. The Livery merely bided their time, and when at midsummer a Common Hall had to be summoned for the election of officers, calmly and defiantly passed the petition as the first item on the agenda. This question of the Common Hall did not remain debatable long, but it is significant that Wilkes earnestly supported the Livery's right.

(3)

While his cause was being fought outside, Wilkes within the prison was not neglected. He was the recipient of unending gifts and letters. Delicacies and money were showered upon him; visitors of both sexes flocked to see him. In short, he had a delightful time, even if his liberty was circumscribed.

Among other incidents, in June 1768 he received a long letter written in perfect copperplate. It came from a maiden lady of fifty, Charlotte Forman, who confessed her age and gave a description of herself not calculated to tickle a libertine: "I am well born and have nothing mean in me but my outward appearance." Her tale was truly pitiful. Four years earlier she had lost the brother who supported her. A second brother had suddenly married his cook and gone away, leaving his sister to starve. She was arrested for debt, thrown into prison, and had to pawn her clothes. All she could earn was nine shillings a week by translating foreign books, and she was in danger of further imprisonment. This destitution was too much for the poor soul; she applied to Lord Hillsborough, a member of the Government, in whose service her brother had been for fourteen years, only to receive evasive answers. "At last", she told Lord Hillsborough, "I found myself on the brink of a precipice. In that extremity I looked up to Him Who alone can save, and begged that He would raise me up a protector. . . . I wrote to John Wilkes, Esq., and at his own desire, was introduced to him by Mr. Meres, Printer of the *London Evening Post*. That gentleman received me with the utmost affability. He passed a compliment on my letters, and desired me to name the sum required. I did so, and I had it." The lady had a garrulous pen, but it made a good point when it continued: "Oh, my Lord, what shall I say to this? Has Benevolence then forsaken the gilded mansions, to take up her abode in a prison? Is it credible, my Lord, that a private gentleman, labouring under the pressure of prosecutions, should display more greatness of soul than the mighty and the affluent? Yet it is so.

The fact is well known." Charlotte Forman became an ardent Wilkite. She took, to use her own phrase, a pleasure in exalting his name; and one may hope that the numerous articles she wrote in his support improved her finances.

(4)

The pause following the Luttrell decision was not of long duration. No riots came, but instead petitions began to flow in from all over the country. According to Walpole it was the Supporters of the Bill of Rights who adopted "a much more decent system; not with the approbation of Wilkes, whose existence depending on heats and riots, has made him afraid of being dropped, and of seeing any grievances in question, except his own". If Wilkes really liked riots, he thought the best way of provoking them was to do his best to prevent them. At all events, he encouraged the petitions, inquiring anxiously after their progress. The fact is that petitioning was entirely in accord both with Wilkes's fears of riots and with his firm belief in democratic government; and it is in the highest degree probable that he himself suggested the move. Had he not been petitioning the King, Ministers, and Parliament for many years past?

So the summer of 1769 was spent in a great campaign throughout the country—perhaps the first of its kind, and certainly the forerunner of many another. It was one more step in the direction of popular government. Success was hardly to be expected, because Society had adopted a cast-iron attitude, which in the case of Horace Walpole—Society's exponent—was reinforced with a crust of logic as tough as it was unreasonable. His mind worked in a sort of one-sided dichotomy that was crushingly conclusive. Either the mob were rioting or they were not. In the former case he was naturally shocked; in the latter case he was glad to record that Wilkes was forgotten. The same specious reasoning could be applied with irresistible force to parliamentary action. If nothing was done, discussion was unnecessary; if, on the other hand, the King was petitioned to dissolve Parliament, this was "inconsistent with the principles of liberty as appealing to the Crown against the House of Commons". The very methods employed were one and all open to suspicion. If the petitions were not promoted by gentlemen, far from regarding them as essentially the voice of the people, Walpole chuckled to think that the "petitions have contracted an air of ridicule from the ridiculous undertakers that have been forced to parade into the different counties to supply the place of all the gentlemen, who have disdained to appear and countenance them". When, on the other hand, the question was agitated in Parliament itself, then "the people are perfectly quiet, and seem to have delegated all their anger to their representatives —*a proof that their representatives had instructed their constituents to be angry*". Nothing, in fact, was of any use; whatever the popular party did, or left undone, Government were put to no trouble in misrepresenting it.

(5)

The Middlesex election was to have a further and much more dramatic effect. Whatever Wilkes wanted or preferred, the fact remained that he had once more raised a constitutional question of the highest moment which the greatest in the land might reasonably take up. And, sure enough, when the jackal had cleared the way, the lion stalked out of his lair to toss his mane in the wind and shake the world with roaring.

On the 7th of July, 1769, all England was electrified to hear that Chatham had appeared at the Royal levee and been closeted with the King. Everyone was agog with excitement; expectation ran on the tips of its toes and the sinners in high places trembled and were ashamed. But alas! the lean, eager years were over; the lion had grown plump; there was more of weight than thunder in his step; the brilliance of olden days had somehow lost its lustre; the majesty was no longer new. True, an explosion followed, but when the smoke had cleared away it proved no more than a flash in the pan—gigantic, huge, but only a cracker.

Chatham's genius and powers thrown into the scale went near to overthrowing Government. Near, but not quite—and the reasons of his failure are not hard to trace. He was always intractable and impracticable; but to those two stumbling-blocks had been added two even greater. The first was that Pitt had sold his birthright for a peerage, and it was vain for Chatham to think of leading the people from the House of Lords. The second was the change in Wilkes. He was no longer the jackal of five years before; he was not working for Chatham, nor interested in him. If Chatham cared to discuss the Middlesex election in the House of Lords, Chatham must do as he pleased; but he would get no encouragement from Wilkes. On the contrary, Wilkes was definitely opposed. In November of this very year Wilkes received an anonymous letter from "a gentleman of the Middle Temple", whose name was Bolton, proposing that Wilkes should give him a franked envelope. As franks could only be given by Members of Parliament, the gift would enable a case to be brought into court for testing Wilkes's right to sit in Parliament. Bolton was prepared to fight the case right up to the House of Lords. But he failed to convince Wilkes, who objected, amongst other things, to the House of Lords deciding who should be a member of the House of Commons. He was here, as usual, showing a profound knowledge of the Constitution and a clear perception of facts. The Lords would not have decided the matter on legal, but on political grounds, and their decision would have proved one more obstacle.

(6)

Wilkes had received notice, through Temple and Almon, of Chatham's views in the preceding February, but the world in general could only surmise until Parliament met in January

1770. Meanwhile, two other events helped to shape the situation. One was that in November his case against Halifax came to an end. The damages were assessed at £4,000, and the crowd hissed the jury for not giving more.

The second was the appearance of a new scourge for Government. January 21, 1769, saw the first letter signed with the dreaded name of Junius. Like so much of the eighteenth century, he was quite inexplicable, flashing over the sky like a meteor—no one knew whence or whither—and leaving in his wake an unclaimed reputation for genius, and a thousand barbs rankling in the highest hearts of the land. Never was an apparition so mysterious, never one so ruthless. And yet he did precisely nothing. The men he tormented fell from other causes; the truths he enunciated were mostly lies; his brilliant epigrams shine nowadays mostly by hearsay. Junius, unlike Wilkes, was a libeller—more than a libeller, a manufactory of libels. His style was more polished, but it lacked the humour which Wilkes could not repress and the truthfulness which was ingrained. He fell, too, far short in profound constitutional knowledge, crumbs of which Wilkes could not help dropping. Junius was bitter, cynical, and unkind; he dealt in gossip, which he dressed up in glittering venom and passed for truth. His letters were like the sting of that particularly vile wasp which leaves its victim alive but paralysed. When all is said, he did nothing but denounce and defame; the nearest approach to constructive criticism is to be found in his letter to the King, where he threatened George III with revolution unless he dissolved Parliament or pardoned Wilkes. This letter, for obvious reasons, was the most polite; some of it was remarkably true—where, for instance, he told the King that Wilkes was hardly serious at first, but had been driven to enthusiasm, and that if pardoned he would become "a silent senator". But all he had to say could have been written in a dozen lines. For the rest, he described his work aptly when he told Grafton, "I do not give you to posterity as a pattern to imitate, but as an example to deter." The best justification of Junius, apart from his glittering style, is that the Ministers were mostly scoundrels and their actions mostly wrong. But whether he were justified or not he plunged into the fray on Wilkes's behalf, and kept all England in a twitter.

(7)

The culmination of Junius's efforts was the letter to the King, which appeared on the 19th of December, 1769, and created an extraordinary sensation. It was in this atmosphere of petitions, unrest, and excitement that Parliament met on January 9, 1770. Never was a King's Speech listened to with greater interest; never was one received with greater disappointment. At least some reference to the petitions for dissolution was expected. Instead, the breathless and bewildered public were treated to a lecture on the diseases of cattle! The storm burst forthwith. Chatham thundered against the infamy of the Middlesex election in one speech after another, apparently trying to out-Wilkes Wilkes; the Constitution was violated, and unless it were restored Chatham for one was eager for revolt. "The English people . . . will never return to a state of tranquillity until they [the complaints] *are* redressed; *nor ought they.*" "If the King's servants will not permit a constitutional question to be decided on, according to the forms, and on the principles of the Constitution, it must then be decided in some other manner; and rather than it should be given up, rather than the nation should surrender their birthright to a despotic Minister, I hope, my Lords, old as I am, *I shall see the question brought to issue, and fairly tried between the people and the Government.*" "When the liberty of the subject is invaded, and all redress denied him, resistance *is* justified." While he was thus openly preaching revolt, his views of Wilkes and the King had undergone a striking change. Wilkes was no longer the blasphemer of his God and the libeller of his King. By this time Chatham had made the remarkable discovery that "the character and circumstances of Mr. Wilkes have been very improperly introduced into this question, not only here, but in that court of judicature where his cause was tried; I mean the House of Commons". Far from looking at him with jaundiced eyes, "for my own part, I consider him merely and indifferently as an English subject, possessed of certain rights which the laws have given him and which the laws alone can take from him. I am neither moved by his private vices nor by his public merits." As for the King, Chatham, in effect, called him a liar and a humbug. "I own I was credulous, I was duped, I was deceived."

To such recantations are great statesmen brought, who allow the itch for power to overcome truth and friendship. But greatness covers a multitude of twists, and so Wilkes remains the blasphemer of his God and the libeller of his King, while Chatham secures an added laurel for his defence of the Constitution!

Certainly his example was infectious. Camden followed in a white sheet. "For some time", he admitted, "I have beheld with silent indignation the arbitrary measures of the Minister; I have often drooped and hung down my head in Council and disapproved by my looks those steps which I knew my avowed opposition could not prevent. I will do so no longer, but openly and boldly speak my sentiments. I now proclaim to the world that I entirely coincide in the opinion of my noble friend, whose presence again reanimates us, touching this unconstitutional and illegal vote of the House of Commons." Even the arch-enemies were stricken dumb; Mansfield could do no better than affirm that he never had and never would express his opinion, which "he had locked up in his own breast, and it should die with him". In the House of Commons Sir George Savile and Edmund Burke both stood up in their places and told the House that they were sitting there illegally and had betrayed their trust. It was only fear of the consequences that prevented Government from hurrying them both to the Tower.

Meanwhile Chatham, eagerly looking round for a party, and

fully expecting the Ministry to fall, made overtures to Rockingham, whom he had so flagrantly insulted but a few years
earlier. Rockingham was too small a man to forgive, and not
big enough to refuse. An awkward alliance took place, much
hampered by Rockingham's anxious care for his reputation.
He was very right, for his reputation was the second biggest
thing about him, the first being his private secretary.

The slashing attack on the Government went home. Though
Camden was driven out of office, no one could be found to
fill his place. Only one man was regarded as fit for the post,
Wilkes's old enemy, Charles Yorke. That bloated bubble had
long since repented his resignation, but the overtures which
he had made to Government had not been kindly received.
At this point he promised Rockingham to stand firm, but his
craving for the Great Seal made his promise taste bitter.
Government offered him the post; he nibbled, withdrew, and
nibbled again; till at last ambition got the better of him and
he accepted. Remorse followed promptly, and three days later
he was dead—of suicide. Resignations followed thick and fast,
culminating in Grafton's. The Ministry was at an end.

In high circles all was excitement, and there were many
pangs of disappointment when the King circumvented all
intrigues by promoting Lord North and continuing as though
nothing had happened. In a sense nothing had—except that
the King at long last had found his perfect tool—because
Wilkes had washed his hands of Parliament and the people
had followed suit. Until their wrongs were redressed they
neither acknowledged the House nor cared what it did; they
were indifferent to the Ministry and the Opposition alike.

This estrangement, induced from without by the example
of Wilkes, was unconsciously aided from within by Lord
North's skill in muzzling the Opposition. There can be no
doubt that as a leader of Parliament North had more than
ordinary talents. It is a pity that his genius for getting his
own way was not exercised on the King. He disarmed opposition and repelled attack with an ingenuity that was at once

humorous and masterly. Unfortunately his skill as a tactician was not allied to statesmanship. Only a few months before attaining the premiership he had admitted in the House that he had voted for every unpopular, and against every popular, measure. A Member of Parliament who goes out of his way to resist the people's wishes can under no construction be regarded as fit to lead an English House of Commons. But he was precisely suited to the eighteenth-century ideas before Wilkes, and admirably fitted to carry out the King's wishes.

P

CHAPTER XX

THE EX-CONVICT

(1)

THE alienation of people and Parliament grew more pronounced as 1770 progressed, and for that reason the efforts of the Opposition, futile in spite of Chatham's fury, matter the less. More important, since in the long run the people were to prevail, is the action of the City. As their petition of the year before had been ignored, they now decided to remonstrate; and on the 14th of March a procession of Lord Mayor, Aldermen, Sheriffs, Common Councillors, and Liverymen, imposing in their numbers and brilliant in their gowns, marched down to St. James's, resolute and grave with a sense of their responsibility.

There was no hissing on this occasion, no dumb peal of bells, no riot; yet the King was not glad to admit these "fellows in furs". The answer was composed before the Remonstrance was seen, and was found to be "too stern and rough" for the dignified restraint of the document itself. Another had to be prepared, which the King with offhand insolence ordered to be "short and dry".

But however simple it might be to meet the Remonstrance with a blank negative, its mere presentation was a matter of moment. Government did their best to defeat its adoption in the City, and having failed, were seriously perplexed. They tried to get an opinion out of the law officers as to whether the City could be impeached, but the Attorney-General kept his mouth obstinately shut. When the Remonstrance and answer came before Parliament, Government obtained a loyal address, but the country members told them frankly that they would withdraw their support if any punishment were attempted. Indeed, the feeling was so strong that North had the greatest difficulty in choking off a Bill to regulate the power of the House to expel its members, and was forced to accept a Bill, introduced by Grenville, dealing with contested elections. Popular clamour had produced a faint echo in the House itself.

(2)

Meanwhile, in April Wilkes was due to be released. In anticipation the Supporters of the Bill of Rights issued a statement of his financial position, from which it appears that the Society had paid or compounded debts to the amount of £12,000, besides nearly £3,000 of election expenses and £1,000 of fines. There still remained about £7,000 to be met. In making the account public the Society declared that Wilkes had contracted a large proportion of the debts by becoming security for friends. Wilkes's debts were thrown in his face the next year by Horne, and have ever since formed a large part of the charges brought against him. Judged as a private man, it would have been better if he had lived within his income. But even private men are allowed to be both extravagant and bankrupt without forfeiting their characters. With public men in the eighteenth century debts were extremely common, and it is as a public man that Wilkes must be judged. The beginning of his money troubles was the expense of the elections at Berwick and Aylesbury. Then came his exile, the mismanagement of his affairs by Cotes, his legal expenses, and his fines. If, as may reasonably be done, his involuntary costs and losses are set against the debts, they do not appear so very large.

But far more important than their size is Wilkes's own attitude and the verdict of History. History is supposed to be impartial, but very rarely is. She has given Wilkes a bad name, and consequently everything he did stinks in her nostrils. A good deal of it should; but History's nose is made in a peculiar way, and in her favourites precisely the same conduct tickles her nostrils with a sweet savour. The great Lord Chatham lived and died in debt, though he held office for many years, though he was granted a pension of £3,000 when he left it, though in his poorest period Temple gave him an income,

though the Duchess of Marlborough left him £10,000, and
Sir William Pynsent a magnificent estate. The fact that he
lived and died in debt does not matter to History at all; the
fact that his debts were due to his hopeless extravagance is a
trifle; the fact that a grateful country discharged £20,000 for
him and double that amount for his son is a feather in both
their caps. So be it. But why are Wilkes's debts treated in so
different a fashion? Many of them were due to elections, misfortune, misplaced confidence in others, and the tyranny of
Government, a catalogue in striking contrast with the good
fortune of the two Pitts. The worst that can be said of Wilkes
is that a proportion of his avoidable debts came from extravagance towards his mistresses instead of, as in Pitt's case,
towards himself—financially, a mere matter of taste. Yet the
fact that a grateful country paid or compounded most of those
debts without waiting for his death is far from being a feather
in his cap. It is somehow a disgrace. The fact that he lived
within his income—by no means large—for the last eighteen
years of his life is simply ignored; and he is actually reputed
to have died insolvent because in an optimistic moment he
left bequests beyond the power of his estate to pay.

His own attitude is even more enlightening. In his youth
Wilkes was careless of money; in his exile he was largely
desperate. But he was never a money-grubber, and on the
whole he was not particularly extravagant. He had been brought
up in an atmosphere of riches, and had married a wealthy
woman; and like many another he found it difficult to adjust
himself to straitened means. But he never attempted to deny
his debts. When the "Bill of Rights" had squared the position,
Wilkes intended to secure a post in the City and live in honest
independence. He was only too well aware of his want of
prudence: "I know", he told Horne when the two were fighting,
"the sin that easily besets me, and I know too where you and
the Ministry expect to surprise me. You will both be disappointed. My friends have with pleasure marked my reformation." The reformation was genuine. As Chamberlain of

London he not only kept clear of debt, but accepted the
moral obligation of helping old friends who had fallen on evil
days. He could even be self-sacrificing. His mother had left
him in her will a life interest in some property which she
possessed at Enfield, with reversion to his brother Heaton.
Before she died Wilkes had become Chamberlain, and Heaton
had bungled himself into poverty. The good lady therefore
asked Wilkes to hand the revenue of the estate over to Heaton,
a proceeding which virtually cut Wilkes out of the lady's will.
But "my dear son John Wilkes in the most frank and liberal
manner assured me my request in favour of his brother Heaton
Wilkes should be strictly performed, and also added that he
would lose no opportunity to render all the services in his
power to his brother". As Heaton had been by no means too
kind to him during his exile, and after his return brought
difficulties on him by his stupidity, Wilkes's attitude was at
once generous and forgiving. He lived up to his promise and
practically carried Heaton on his back. So much for his debts.
Many a man's financial record has been worse—but of that
History takes no account.

Incidentally the same misrepresentation is true of his moral
and political life. Wilkes's vices were confined within limits,
yet they have swamped his greater virtues; while others who
had greater vices and smaller virtues have somehow managed
to shed the ill. So of his politics. Because he spent his time
fighting for the people's rights he is a demagogue, though
his addresses to the mob were mostly attempts to keep
them quiet when others were stirring them up by folly, by
oppression, or by stupid contempt.

(3)

On the 17th of April Wilkes was due to be released. Government, quaking with fear at the thought of this firebrand flaming
through the City, made preparations commensurate with the
danger. The town was filled with constables and troops; money

and trouble were lavished in profusion. The mountains laboured, and before the mouse could be brought forth Wilkes had slipped off quietly to the country. Horse, foot, and artillery were called upon to face—illuminations! Government were so much relieved at the orderly nature of the proceedings that they failed to realize how widespread were the rejoicings and what they signified. Walpole mentions celebrations "at Lynn, Norwich, Swaffham, Bristol, and a few other towns", but betrays the general blindness of Society when he adds "but not universally". The fact is that, with or without Chinese lanterns, whether they understood his aims or not, the whole people regarded Wilkes as their champion. Even the entirely ignorant and those well-affected to the Crown heard good reports of him and took him to their hearts. "A few months ago", wrote John Newton to Lord Dartmouth, "I heard that some of them [his parishioners] in their prayers at home had been much engaged for the welfare of Mr. Wilkes. As the whole town of Olney is remarkably loyal and peaceable with regard to the Government, I was rather surprised that gentleman should have partisans among our serious people. Upon inquiry I found they had just heard of his name, and that he was in prison. Comparing the imperfect account they had of him with what they read in their Bibles, they took it for granted that a person so treated must of necessity be a minister of the Gospel, and under that character they prayed earnestly that he might be supported and enlarged."

Amusing as the extract may be, it is not altogether without point. On his release Wilkes published addresses to the electors of Middlesex and the ward of Farringdon. "In those and former addresses", sneers Walpole, "he had the assurance to talk of protecting our *religious* as well as civil liberties. When Lord Sandwich informed against the *Essay on Woman*, *he* too talked religion. It is impossible to decide which was the more impudent, the persecutor or the martyr."

In spite of Walpole there was a world of difference between Wilkes and Sandwich. While he could not by any stretch of imagination be called a religious man, he was far from being irreligious. His mother's example and the pious atmosphere in which she had brought him up had borne their fruit, and Wilkes had a strong religious sense ingrained in his composition. As a practical man, however, he was impatient of dogma. "I have been this morning at church", he once wrote to his daughter, "and heard a really good sermon on Faith, Hope, and Charity, three sweet sisters, the eldest of which, however, I know little of; but the other two good girls are my favourites, and I wish always to dwell with me." No better description of his attitude could be given. Although his satirical humour induced him to poke fun at the tenets he could not accept, he always had an affection, half sneaking, for the underlying truths and a genuine appreciation of saintliness. The one made him a regular churchgoer, and the other led to such passages in his private letters as "the good, benevolent Paice I see continually. He really *goes about doing good*, like his great Master, and his worthy disciple the Moravian." He prided himself on belonging to the Established Church, acted as churchwarden, instilled religion into Polly, and supported religious societies. A Roman Catholic once asked Wilkes, "Where was your religion before the Reformation?" Wilkes replied without hesitation, "Where was your face before you washed it this morning?"—which was not only the retort of a wit, but of a man who knew something of the subject.

In maintaining religious liberty he was thus acting strictly in accord with a certain element in his nature. But he might very well have done so had he been as atheistical as is usually supposed. Religious liberty was not a fact in the eighteenth century, and one of its chief opponents was George III. The Established Church was dead spiritually, and its leaders were busy driving out Wesley and Whitefield. Roman Catholics and Nonconformists alike suffered under many disabilities, and a man of Wilkes's breadth of view was just the man to observe the absurdity of a dead Church oppressing the live spirit of religion. Moreover, he had a certain debt of gratitude. He numbered several highly disreputable parsons, such as Churchill and Lloyd, among his intimate friends; but many parsons of a very different stamp supported him. Dr. Somerville, in a conversation with the well-known Dr. Price, declared that the gross immoralities of Mr. Wilkes rendered him unworthy of popular favour. Price, however, was of a different opinion: "he said he [Wilkes] was a man he could trample under foot, but the question he had been the occasion of moving was of such constitutional magnitude, that his private character ought to have no influence on the decision of it". Apparently he induced Dr. Somerville to change his opinion, for that worthy man "spent part of a day in the King's Bench with a jovial company of prisoners", including Wilkes.

(4)

This April of 1770 was to be famous for two more events. Shortly after Wilkes was released, Chatham moved for a Bill to rescind the various resolutions of the House of Commons on the Middlesex election, and was defeated. About the same time there appeared a new and formidable pamphlet from Burke's pen, the *Thoughts on the Cause of the Present Discontents*. This pamphlet was a reasoned and very powerful attack upon the plan of Government which the King was pursuing. Burke, like Wilkes, believed that "the virtue, spirit, and essence of a House of Commons consists in its being the express image of the feelings of the nation"; and found nothing but discontent, precisely because Government was carried on by Royal favour alone. To bolster up this system "popularity was to be rendered, if not directly penal, at least highly dangerous". Such was his view of Wilkes's treatment. More interesting is his view of Wilkes himself. Burke had come into touch with Wilkes during the negotiations of 1765; he had remained friendly ever since. With a full knowledge of the man, he wrote: "A violent rage for the punishment of

Mr. Wilkes was the pretence of the whole. This gentleman, by setting himself strongly in opposition to the Court cabal, had become at once an object of their persecution and of the popular favour. . . . A strenuous resistance to every appearance of lawless power; a spirit of independence carried to some degree of enthusiasm; an inquisitive character to discover, and a bold one to display, every corruption and every error of Government; these are the qualities which recommend a man to a seat in the House of Commons, in open and merely popular elections." These last words are not given as a direct description of Wilkes, but by inference and position clearly apply to him. A little farther on Burke continues: "I will not believe, what no other man living believes, that Mr. Wilkes was punished for the indecency of his publications or the impiety of his ransacked closet. . . . Does not the public behold with indignation, persons not only generally scandalous in their lives, but the identical persons who, by their society, their instruction, their example, their encouragement, have drawn this man into the very faults which have furnished the cabal with a pretence for his persecution, loaded with every kind of favour, honour, and distinction which a Court can bestow? . . . I must conclude that Mr. Wilkes is the object of persecution, not on account of what he has done in common with others who are objects of reward, but for that in which he differs from many of them: that he is pursued for the spirited dispositions which are blended with his vices; for his unconquerable firmness, for his resolute, indefatigable, strenuous resistance against oppression."

It is remarkable, it is worth remembering, that in 1770 at least three men of genius defended, supported, and even praised Wilkes—Chatham, Burke, and Junius. All three admitted certain serious flaws in his character, certain limitations in his abilities, which gives the greater weight to their words. Why their testimony should be outweighed by the overweening bile of Walpole or the acrid abuse of Brougham is one of the mysteries of fate.

(5)

Immediately on his release Wilkes set about the fulfilment of his promise. He told his constituents in the addresses at which Walpole sneered that the existing House of Commons was illegal and ought to be dissolved. When that happened, they might expect "in a future honest Parliament, the three essential, and only effectual remedies of this distempered state—acts for the exclusion of placemen and pensioners, for the short duration of parliaments, and for equal representation". So he sketched a system of reform which was ultimately accomplished, though he never lived to see it, and for the moment washed his hands of politics. "I have not yet", he remarked in a letter to Polly, "been at either House; to avoid every pretence of a riot, or influencing their debates by a mob."

Coincidently he took up his duties as an alderman, first thanking the inhabitants of Farringdon Ward, in an excellent and inspiriting address, for their patience while he had been unable to attend to his duties, and congratulating them that "the high spirit of liberty, joined with prudence, temper, and intrepidity" animated the whole people of London. He reminded them of the part which the City had played at the Glorious Revolution, and declared that trade and commerce had "never arrived at perfection but under the patronage of liberty". So he proclaimed his faith, and forthwith plunged into the press of business.

Most of it was of the normal, routine type, but there was one excitement. In May the City presented a second Remonstrance to the King, and the whole Court was startled out of its wits by the daring of Beckford, the Lord Mayor, who, when the King returned the usual *non possumus* answer, made an impromptu speech, which the curious may read on his statue in the Guildhall. Wilkes, anxious to avoid hurting feelings, kept away, and his enemies, with more malice than logic, seized the occasion to accuse him of truckling to the Court. He defended himself on the ground that his presence might have provoked a further massacre, and felt obliged to prove his *bona fides* by watering down a congratulatory address on the birth of a princess. Not that Wilkes really enjoyed his own proposal, which was an unnecessary affront, and he tried to atone for it by urging the City to be as complimentary as possible to the Queen.

Otherwise affairs in the City were progressing "according to my most sanguine wishes". The two new Sheriffs, elected at midsummer, were his friends, and when Beckford died in the middle of his term of office, another friend, Trecothick, was elected Lord Mayor in his place.

(6)

Amongst other joys which awaited him on his release was the possibility of making a home for Polly, now nearly twenty years of age. Early in August he met her on her return from a visit to Paris, and the two of them spent the remainder of the month very pleasantly making a tour through Kent and Sussex, which turned into something of a royal progress, with bunting, bells, and cannon. Then they returned home to London, to remain together in perfect harmony and love till Wilkes's death.

The understanding which existed between them was not only beautiful in itself, but was based on the surest of all foundations—absolute confidence. Wilkes had from the beginning solved the great problem of parents, the problem of retaining their children's respect without forfeiting their love, and his method may be worth recording. When Polly was only twelve years of age he placed her in a French family to be educated, and wrote her a letter remarkable in many respects. Polly was allowed unlimited discretion, because she would not abuse it. "I wish that my sweet girl may have every reasonable pleasure; and I am sure that her good sense will desire no other." She was given the same *carte blanche* with money. As for advice, it was short and may seem surprising from Wilkes: "When you are well, I beg you never to miss the embassador's chapel on Sunday." He imposed no further injunctions, "because you have as much sense as anybody I know; and I am sure will conduct yourself in everything so as to win the esteem and love of everyone"; but by way of keeping a watch over her he asked her "to write your opinion to me on everything". He pursued the same policy of encouragement and trust in the matter of education: "you have an excellent genius given you from Heaven; and it will be your own pleasure to cultivate it. Read the best books, and they will be your pleasure through life. . . . God has given you excellent understanding; but the best land requires cultivation." The treatment was amply justified in the results. Polly grew up to be a charming and accomplished girl, and remained throughout life devoted to her father. Wilkes, on his side, remained her guide and protector, full of encouragement and praise, and showing a tender love which never varied. His pride and joy in her grew with time, and when the tide of abuse and misrepresentation was strong against him he would end his letters with a half wistful "continue to love me". He clung to this one constant beacon in a stormy life, and it never failed him. She was "a more than balance against the misfortunes and miseries of life", for "the greatest blessing which Heaven can bestow on any man, is a daughter like you", and so he "must always add, happy, happy father in such a daughter". Always generous, he would send little presents to his "Euphrosyne", and if they were small, "we poor patriots have little to give except wishes, but to you they come warm from the heart which is your empire". His misfortunes he kept to himself, but his pieces of good luck must be shared, even down to so simple a point as new clothes: "Polly, dear, sweet Polly, I have got a new coat, and it is all blue, and it has a fine gold edging, and I have a fine silk waistcoat, and it is all ribbed, and is blue, and has likewise a gold edging, and I have small-clothes all blue, and fine mother-of-pearl buttons, in every one of which you might see your pretty face. Now I intend to go to Ranelagh, with you, in this same fine waistcoat and coat, but then you must have a new gown, or all the fine folk will jeer me; therefore, as I am preparing for my return, you must call at Mr. Redhead's, and have a fine new gown made immediately, and then I will go with you the first day you choose." Their life together was a gentle record of happy domesticity and small pleasures.

Meanwhile, soon after their return to London, the seeds of fresh victories for Wilkes were being sown. The first sprang out of the threatened trouble with Spain over the Falkland Islands, and the second out of Woodfall's trial for publishing Junius's letter to the King.

CHAPTER XXI

HOSTILITIES

(1)

By the middle of 1770 England's reputation had fallen so low that Spain plucked up courage to attack her in the farthest corner of the world. Five frigates and sixteen hundred men appeared before Port Egmont, a tiny English settlement in the Falkland Islands, and solemnly captured it. When the news arrived Lord North was startled into firmness, and not only demanded restitution, but began busying himself with preparations for war—preparations that were necessary enough in all conscience, since the miserable system of bribery had long since sacrificed the Navy to rascally contractors. Among other steps press-gangs were set in motion.

Press-gangs were an infamous institution, whose only possible justification was necessity, but they were smeared over with a whitewash of legality by Press Warrants. It so happened that in 1763, when making his famous pronouncement on General Warrants, Pratt had included Press Warrants as equally illegal. Wilkes had too good a memory to forget the fact, and was at once too humane to like the method and too clever not to see an opportunity. He could not take action in Parliament, being debarred entrance, but parliamentary action was unnecessary; the warrants were at least of doubtful legality, and so far as the City was concerned could be made illegal beyond doubt if the City magistrates refused to back them. Here was a position made for Wilkes, the magistrate and man of action. He not only refused peremptorily to back them himself, but did his best to bring the other magistrates round to his view. More than that, on his own responsibility—and responsibility was a thing Wilkes never feared—he released a man who had been impressed within the liberties of the City.

His action at once gave life to the matter, and Trecothick, too timid to follow Wilkes's lead, found his popularity waning.

In November he was succeeded as Lord Mayor by Crosby, who consulted Chatham. Chatham very discreetly referred him to the lawyers, who with equal discretion advised that Press Warrants were respectable from hoary precedent though their form might be objectionable; and that Crosby was not forced to back them, but by doing so might prevent abuses.

Wilkes had a profound contempt for timid discretion; he recognized its advantages, but preferred the courage of his convictions. But he was too patriotic to be merely obstructive. Clearly the Navy must be manned, especially as war seemed imminent; and if Press Warrants were to go, something must be put in their place. Accordingly he persuaded the City to offer larger bounties for volunteers, and the precedent was followed by a number of towns, as well as by the Brethren of Trinity House.

Here was an excellent reform, but the mere fact that it was promoted by Wilkes damned it from the start. The Court aldermen went out of their way to back the warrants, which so disgusted the Common Council that they passed a resolution ordering their solicitor to prosecute at the City's expense any magistrate who backed a warrant in the City and any constable who executed it. The struggle was short, because the Falkland scare soon blew over, but the result was much the same as in the case of General Warrants. Wilkes's views were not adopted officially nor was the press-gang immediately abolished; but in fact the system had received a death-wound and in due course died. Wilkes had struck another blow for freedom and decency in the way peculiar to himself.

(2)

The events which arose out of Woodfall's trial were at once more exciting and more amusing. They display Wilkes at the top of his form and are altogether honourable to the City.

Junius's letter to the King was published by Woodfall in December 1769. It created extraordinary interest, and in the prevailing fashion was copied into all the other papers. Perfectly furious at the production, the King insisted on prosecutions for libel, but as Junius himself was beyond discovery, action could only be taken against the publishers. The first victim was Almon, who had republished the letter in *The London Museum*. Mansfield, before whom the case was tried, held very high notions of legal prerogative, and was as touchy at all infringements of it as ever the King could be over the Royal prerogative. In his view the only function of the jury was to decide the question of printing, and, if there were blanks or asterisks, the actual words or names which were intended. Whether the article were libellous or not was a matter for the bench alone. It was his invariable habit to sum up on these lines, and in Almon's case the jury accepted his ruling. Mansfield was therefore at liberty to decide on the point of libel and found Almon guilty.

There can be little doubt that Mansfield was straining the position. Juries had the right of bringing in either a special or a general verdict, the former being confined to the question of printing and the latter covering the question of libel—or as Mansfield preferred to call it, the question of law. Had justice been divorced from politics, it would probably have mattered little whether the jury brought in special or general verdicts; but in the eighteenth century the judges were much entangled with the Government, and libels were mostly questions of politics. It was intolerable that attacks on the administration should be judged solely by Mansfield, who was one of the leading lights of the Cabinet, and as often as not responsible for the actions criticized. Moreover, this limitation of the rights of juries was one of the points which had been fought and won in Wilkes's early days.

Wilkes and the popular party took up the question with vigour, and when in due course Woodfall was brought before Mansfield the jury ignored his ruling and returned a verdict of "guilty of printing and publishing *only*", which was in effect an acquittal. Wilkes, however, was not content with this.

Mansfield's attitude involved more than the question of libel; it struck at the whole liberty of the Press, and was intimately bound up with the decision of Parliament that their proceedings should not be published. To Wilkes, with his conviction that representatives should represent and that the public were entitled to full information, it was far more than a scandal, it was definitely unconstitutional that the Commons should be able to impose penalties on publishers for printing the debates and prosecute their critics before a judge who was virtually no more than a member of the Government. He decided to bring the matter to an issue, and concocted a trap into which Government promptly jumped.

His method was simplicity itself. He encouraged printers within the bounds of the City to publish the full debates, promising them his protection as a magistrate. Exactly how the matter would develop must depend upon the degree of Parliament's folly, which Wilkes had not over-estimated.

The first sign of movement came from the Lords, who were particularly anxious to confine Chatham's speeches to their own four walls. One of them suddenly moved that the House should be cleared of strangers. There were protests which ended in a brawl. The peers emulated pandemonium; everyone was shouting, and a certain number using their fists; all strangers were forcibly ejected and—amongst others—a deputation from the Commons who in the normal course of business were bringing a Bill up to the Lords for their consideration. This flagrant, though unintentional, violence practised upon their own members infuriated the childish Commons, and for some time both Houses shut their doors against one another, and some bright sparks in the Lower House suggested that none but the eldest sons of peers should carry up Bills, so that if the ferocious Lords were bent on murder, the victim should be one of their own kin.

With so much electricity in the air it was only to be expected that before long the Commons should complain of the printers. Onslow started the game in February 1771, and on his motion two men, Thomson and Wheble, were ordered among others to attend at the bar of the House. In spite of all orders, however, Thomson and Wheble remained obstinately within the confines of the City, and even added fuel to the fire by a sarcastic note making fun of the slipshod English of the order. To maintain their dignity the House ordered the Serjeant-at-Arms to arrest them, and on the 8th of March Government issued a proclamation offering rewards of £50 for their apprehension.

Wilkes had laid his plans on the assumption that the Serjeant-at-Arms would be brought into the picture, but the proclamation gave him an opportunity beyond his wildest hopes. Negotiations were rapidly begun with the two printers to extend the plot, and both were persuaded. On the morning of the 15th of March the comedy began. Wilkes was sitting as magistrate at the Guildhall when Wheble was arrested by his own workman, one Carpenter, and haled before Wilkes. The grave alderman solemnly examined Carpenter on the charge which he brought against his captive. Carpenter brought none; Wheble was an excellent master, but here was a proclamation by virtue of which as a law-abiding citizen Carpenter had laid hands on his employer. Wilkes studied the proclamation, found it was out of order, and extremely shocked at the whole proceeding promptly discharged Wheble and bound him over to prosecute Carpenter for assault and illegal imprisonment. Carpenter, in no way abashed, asked Wilkes for a certificate so that he might claim the £50 reward, which Wilkes readily gave him.

At seven o'clock that same evening Thomson was seen entering his own door in Newgate Street. A zealous citizen arrested him and haled him before Alderman Oliver at the Mansion House. The same gravely proper proceeding followed as had taken place at the Guildhall in the morning.

All this, of course, was by-play, the main effect of which was to make a laughing-stock of Government, and to remind the world in general that no Englishman could be arrested merely on the strength of a proclamation. The serious business was to follow, and it followed quickly.

Among the printers marked down for punishment was one John Miller, of the *London Evening Post*. There was an order out for his arrest, and a messenger proceeded to put it in force. John Miller had been coached in the part he was to play, and finding that the messenger had no warrant from a City magistrate, not only refused to accompany him, but handed the messenger over to a City constable on a charge of assault. The constable, printer, and messenger repaired to the Mansion House, where an examination was conducted by Brass Crosby, the Lord Mayor, supported by Wilkes and Oliver. The news spread like wildfire, and before long the Serjeant-at-Arms was hurrying to the City to release his messenger. But the City magistrates were quite sure of their ground. Crosby in his gravest manner declared that so long as he occupied the high office of Lord Mayor he looked upon himself as the guardian of the liberties of his fellow-citizens; that no power on earth had the right to seize a citizen of London without a warrant from himself or some other City magistrate, and that the arrest of Miller was illegal. Miller was accordingly set at liberty, and when evidence of assault had been given, the messenger was asked if he would give bail. Both messenger and Serjeant-at-Arms refused, whereupon the three magistrates signed an order for his commitment. At that point, realizing that they were in earnest, the Serjeant-at-Arms gave way and offered bail, which Crosby accepted, though at the same time he rebuked the Serjeant-at-Arms for trifling with them.

The die had been cast. Parliament and the City had crossed swords over the high question of privilege and the liberty of the Press.

(3)

Being thus deliberately thwarted, the Commons had to do something in mere self-defence. Ministers were not at all sure what that something ought to be, and their hesitation was the more pronounced as one of the offenders was Wilkes. They had burnt their fingers at his flame often enough to fight shy of him. The King, however, came to their aid. In February he had written to North: "I do in the strongest manner recommend that every caution may be used to prevent its becoming a serious affair", and suggested that if a messenger were sent to arrest printers in the City, he should be instructed not to find them. But a good deal of water had flowed under the bridges since then, and George III, who never lacked courage, now told North that "the authority of the House of Commons is totally annihilated if it is not in an exemplary manner supported to-morrow by instantly committing the Lord Mayor and Alderman Oliver to the Tower; as to Wilkes, he is below the notice of the House".

With some trepidation the Ministers ordered the three sinners to attend the House. Wilkes replied at once that he would attend only if he was allowed to take his seat; Crosby was genuinely ill, and his case had to be put off. Oliver, therefore, was the first to meet the blast. He was young; he was obviously not the chief offender; and whatever was done to him would prove an embarrassing precedent. For all reasons, therefore, the Ministers were anxious to show moderation, and not the less so because their case was bad. He was told time and again that it would be sufficient if he apologized; but, young as he was, Oliver simply replied that he had done what he thought right and would do it again. After a debate which did not end till four o'clock in the morning, Oliver was sent to the Tower.

Two days later Crosby managed to get down to the House, swathed in flannel and suffering badly from gout. Much more formidable than his appearance were the cheering crowds that accompanied him the whole way from the City. The Ministers tried to run away from their own actions and proposed that because of his illness Crosby should be placed in the custody of the Serjeant. But Crosby would have none of it; he was well enough to suffer the fate of his junior, and if he could not get justice, he refused to accept favours. So to the Tower he was sent in the custody of two trembling attendants, who would have been lynched by the crowd there and then if Crosby had not protected them. Crosby and Oliver remained incarcerated till the end of the session, when they were automatically released.

As for Wilkes, he was twice more summoned to attend, and as he obviously had not the least intention of complying, the Commons got out of the hopeless impasse by adjourning over the date on which he ought to have appeared.

Here again Wilkes had gained his end in his own way. The right to print debates was not admitted, but it had in effect been obtained.

(4)

Wilkes had been showing a bold front, and at this point seemed to have rallied the whole City to his side. But his enemies had not been idle, and underground intrigues were at work.

Partly they were due to jealousy and partly to extraneous events. The first check to his triumphant career had occurred before his release from prison. In October 1769 the weavers, who had played so prominent and so unsolicited a part in Wilkes's affairs, came once more on the scene. In Walpole's words, "the weavers mutinied against their masters and many were killed by the Guards". The ringleaders were condemned to death, and though the Sheriffs tried to save them, suffered the penalty. The angry mob replied by destroying the looms of the prosecutor. This sudden uprising was the result of economic pressure; it had nothing to do with Wilkes or the causes for which he stood. But no one was calm enough, or skilled enough, to delve into the causes of different riots. The people and the Government were at loggerheads, and any manifestation of unrest was put down to Wilkes. Here apparently he was urging his followers to destroy property, which was not a form of liberty with much appeal for City merchants. Hence the opposition to Wilkes gained strength, and the popular party even lost the next election for an alderman.

Side by side with the natural suspicion of the wealthier men came the machinations of Horne, whom jealousy was turning from an ardent supporter into an inveterate enemy. When he had first met Wilkes towards the end of 1765, Horne had been a clever, restless young man, with a taste for fine clothes and an itch for notoriety. With that mixture of hero-worship and disdain typical of immature brains, Horne had regarded Wilkes with mingled awe and contempt. The combination resulted in a ridiculous letter, full of gross flattery, impertinent advice, and silly bravado. The letter was completely foreign to every sentiment that Wilkes possessed; he disliked flattery; was more accustomed to asking than giving advice; and avoided bravado, especially towards comparative strangers. He never answered the letter, and probably betrayed his feelings when next the two met. At all events Horne subsequently maintained that on the next occasion "I saw reasons sufficient never more to trust you with a single line". This incipient hostility grew, and though Horne played an active part in the Middlesex election, it was more by way of bringing himself into prominence than out of real friendship. Similarly, he took a large share in the foundation of the "Bill of Rights", mainly with the hope of gaining importance under the shadow of Wilkes's name. On Wilkes's release, however, he had sunk from virtual leadership to a minor position, and his self-conceit, inflamed by Wilkes's coolness, inclined him to try a fall with his nominal chief. What most restrained him was fear of his silly letter becoming public. By this time Horne was old enough to know better, and sufficiently thin-skinned to be afraid of exposure. But the knowledge that Wilkes held this weapon of his own forging embittered his angry jealousy and made him the more ready to foment trouble by backstair methods.

It did not take Wilkes long to discover Horne's double-dealings, or to trace to him the anonymous attacks in the papers and the insinuations covertly circulated. Holding such men, as he said, "infinitely less dangerous as open enemies than as professed friends", Wilkes tried within six months of his release to force Horne into the open. But Horne had eluded him, preferring to choose his own time and method. He continued his scheme with some success, keeping Wilkes continually engaged in soothing friends who had been incensed in one way or another. In January 1771 in particular, Wilkes was nearly involved in a duel with his old friend Lauchlin Macleane, because of an anonymous attack which Macleane believed to have emanated from Wilkes. As a matter of fact Wilkes was not responsible, but had some difficulty in making up the quarrel.

The affair of the printers gave Horne a new opportunity. He summoned a special meeting of the "Bill of Rights", at which he proposed that money should be voted to the printers out of the Society's funds. There was no sort of reason for this. The three printers mainly concerned had been forgotten by Government in the subsequent turmoil; the others had suffered nothing worse than a reprimand. While there was thus no solid ground for giving them money, it was very certain that the funds of the Society had been contributed by Wilkes's admirers for his own benefit and to meet his debts. Wilkes protested, as he had some right to do; but he was placed in an invidious position, where he could be accused of insensibility to the needs of everyone but himself. It was an astute move and alienated individuals, more particularly the well-to-do, though it did not affect Wilkes's real popularity.

Among others who were influenced was Alderman Oliver. Wilkes, unaware of this changed mood, asked Oliver to stand with him for the office of Sheriff, and received a blank refusal, Oliver preferring to stand alone. It seemed to Horne that no more favourable moment could arise for an open break. Oliver at the moment was floating on a flood-tide of popularity, sharing with Crosby the honours of the battle with Parliament, and being daily fêted in his prison within the Tower walls. He would certainly defeat Wilkes at the election for Sheriff, and if Horne let loose the onslaught he was meditating, Wilkes would be driven from public life. In May and June 1771, therefore, while Wilkes was conducting his canvass, Horne published a series of twelve letters designed to crush his rival finally and for good.

The attempt was a dismal failure. It is universally admitted that Wilkes got the better of the exchange. But these controversial letters are of more than passing interest; so far from damaging Wilkes, they provide a full vindication. In his first letter Horne declared that he did not intend to attack Wilkes on the score of private character, but only on his public conduct. From beginning to end the nearest approach to a public charge is that Wilkes wanted to make his friend, Reynolds, Town Clerk, and to get his brother Heaton appointed Chamberlain. If this is really the worst that can be said of Wilkes's public career, it was easily the best and purest of the age.

The remainder of these letters deal with nothing but Wilkes's private character. Horne was very much in earnest and allowed nothing, however trifling, to escape his notice. Yet the length and breadth of his discoveries was that Wilkes was uncommonly hard up and was put to all manner of shifts to avoid duns. If Horne had possessed a lighter pen, he might have made his letters extremely funny at Wilkes's expense, but he thought indignation better than ridicule, with the result that he made mountains out of molehills. Many of the individual charges, quite unimportant in themselves, were shown to have no foundation, and in effect the substance of his case was that Wilkes had for a few weeks pawned some clothes which Horne had left in his care, and avoided paying a debt of a few pounds to Horne's brother-in-law, an innkeeper. Wilkes denied both these charges, and no other evidence is forthcoming. The rest of the letters were filled with details of the debts discharged by the "Bill of Rights".

Wilkes did his best to avoid replying, but when it became inevitable, did so with devastating effect. He doled out Horne's letter piecemeal—to Horne's impotent fury—and let the shafts of his wit and sarcasm play about the devoted parson's head. If Horne had not begun the attack, Wilkes's letters would have been cruel. The controversy was the end of Horne for the time being, but it also caused a split in the popular party, which weakened Wilkes without doing the least good.

CHAPTER XXII

BITTERNESS

(1)

WILKES continued his canvass for the post of Sheriff unperturbed by Horne's damp squibs or Oliver's surly refusals, and found a colleague in Frederick Bull, a rich, amiable tea merchant devoted to Wilkes and full of good intentions. These two easily headed the poll, while Oliver was a long way the last of the five candidates.

Meanwhile, as though determined to show that obstruction merely fired his activities, Wilkes branched out in a wholly new direction, putting forward proposals on the 18th of June to prevent profiteering in food-stuffs. The country was passing through an exceedingly rough patch, when bad harvests combined with economic pressure to make life difficult for the lower classes. The Ministers were too busy at Newmarket, and Society too taken up with masquerades, to find a remedy, and Wilkes accordingly urged a form of control within the City. Whether his proposals had much direct success does not appear, but he does seem to have produced an entirely new spirit. This was reflected a few months later when the journeymen tailors, instead of rioting, petitioned the City magistrates for an increase of wages on the ground of the cost of living. Their petition was not only granted, but they were publicly commended for their behaviour.

At the same time Wilkes rallied those members of the "Bill of Rights" who had remained loyal, persuaded Crosby to stand as Lord Mayor for the second time in opposition to Sawbridge—one of the seceding members—and issued a manifesto containing a test for parliamentary candidates, by which they would be sworn to press for shorter parliaments, the removal of placemen, and a more equal representation. The manifesto was the more interesting because it touched upon the shocking state of Ireland and the illegality of American taxation. Wilkes was rapidly taking within his sphere every form of grievance, besides setting an example of good administration in the City.

His prompt decisiveness brought him a letter from Junius, which was followed by a regular correspondence. As Junius was here trying to be constructive, he was uncommonly dull, but the letters throw a flood of light on Wilkes's political standing.

Junius, knowingly or unknowingly, took up Chatham's attitude. For all his protestations, at heart Chatham was an oligarch. He wished to live and die in Whig principles, and was not prepared to sweep away the political entrenchment built up by the Whig magnates. True it was the rotten part of the Constitution, but on it depended the influence of the oligarchs in the Lower House, and if that went, the Constitution went with it. The voice of the people was at present a trifle swamped; it might without harm, perhaps with advantage, be made a little more important. So Chatham rather doubtfully proposed to increase the number of county members, and more vigorously decided to leave the rotten boroughs alone.

This was the compromise which Junius now put forward. But Wilkes was too honest to accept it. He had long since maintained that the King was merely the chief magistrate, appointed by and for the people. The peers were useful as a second chamber; but the final word lay with the people. This was what he meant when he declared that the voice of the people was the voice of God. There was no appeal beyond. Nominally the people had the last word, but in practice they had no voice at all. Nor would they get it by any tinkering with the existing plan. A reformation was needed from top to bottom. Individually his proposals might lead to greater trouble, perhaps to more corruption—as Burke pointed out on Sawbridge's motion for shorter parliaments—but taken as a whole they would give a real meaning to what were now mere words. Wilkes was not interested in patching old garments with new cloth; he wanted a new suit to fit the proverbial John Bull.

Again, Chatham liked to have respectable names about him, and thrilled with emotion in the Royal presence. He could never have echoed Wilkes's remark, "I am not fond of the air of a Court". Junius, following his example, besought Wilkes to be reconciled with Sawbridge, a thoroughly respectable man. He put forward a specious argument: by making it up with Sawbridge, Wilkes would rout Horne and reunite the "Bill of Rights"; on the other hand, by remaining an enemy, he would split the popular vote, fail to bring in Crosby, and very probably let in the Court candidate as Lord Mayor; if so, all would be lost.

For immediate purposes Junius was right. Sawbridge and Crosby received practically the same number of votes, and were respectively second and third on the poll. The Court candidate, Nash, became Lord Mayor. But in the long run Wilkes was right. Nash's election drove home the danger of a split vote; the popular party realized in time that they must choose between Wilkes and Horne—and Horne disappeared. All was by no means lost, and thenceforward Wilkes ruled the City.

But this is looking too far forward. The receipt of Junius's letter, thrust into his hand one August afternoon by a sedan chairman, gave Wilkes much food for thought. With views so divergent, Wilkes could not possibly follow its advice; but refusal was dangerous. Junius exerted tremendous influence, and his style was uncommonly pungent. It was only a month or two since Wilkes was tossing in a rough and tumble with Horne, and he was by no means anxious for a new and fiercer assailant. At all costs Junius must be placated.

In times of danger Wilkes was always inimitable, and he now proceeded to twist Junius round his little finger. Without receding an inch from his principles or his determination, he professed the greatest veneration for Junius, and proposed to ask his advice on a number of schemes. The first, which he doled out after some delay, was purely fantastic, and was invented simply to be turned down. Wilkes proposed to send an insulting note to the Lord Mayor, refusing to attend the official service at St. Paul's. Such a suggestion was wholly unlike Wilkes; it was merely an affront; it was based on no principle; it would lead nowhere and help nobody. Wilkes undoubtedly expected Junius to advise against it, and when he did so, Wilkes very humbly accepted the advice. Thereafter he hinted at vast schemes on which he would be grateful for further advice—schemes which he never unfolded, and never meant to unfold, even if they existed. But they kept Junius in a good temper. Meanwhile Wilkes boasted to his friends that he was in touch with the Great Unknown, thereby gaining a larger measure of influence and respect. The possible danger had been turned into a positive asset.

(2)

Wilkes was sworn in as Sheriff on the 29th of September, 1771. Here was a new field of endeavour much more congenial to his talents. As Sheriff he would be definitely engaged on administration, and he made haste to give practical examples of reform. His first official duty was to preside over the polling for the Lord Mayor, and he at once proclaimed that the voting would be secret—a declaration which, says Thornton, the City historian, was received "with the greatest applause".

A fortnight later Wilkes moved again. In conjunction with his colleague Bull, he issued instructions to the keeper of Newgate, requiring him to rectify two abuses. The first was the system of keeping prisoners in irons during their trial. "This", said the instructions, "we conceive to be equally repugnant to the laws of England and of humanity." The second was the taking of money for admission to the trials at the Old Bailey. "This, likewise," ran the instructions, "we hold to be contrary to law." To the delight of Wilkes's detractors this second order led at the next sessions to an immense crowd, which rushed into the building and caused the utmost confusion. It is usually in her children that Wisdom is justified; and to-day the spirit of Wilkes has the last laugh.

Many other reforms were introduced, mostly in connection with prison affairs. Wilkes had great sympathy with the under-dog, which was not to be choked by his love of order and decency. Justice should be tempered by mercy, and Wilkes made personal inspection of the gaols to see that criminals were treated with humanity. Supervision was only too necessary when prisons were hotbeds of disease and prisoners were objects of prey if they had money, and mere carrion flesh if they had none. Wilkes's efforts at reform were so conspicuous and so successful that friends and foes alike were forced to join in a unanimous vote of thanks at the close of his term of office. It was probably also Wilkes's doing that the City's annual petition was not addressed to the King, but to the House of Commons, and dealt, not with the political situation, but the much more pressing matter of food. The City urged Government to allow the free importation of corn.

Meanwhile, if Wilkes had time to chuckle over revenge, it came in a peculiarly sweet fashion in November 1771. In that month the King learnt to his horror that his younger brother, the Duke of Cumberland, had married a widow, Mrs. Horton, the sister of the notorious Colonel Luttrell. The Ministerial Member for Middlesex did more than keep Wilkes out of Parliament; he brought in the Royal Marriage Bill—the King's indignant reply to the insolence of the Luttrell family. To add to the irony, Luttrell, who had been rewarded for past services with a post in Ireland, began about this time for his own purposes to develop qualms about retaining his seat for Middlesex, and threatened to return to England in order to resign it. More terrified than ever at the thought of a new Middlesex election, the King wrote to North: "I had heard a week ago a report of it, but thought it was too absurd to give any credit to it; I do not yet see how he can effect it; but would insinuate whether Lord Townshend [the Viceroy] might not

receive a private intimation from you not to give him leave to
quit his attendance in Ireland, which will at least postpone
what might occasion some noise." Wilkes needs no further
justification than the despicable methods of his opponents.

(3)

Wilkes had mapped out his career in the City with great care,
and so far had succeeded to admiration. He was now to experience his first rebuff. According to plan, he stood as candidate
for Lord Mayor in 1772. At these elections the first two names
on the poll are presented to the Court of Aldermen, who
choose between them. In the eighteenth century, when the
elections were more than formal, contending parties put up
two candidates, so as to shut out their opponents altogether.
In the prevailing fashion the Court party put forward Aldermen Shakespeare and Halifax. Wilkes had no doubt that he
would head the poll himself, but he knew that the majority
of the Aldermen were on the Court side, and unless he could
secure some candidate to stand with himself, either Shakespeare or Halifax was bound to be elected. Unfortunately the
split in the popular party had left him very little choice.
However, James Townshend allowed his name to be put
forward.

Townshend was a curious, pig-headed man, of considerable
wealth and strong convictions. Originally he had been an
ardent supporter of Wilkes, fighting manfully at his side through
the Middlesex election. In the debate about Crosby and Oliver,
he had electrified the House by appearing suddenly from a
bed of sickness, pale-faced and in bandages, to declare that all
their proceedings were due to "the baneful influence of the
Princess Dowager of Wales". Subsequently he had refused
to pay his taxes on the ground that Middlesex was not legally
represented, and therefore Parliament had no right to levy
taxes—a method of turning himself into a martyr that left
the nation cold. Recently he had come under the influence of

Horne, and at this election behaved in a curious manner, refusing to canvass or to appear on the hustings. None the less he was supposed to be loyal, and Wilkes's supporters very gladly voted for him.

If Townshend took no interest in the poll, the King followed it with breathless anxiety. For the first few days Halifax and Shakespeare led by a comfortable majority; Wilkes was last. The King sighed happily. A day or two later he was a trifle uneasy at the fact that the mob were "less quiet". Another day or two, and the "unpromising appearance" of the polls led him to the conclusion that "Wilkes is not bound by any tyes, therefore would poll non-freemen rather than lose the election". When Wilkes came out triumphantly on top, North and the King comforted each other with the belief that a scrutiny would bring to light "his little regard to true votes". Why they never learnt the utter groundlessness of their views is a pretty problem in psychology.

But now came the surprise. Wilkes and Townshend were returned to the Court of Aldermen, and it was considered certain that Wilkes would be elected. Oliver, however, as Sheriff, suddenly bestirred himself, collected a Court of Aldermen in a hurry, and before Wilkes's supporters could put in an appearance triumphantly elected Townshend, who as triumphantly accepted the post. Wilkes had been outwitted.

"Wilkes", says Walpole, "was thunderstruck, and for once angry in earnest." He was a great deal more than angry; a touch of real bitterness appeared in his conduct. On the whole it was not surprising. More than fifteen years earlier he had entered politics rather against his will to support his friends. After doing yeoman service he had been cast off and ruined; yet he had accepted the buffet without rancour, trusting that those same friends would do him justice. Time and again they had played him false, till at last he had determined to cut himself adrift and carve out a new career for himself. He had entered on that new career at forty years of age, a time of life when most men have either failed or planted their feet firmly on the road to success. In a few brief years he had made a remarkable "return"; everything seemed set for a brief and brilliant passage to prosperity and peace. And now, inmid career, he was checked. What would be the result? Years before he had told Cotes, "I have in my own case experienced the fickleness of the people. I was almost adored one week— the next neglected, abused, despised." Was the same to happen again? Was this check the turn of the tide? Would his second effort fail, and Wilkes the Alderman fizzle out as dismally as Wilkes the Politician? If so, he saw no prospect of another return. What he had been able to do at forty, he could hardly hope to repeat at fifty. There was reason for his bitterness.

Wilkes was not the only man that was angry; the whole City was up in arms. The Lord Mayor's procession turned into a harassed retreat with the windows of most of the carriages broken; and during the usual festivities in the evening the mob surged round the Guildhall, yelling and snarling at the doors. Livid with rage, Townshend dashed out, sword in hand, and arrested all the rioters he could reach. Subsequently he accused Wilkes of setting the mob on, and tried to push the charge home. He failed utterly, his own witnesses turning against him. And indeed he was wrong; all Wilkes had done was to withdraw his restraining hand.

Meanwhile, in all the petulance of defeat, Wilkes took every step to thwart and harass Townshend during the whole of his mayoralty, his bitterness leading him into actions which can only be deplored. He made the quarrel personal, insulting Townshend in the Council Chamber and attacking him by anonymous paragraphs in the papers. He nosed out every slip that Townshend had made, and was overjoyed to find evidence that he had horsewhipped two small children who were collecting firewood on his estate—a matter that would have disgusted Wilkes in any case, but one that was ferreted out for purely personal reasons. When he had discovered the facts he published them anonymously, but had no hesitation in admitting authorship, and by calling Townshend a liar and a bully to his face, did his best to goad his antagonist into a duel.

It is not a pleasant episode in Wilkes's life, though he managed to introduce one touch of rather grim humour. When the time came for the yearly Remonstrance to the King, Wilkes did the drafting, and produced the most flaming document the City had ever presented. Townshend, Wilkes remarked cynically, would be undone at Court if he presented it, and stoned by the people if he did not. Probably it was by his machinations that the City as a whole, though adopting the draft, showed very little interest in its presentation. Townshend, who had betrayed his apprehensions by taking legal advice, found himself obliged to hand the Remonstrance to the King with a very small company to support him. Fortunately for him, Wilkes's hand in the affair was known to the authorities. How personal and how bitter was the quarrel can be seen by a comparison with Wilkes's moderation during the mayoralty of Nash, who belonged to the opposite party.

(4)

The opening months of 1773 gave Wilkes an opportunity of working off his bottled rage in another direction. The Commons were summoned to meet on the 26th of April, and in accordance with their usual practice the Sheriffs of Middlesex sent the summons to Wilkes instead of to Luttrell. Still smarting at his recent defeat, Wilkes wrote a vigorous letter to the Speaker, asserting his right to attend, and included in it one of his very rare declarations of future conduct: "I will never cease to support with spirit the clear right I derive from them [the freeholders of Middlesex] by all constitutional modes of redress, till every the most minute trace of the late flagitious proceedings be utterly done away, and the guilt fully expiated."

On the 26th he appeared at the Crown Office to demand his writ, and when it was refused, marched at the head of a large crowd to Westminster. This was the first time that Wilkes had deliberately led a mob to the doors of the House, and his action betrays the strength and bitterness of his feelings. He was definitely making a bid to regain the popular favour which he feared he was losing. Yet it was typical of him that even at this desperate moment he kept the mob under control, and certainly had no thought of more than moral suasion—perhaps not so much, perhaps only a public gesture. The Guards, who had been kept under arms, were not needed.

While Wilkes was marching up and down outside, Glynn informed the House that Wilkes desired to be heard at the bar of the House on a complaint against the Clerk of the Crown for refusing the writ. Sawbridge, who in spite of a temporary estrangement, respected, and was respected by, Wilkes, seconded the motion. It was, of course, rejected; but the sore, which Government had hoped that time would heal, had broken out again, and a few days later the freeholders of Middlesex met at Mile End to pass resolutions in favour of Wilkes, and a vote of thanks to Glynn and Sawbridge.

There was little of interest after this until the elections for Lord Mayor in October. In the intervening months Wilkes managed to pick a quarrel with a Mr. Lane, whom he called a "tricking attorney", and challenged to a duel, but the man of law very prudently would "never stoop so low". The incident is of no interest except as further proof of the irritable state of Wilkes's nerves. In May he received news that a certain William Temple had left him a legacy of £500, but in keeping with the cross-grained nature of this period of his life, the legacy was not to be paid for twelve months.

The elections for the Lord Mayor were stormy. Wilkes stood once more as candidate with his friend Bull. The Court did not oppose him, but Horne's faction put up Sawbridge and Oliver, the former of whom accused Wilkes of slandering him anonymously. Wilkes made a spirited reply, which he published in the papers, and he had the solid support of the people. As ever, he headed the poll, with Bull second. Even the Court of Aldermen were equally divided. But Townshend, as Lord

Mayor, gave his casting vote for Bull, and so got some of his own back.

If the Court party still thought, as apparently they did, that this continual thwarting would destroy Wilkes's popularity, they were much deceived. Quite the contrary; the people felt that he was being baulked of the honour they intended, and were accordingly the more eager to serve him. A month or so later, when one of the City members died, they had an opportunity of testifying their doglike devotion. Wilkes nominated Bull, and the Court had the greatest difficulty in finding anyone who would oppose—a fact which induced the King to complain that "it is melancholy to find so little public virtue remaining in this country". At last they persuaded one Roberts to stand. This Roberts had been a director of the East India Company, but had been turned out for mismanagement, which lends piquancy to the King's description of him as "an eminent merchant". The electors simply brushed Roberts aside, and Bull was returned.

For the remainder of the year Wilkes remained quiet. He had no wish to annoy Bull, and was as a matter of fact in rather poor health. In October, however, he was again candidate for the post of Lord Mayor, and chose Bull as his colleague. He headed the poll for the third time, and the Court of Aldermen gave up the contest. Wilkes was elected.

At almost the same moment Parliament was dissolved. In spite of his preoccupations in the City, Wilkes managed to bestow a good deal of attention upon the General Election. His successes were not as widespread as some people had at first feared, but he himself was returned for Middlesex unopposed, and about twelve other members were definitely pledged to support him—a band whom Wilkes irreverently nicknamed his Twelve Apostles.

CHAPTER XXIII

THE WAR WITH AMERICA

(1)

Wilkes meant his mayoralty to be a success. When his election was announced, there were deafening cheers in the Guildhall, which were caught up and re-echoed through all the City streets, while the bells were set pealing from every steeple. The exuberance of delight was renewed at the Lord Mayor's Show, which was the most magnificent within living memory. The dinner at night was not quite so successful because the worthy bidden guests refused to come. But Wilkes was nothing daunted. For all his reputation he had moved in the highest circles at home and abroad; he knew how to make a success of parties, and he had an incomparable hostess in his Polly—now a charming, vivacious young woman of twenty-four, with much of her father's sparkle and the polish of a Parisian education. It did not take the great world long to discover the fascination of the City banquets under the new Lord Mayor, and their haughty standoffishness soon gave way to an eagerness to be asked.

His term of office was no less remarkable on the business side. He continued the reforming zeal which he had shown as Sheriff in caring for the poor and oppressed and overhauling the administration of justice. Everyone, except his old enemy Harley, was delighted; and even the Court of Aldermen, who were never afraid of giving blame, awarded him unstinted praise, thanking him "for his indefatigable attention to the several duties of that important office; for the particular regard and politeness which he was pleased at all times to show to the members of this Court; for his wise, upright, and impartial administration of justice; for his diligence on all occasions to promote the welfare and true interests of this City; and for his unblemished conduct and exemplary behaviour during the whole course of his mayoralty".

In matters of entertaining and City administration Wilkes might be expected to shine. The real proof of statesmanship was the guidance of the City in its attitude towards the wider affairs of State. Wilkes had been responsible for the tension already existing, and the question in people's minds was whether he would use his new authority to aggravate the position or allow the sense of responsibility to damp his ardour. It was characteristic of Wilkes to do neither. His term of office increased the weight and importance of the City; all that was shed was the noisy incompetence.

He was soon given an opportunity of showing his firmness and tact. In February 1775 the Lords thought fit to order the arrest of a printer for publishing their debates. It must have been difficult to be patient with such foolishness, but Wilkes was saved by his humour. He told the printer, who lived within the liberties of the City, to write to the Serjeant of the House of Lords, Sir Francis Molesworth, fixing a date and time when he would be at home, awaiting arrest. Concurrently Wilkes let it be known that if the Serjeant accepted the invitation he would find himself in prison on a charge of assault. The Lords, or perhaps Sir Francis Molesworth, thought discretion the better part of valour—and to this day the reports are published for all the world to read.

The next problem was the petition to the King, which by this time had become a hardy annual. Wilkes could not decently hold back, and in April a petition was duly prepared dealing with the really vital matter of America.

The thought of meeting Wilkes face to face disturbed the King, who suddenly recollected that while he was bound to receive the City in its corporate character, he was not bound to receive a petition from the Livery. He propounded this view to North, who realized the danger of altering the method of procedure "in the mayoralty of Mr. Wilkes". The King reluctantly acquiesced, but his nervousness was shown by the warning given to Wilkes at the palace gates that he was not to address the King personally. The caution was quite unnecessary; Wilkes, as usual, behaved in a quiet and orderly fashion, so that the King was forced to admit that "he had never seen so well-bred a Lord Mayor". His moderation, however, did him no good. The King merely looked on it as a sign of weakness, and at once ordered the Lord Chamberlain to inform Wilkes that he would not in future receive any petitions from the City unless they came from the Corporation. This was a piece of petty spite, but not without a reason, nor yet quite without a sting. Wilkes's encouragement of the Livery was a democratic move, and as such distasteful to the King. Wilkes neither could nor would suffer an insult to the Livery. He first published a reply to the Chamberlain's letter, and then arranged for a fresh petition to be voted. When the King refused to receive it, Wilkes obtained a resolution to publish the petition and a protest against the King's attitude. Finally, a petition on the same lines was passed by the City in its corporate capacity, which the King was obliged to receive. In a word, the only result had been two petitions instead of one, besides resolutions and a protest.

(2)

Towards the end of his term of office came one of those disasters that are liable to overtake sinners. Among the most faithful of Wilkes's friends was a certain John Barnard, a wealthy old man, but one who, apart from his riches, seems to have been more than a trifle unfortunate. His health was bad, he had lost his wife, and his daughter had run away with a music-master and subsequently died. Before his daughter ran away he married again, his second wife being much younger than himself. Barnard and his second wife had visited Wilkes in the King's Bench prison, and had been intimate ever since.

On the 6th of October, 1775, Mrs. Barnard burst into her husband's room in the middle of the night, but left again without speaking. The next day she was in the greatest agitation and refused to come down to dinner. When the old man went up to see her, she burst into tears and declared that her stepdaughter's ghost haunted her, threatening that she would suffer the torments of hell unless she confessed all to her husband. The confession was a pitiful affair. Some years before her marriage she had been Wilkes's mistress. Their intercourse had ceased in 1762, but through Horne's influence had begun again while Wilkes was in prison. After his release they had once more parted, but meeting accidentally in a shop, the old passion had revived, and they had been together three or four times in Barnard's own house. Thereafter the affair had ended, but her conscience pricked her, and her dreams had now terrified her into confession.

The old man wrote in extreme agitation to Wilkes: "I am not master of words to express my thoughts. I hardly know why I am writing to you; I wish to see you, and I shudder at the thought of it; for God's sake give me some satisfaction; I don't mean what is commonly called so, since from my age and great infirmities Honor does not require me to demand it, or you to give it if I did; for alas! you may now almost blow me down with your breath."

Wilkes, greatly perturbed, tried to get the old man to the Mansion House, but Barnard refused to see him anywhere but at his own home. To Berkeley Square, therefore, Wilkes went, reluctantly enough, denied the accusations, and suggested that the lady must be suffering from delusions. Barnard replied simply by offering to bring his wife down. Wilkes changed colour, excused himself as best he could, and very abruptly left the house.

Barnard tasted the sweets of legitimate revenge by informing Wilkes that he had altered his will, in which he had previously left him £5,000 and a valuable collection of prints. Perhaps a touch of harshness mingled with his further action in reducing the provision for his wife. At all events he treated the sa - hearted lady with a severity which drove her from his house a year or so later, to die poor and alone in March 1777.

It was a miserable story that did little credit to any of the three—least of all to Wilkes. Intrigues were common enough in his life and as such are hardly worth recounting. Yet this one has its use for the understanding of his character. Through all the turbulent scenes of his career Wilkes presented a bold front—in duels, in courts of law, before the Commons and the mob, and in the presence of the King. Yet he trembled before a helpless old man and ran away from a weeping penitent. Here it was conscience that made a coward of him. What gave him his courage everywhere else?

(3)

The glories and stains alike of his mayoralty were swallowed up in the more exciting fact that he had hardly become Lord Mayor before he once more took his seat in Parliament, from which Government had now no excuse to expel him. His return was triumphant; he came not only as Member for the County of Middlesex but as Lord Mayor of London; he appeared not as a humble follower of others but with a strong programme and a compact party. Government were apprehensive and the nation waiting. Yet Wilkes achieved exactly nothing.

His failure is usually explained in one of two ways—either that he was a worthless demagogue, who sank at once to his proper level, or that he was at least fifty years in advance of his time. Both overlook one startling point—Wilkes never tried to do anything—and neither accords with facts. Wilkes was not a ready speaker, and his morals might certainly have been better, but it is the merest nonsense to describe him as a worthless demagogue. No man is worthless who proves himself the best Lord Mayor of a century and the author of a scheme of parliamentary reform which succeeding generations adopt. In any case he was admittedly fearless, and as a demagogue it was obviously his cue to make a fuss—some pretence, at least, of living up to his promises. Why did he fail in this primary duty? How came it that the fearless John Wilkes, who had been fighting King, Peers, Parliament, and Judges for over a dozen years, suddenly went out like a pricked bubble? Not that he was entirely silent; he lifted up his voice vigorously against his opponents, only he steered carefully clear of reform. There was but one point on which he touched, and that with a steady perseverance which at last achieved success—the reversal of the resolutions on the Middlesex elections. This solitary pawn is proof of his indomitable will. Why was he so feeble in other directions?

To say that he was fifty years in advance of his time is also to blink the facts. Reform was in the air; Chatham had touched upon it; so had the Rockinghams; Grenville had actually forced a Bill through Parliament dealing with contested elections. The country as a whole was profoundly stirred and the question cropped up from time to time. Wilkes may have been the most thorough exponent; but if he led the field, at least the field was at his back. He might easily have failed to secure his whole programme, but there was nothing in the age to prevent a beginning.

The suddenness of his failure is the more strange in view of the care and skill with which he had prepared the ground. During the years that Parliament had shut its doors upon him he had perfected his plan. He was proposing to carry on a vigorous campaign throughout the country, using the irresistible weapon of popular demand. It was his merit to realize the possibilities of that popularity on which Pitt had rested. The will of the people—that new middle class created by Walpole and Pitt—was to be organized and controlled; it was to influence, not one man's election, but all; it was to sway the House itself by petitions and addresses. The struggle was likely to be long, but Wilkes had never been dismayed at the mere magnitude of opposing forces, and he knew well enough the tedious process of persuasion. Yet he had no sooner set his foot on the threshold than he tossed aside his own preparations. Why?

The answer is writ large in the events of the time and in Wilkes's own speeches. It was the war with America.

(4)

The American war was England's biggest disaster, and as such has rightly been discussed with heat. There was a time when George III was generally held to be the villain of the piece. Nowadays there is a laudable effort to prove the colonists even more villainous. The one drawback to this otherwise excellent theory is that it lays most of the blame at Pitt's door. The Americans, so the theory runs, full of black ingratitude, were always nursing dreams of independence, but so long as the French were in Canada and showed a disposition to overflow, British aid was necessary. Pitt, in a moment of aberration, drove the French from Canada, with the inevitable result that the Americans were free to demand independence, and seized the first excuse.

Those to whom this theory appeals will no doubt cling to it. Pitt undoubtedly presented England with a magnificent empire, and was intent on doing a further signal disservice by conquering South America. It is equally certain that in his mania for pushing out one colony by collecting another, he had not given much attention to the thousand problems of administration which success brought in its train. Yet it is possible to believe that he was not entirely blind to the task before him, since he set apart the most brilliant of his coming men to tackle the job—Wilkes himself. How Pitt and Wilkes would have fared is now a matter of mournful conjecture. Before they had begun their work, George III had done his! But it is incredible to suppose that Pitt and Wilkes could have produced a sorrier scheme than their successors.

Bute did precisely nothing but conclude an ineffective peace, which created discontent on both sides of the Atlantic. With that to his credit he passed on the torch, and Grenville applied it neatly to the straw. Peace brought the problems to a head— the difficulties of a transitional period, the chaos of finance, demobilization, high prices, and above all the sudden relaxation of overstrung nerves. There was bound to be a period of unrest and it was made no more peaceful by the dismissal of Pitt and the King's policy of parliamentary chaos. There is no need to impute Machiavellian motives to anyone. The trouble sprang naturally out of the feeling of unrest combined with the mediocrity of England's rulers. The best of statesmen might have failed; the nincompoops to whom the task fell could hardly hope to succeed.

The fact is that Grenville, like any Chancellor of the Exchequer in need of money, was looking round for the tax which would cause the least discontent, and the turmoil of the times lent wings to his imagination. He hit upon America, which was a long way off, and easily justified his action on the ground that the colonists should contribute to a war waged largely on their behalf. The argument was not only specious, but just. It was the method that was wrong. Whether he had a case or not, Parliament was only too likely to jump at a plan which reduced their own burdens. There lay the inherent badness of the scheme. America had no voice in the matter, and if once the principle went, the tendency must be for the taxes to grow. Whatever Grenville meant, and whatever Parliament thought—not that it did think; the proposals went through without debate—Grenville's Stamp Act was infallibly the thin end of the wedge, and must have been till all men were altruistic and Utopia had come.

Whether the Americans thought of principles or probabilities hardly matters. It is only human nature to dodge the tax-collector, and any argument would have been stressed to the utmost. After all, they too could make out a good case. Why say that the war was waged for them when it had given England the whole of Canada and most of the islands? Why insist on taxes when England controlled the trade and grew rich on American products? And anyhow it was an axiom of the English Constitution that there should be no taxation without representation. They put their case forward in a long series of petitions, addresses, and remonstrances, until at last, in 1765, Rockingham repealed the obnoxious Act. His action largely

appeased ruffled feelings, and might have soothed them altogether had he not foolishly kept the sore open by a Declaratory
Act affirming Parliament's right over the Colonies. Americans,
as hard-headed men, were not unduly alarmed by a declaration,
provided it was not followed by actions; but the mere fact of
the declaration kept them anxiously on the look-out. Their
anxiety was justified; two years later Charles Townshend, that
unruly meteor rushing in a blaze of promise to an early grave,
revived the scheme of American taxation in a moment of irre-
sponsibility, and the ferment began anew. He died shortly
afterwards, and succeeding Ministers were by no means sure
if they would follow in his steps. Unfortunately the King
held very strong opinions on the subject—the same opinions
that he held about Wilkes. In his eyes the Americans were
insolent, revolutionary, unprincipled, and all that was bad. It
was their duty to obey their King, and until they returned to
their duty and begged their Sovereign's pardon they should be
treated with the utmost severity.

When North became Prime Minister he did his best to
tinge the King's obstinacy with logic. He argued the case of
what he called "common defence". His argument, however,
was not so good as he thought. Common defence implies a
common policy, and America had no voice in government.
Moreover, the threat to give no protection unless America
contributed to the expense came too late. It might have meant
something in 1760, while the war was being waged; in 1770,
when the war was over, it was either mere words or an offer
of independence. His Whig opponents were more logical;
they demanded a policy of conciliation, and when that seemed
impossible declared frankly that they preferred the loss of
America to a military occupation.

But arguments and justifications were quite beside the point.
The King was mainly concerned with his own dignity; he had
no desire to go to war, but he was none the less determined
that the Colonies must submit. His attitude was by no means
unique. Parliament was equally determined to assert its dignity,

and the people as a whole were frankly contemptuous of the colonists and only too anxious to save their own pockets at the expense of others. Government suggested taxes and coercion; Parliament and the people agreed; the King opposed any concession that was worth the name, and when the Americans protested, assumed his haughtiest mood. It was a stupid course; either he should have climbed down as gracefully as he could or he should have acted with all his strength. As it was, he attempted a clumsy compromise which gave neither money to England nor security to America, and while apparently saving his own face landed England in a war.

There is no need to narrate the various details. Suffice it to say that war was hovering on the verge when Wilkes entered Parliament, and the first shot was actually fired at Lexington on the 18th of April, 1775.

Wilkes had early made up his mind. From the beginning he had strongly supported the Americans, denying Parliament's right to tax them. He had friends in America and the West Indies. As early as 1758 he was receiving letters of congratulation from New York and Antigua on his election to Parliament, and when his troubles began they were followed with intense interest across the Atlantic. In 1768 the "Sons of Liberty" in Boston began a correspondence with him. "Illustrious Patriot," they wrote, "the friends of Liberty, Wilkes, Peace, and Good Order to the number of forty-five, assembled at the Whig Tavern, Boston, New England, take this first opportunity to congratulate your country, the British Colonies and yourself, on your happy return to the land alone worthy such an Inhabitant"; they told him of their own plight, and declared that "to vindicate Americans is—not to desert yourself"; and implored him to be steadfast, since "'tis from your endeavours we hope for a Royal '*Pascite, ut ante, boves*'; and from our attachment to 'peace and good order' we wait for a constitutional redress"—a curious confirmation of Wilkes's moderating influence—and they sent him a copy of the *Farmer's Letters*. Other friends in America sent him turtles, and the inhabitants of South Carolina a gift of £1,500.

Wilkes responded gladly, promising that "as a member of the legislature, I shall always give a particular attention to whatever regards the interests of America, which I believe to be immediately connected with, and of essential moment to, our parent country, and the common welfare of this great political system". "I will ever", he added, "avow myself a friend to universal liberty. . . . Liberty I consider as the birthright of every subject of the British Empire, and I hold Magna Charta to be in as full force in America as in Europe. I hope that these truths will become generally known and acknowledged thro' the wide-extended dominions of our Sovereign, and that a real union of the whole will prevail to save the whole, and to guard the public liberty, if invaded by despotic Ministers, in the most remote equally as in the central parts of this vast empire." In a further letter he declared that "if I had been permitted to take my seat in the House of Commons, I should have been eager to move the repeal of the late Act, which lays the new duties on paper, paint, and other articles. I would have done this from the full persuasion not only of its being highly impolitic and inexpedient, but in my idea likewise absolutely unjust and unconstitutional, a direct violation of the great fundamental principles of British liberty."

These letters were written while he was still in the King's Bench. After his release he was mainly wrapped up in City affairs, but he kept the colonists in mind, and induced the City to petition on their behalf. There were many merchants in the City whose interests in America were seriously threatened by the Government's policy, and it was not therefore difficult to obtain remonstrances and petitions. It was, however, an achievement to bring the whole City over to the American side, since in general the country was anti-American, and became more so as the threat of war drew nearer.

On his return to the House Wilkes had a difficult choice to make. He had been elected as the champion of reform. With no friends at Court or among the Whig magnates, with no means of supporting himself, mere prudence made it essential to preserve his popularity. As a demagogue he would have done so. But Wilkes was a man of startling honesty. Boswell had once said he was good without principles. Morally that may have been true, but it was quite false of Wilkes the statesman. Never once did Wilkes betray his principles, though at his lowest ebb he would have been content to retire. So at this turning-point Wilkes had no hesitation about his course.

Popular feeling at the moment was rather divided. On the one hand there was still the old demand for reform; on the other the resistance in America was arousing the Jingo spirit. Wilkes denied the right of England to coerce the Colonies, and he refused to budge from this principle. At the same time he realized that war was only too likely, and that war is not the moment to press reform. Hence he was obliged both to drop his cherished plans and to oppose the rising clamour for an American war. Such a course could only mean a sharp and sudden drop in his popularity just when it was most needed. But Wilkes never hesitated. His brother-in-law, Hayley, was connected with the City merchants trading to America, and through him he promoted two petitions to the House in January 1775. A little later on, as Lord Mayor, he used the City's annual petition to the King to plead for peace. Meanwhile, in Parliament itself, he urged his views on every possible occasion, spending endless time in the preparation of speeches that did not come easily to his tongue.

(5)

Wilkes took his seat on the 2nd of December, 1774. Shortly afterwards the House adjourned for the Christmas holidays. It met again in the middle of January, and a few days later Wilkes broke his first lance in a little gibe at the anniversary of Charles I's death, a day which he protested should be held as a festival rather than a fast. His first serious speech was made on the

WILLIAM PITT, EARL OF CHATHAM

After a painting by R. Brompton in the National Portrait Gallery

3rd of February in support of Sawbridge's annual motion for shorter parliaments. Wilkes could hardly have avoided speaking, but it is significant that even in this short speech he managed to bring in the Americans. As proof that members were only too ready to betray their trust he cited the fate of Hayley's two petitions, and expressed a fear that unless the motion were carried, the Parliament in which he sat would be employed for seven years in destroying the rights of their constituents "and that of our fellow-subjects in America".

Three days later he spoke again, against a motion to proclaim the Colonies in a state of rebellion. It was a great speech, greatly delivered, with force, eloquence, and deep feeling. "The address now reported from the Committee of the whole House appears to me unfounded, rash, and sanguinary. It draws the sword unjustly against America; but before administration are suffered to plunge the nation into the horrors of a civil war, before they are permitted to force Englishmen to sheathe their swords in the bowels of their fellow-subjects, I hope this House will seriously weigh the original ground and cause of this unhappy dispute, and in time reflect whether justice is on our side, and gives a sanction to the intended hostile proceedings." The ground of the quarrel was the assumed right of taxation without the consent of the subject, and as such was unjust and unconstitutional. Were the Americans then to be protected without contributing a penny? "The Americans themselves have given the fullest answer to this objection in a manner not to be controverted, by their conduct through a long series of years, and by the most explicit declarations." He commended Chatham's plan for reconciliation and added details of his own, and then warned the House that they were attempting the impossible. "Is your force adequate to the attempt? I am satisfied it is not." Massachusetts alone could hold out against Britain. "Boston will be like Gibraltar. You will hold in the province of Massachusetts Bay, as you do in Spain, a single town, while the whole country remains in the power and possession of the enemy. . . . In the great scale of empire you will decline, I fear, from the decision of this day, and the Americans will rise to independence, to power, to all the greatness of the most renowned States, for they build on the solid basis of general, public liberty." It was the voice of prophecy crying in the wilderness.

Again and again he returned to the attack, denying both the justice of the war and the possibility of success; and whenever he spoke on the subject it was always in the same tone of earnest argument and deep seriousness.

(6)

With the return of Wilkes there reappeared another great figure on the political stage—the Earl of Chatham. He was an old man now, old and lonely. The Ministers treated him with a touch of contempt, as well they might, seeing that they were to prove themselves as great as he—only in failure instead of success. The Opposition grudged him his fame and distrusted his lofty genius; they eyed him suspiciously from afar, intent only on filching his mantle for themselves. So after the Middlesex campaign the wounded lion lurked for nearly three years in Somerset, racked with disease, buffeted with the gusts of his fiery temper, watching in impotent fury while mischievous pigmies quenched the beacon he had lighted. Diffidence and despair were torturing his once proud soul, and ran like a threnody through all his letters—"farthest from such a scene of things is best for a man who is sure he can do no good"; "*fuit Ilium*, the whole Constitution is a shadow".

Yet the lion had had a disciple; one who had sat in admiration at his feet during those four glorious years; one who alone of all his friends had battled for him when he had fallen; one who had schemed single-handed for his return to power, and had failed only by inches; one whom he had grossly betrayed and deserted. That same disciple had disappeared, ruined and undone, and now by some marvellous chance had accomplished what Chatham had never been able to achieve—he had rehabilitated himself and returned to Parliament more powerful than before, the chief magistrate of England's capital, the representative of England's premier county, the avowed champion of the common people. Perhaps—perhaps—Something stirred in the sick lion's heart, some feeble flutter of hope. Whatever else Wilkes might be, he was a patriot. Chatham knew it—Chatham, who had denied friendship with him; and Chatham knew also that he bore little rancour. They might toil again for England's greatness—the lion and the jackal, so strangely assorted, so nebulously yoked, ignoring one another openly and yet so closely connected underneath.

It was no mere coincidence that Chatham, who had written but a few months earlier: "I have too long seen my no-weight to dream any longer on that subject; nor have I the least ambition left to be talked of any more, in a world I am unable to be of service to", should have dragged himself up in May 1774 from Somerset to Hayes; it was no mere coincidence that he treated Rockingham coolly and refused to see Camden, while he granted an interview to the Sheriffs of London— Wilkes's creatures, as Walpole called them. Twice after that interview Chatham had appeared in the House of Lords, in May and June of 1774, to speak on American subjects. But the time was not ripe; Wilkes was still struggling in the City, and Chatham retired to watch and wait. Sooner or later Wilkes would triumph, and then this couple whose lives had been interwoven in so curious a manner would strike one more blow for the country of their pride. They were to fail—Chatham most gloriously, breaking his heart in one last summons to the high spirit he had raised in years gone by; Wilkes in his more humdrum fashion, letting drop a seed which sprouted and grew, till it spread over the whole country and Wilkes was forgotten in the shade of his own tree. They were to strike one more blow and to fail. But better that than the bitter record of bungling and defeat, in devious ways and by crooked paths, that was to be the epitaph of their opponents.

In January 1775 the hour struck. Wilkes had returned to

hold aloft the banner in the House of Commons, and Chatham would sound the trumpet in the House of Lords. Seemingly distinct, seemingly divided, they found their own lines of communication. Chatham awoke suddenly. For some reason a wave of hope, almost of optimism, swept over the desert places of dismay. "I trust", he wrote on the 24th of December, 1774, "that the minds of men are more than beginning to change on this great subject, so little understood; and that it will be found impossible for freemen in England to wish to see three millions of Englishmen slaves in America." What was that change in men's minds but the excitement of the recent election, the main feature of which was the return of Wilkes and his "Twelve Apostles"? And how was it that, when the one point of interest seemed to be the question of reform, Chatham saw a change in the attitude towards America—a change more strikingly reflected in Wilkes than in anyone else?

Chatham's wave of optimism swept upward. On the 18th of January, "being deep in work for the State", he could find time for "a word only" to his wife, but it was a word of tremendous and triumphant sound: "Be of good cheer, noble love—'Yes, I am proud—I must be proud—to see Men not afraid of God, afraid of me.'" Two days later he made a great speech, and the next day wrote urgently to Shelburne, "I hope to be in condition to attend the House on Monday, if the Merchants' petition is certainly to come to us on that day." If it were not to come on Monday, Chatham entreated to be told the exact date, "to which I would on no account be wanting, by failing in personal appearance". The merchants' petition loomed large in his thoughts. "I do not wonder", wrote Chatham four days later, "that the merchants are grown *in earnest*." How could he, when the merchants were being stirred up by Hayley, Wilkes's brother-in-law, at the express wish of Wilkes himself? Chatham was driven on by the goad of a divine impatience, which swept aside the sad reluctance, the old hesitations. "Not a moment can be lost", he told Shelburne on the 31st of

January, "for whoever has anything to offer to the public, for preventing a civil war, before it is inevitably fixed."

On the 1st of February, 1775, Chatham presented his Bill for settling the troubles in America. It was rejected, but on the 6th Wilkes supported and embellished it in the House of Commons, and on the 10th the City of London, with Wilkes as Lord Mayor, passed a vote of thanks "to the Right Hon. the Earl of Chatham, for having offered to the House of Lords a plan for conciliating the differences which unfortunately subsist between the Administration in this country and its American Colonies; and to all those who supported that noble Lord in so humane a measure".

It seemed for one moment as though Chatham and Wilkes had succeeded. Government entered into negotiations with Benjamin Franklin, who was in England to plead America's cause, and on the 20th of February Lord North laid before the Commons a scheme of conciliation. Unfortunately he coupled it with coercive Bills, and the effort led to nothing. Meanwhile the physical strain had been too great for Chatham, who retired for the time being; but the strenuous will remained, and in July 1776 he adjured Dr. Addington to bear testimony to his views and gave him a declaration of his *"unshaken"* opinion.

Perforce he left Wilkes to bear the burden, with such help as he could get from a hesitating Opposition and Charles James Fox, who chose this point to interlard a period of repentance between a misspent youth and an act of gross betrayal. But Wilkes was as unshaken as Chatham. The Americans recognized his efforts, and in June sent him an address. Meanwhile he spoke from his heart in the House and stirred up the City to petitions, and when in August the King issued a proclamation declaring the Americans rebels, Wilkes allowed no official but the common crier to attend the reading of the proclamation.

CHAPTER XXIV

THE DARKEST HOUR

(1)

So Wilkes made his choice of set purpose, though it led him into paths that were far from popular, and pushed into the background his cherished plan of reform. Not that he let it go without a pang or without an effort. When he first entered the House, war was not inevitable, and even if it came would not last for ever. He could therefore legitimately prepare the ground, so that with the occasion the plan might be resumed. His methods lacked nothing of the old masterly touch.

America came first, but when North had introduced his scheme of conciliation, Wilkes was free to turn elsewhere. He turned automatically to reform, and on the 22nd of February—two days after North's speech—moved to expunge the resolutions of 1769 dealing with the Middlesex election. His choice is illuminating. For all practical purposes the Middlesex election was dead. To expunge the resolutions would do no good except as confirming the principle of representation in which Wilkes believed. From that point of view it was a proper jumping-off ground for future reform. From another point of view it was peculiarly appropriate to the times. In itself it was a condemnation of past sins rather than the preaching of a new way of life. Even in the midst of war sins may be condemned; even when a forward movement is out of place it is legitimate to protest against retrogression.

His speech was temperate, but convincing; he dealt faithfully with all the arguments of the Court party, and dealt with them in the curiously impersonal way peculiar to himself. Wilkes, for all his exuberant wit and light-hearted badinage, perhaps because of it, was full of a decent reticence. He never carried his heart on his sleeve, and disdained to clear himself of false charges. When he discussed his own case he was in the habit of referring to "Mr. Wilkes" in a detached way that almost wore an air of indifference. Perhaps it was a pity, since it laid him open to a charge of insincerity. But it was all of a piece with his habit of depreciating himself, and was, in fact, a form of shyness which often goes with a puckish humour.

Needless to say, Wilkes's motion was lost. Walpole tells a story of the debate which has often been repeated. "Wilkes", says Walpole, "opened the question with temper, and adhered to it. In truth he was sick of his part; and though he called the resolutions of the last Parliament a violation of Magna Charta, he said, in a whisper to Lord North, he was forced to say so to please the fellows who followed him." The story as told by Walpole is quite incredible. If Wilkes was fond of shocking people, he was not a born fool. But without calling his prudence in question, it is in the highest degree unlikely that Wilkes, a member of the Opposition and an independent member at that, would have been sitting near enough to the Prime Minister for whispered asides. The story, in short, falls into the same category as that even more familiar story of Wilkes and Luttrell at the Brentford election. Wilkes, so Lord Brougham relates, asked Luttrell whether he thought there were more fools or rogues among the electors. Luttrell threatened to repeat his words to the crowd, upon which Wilkes replied with a shrug, "I should merely say it was a fabrication, and they would destroy you in the twinkling of an eye." The yarn is amusing, but its veracity is somewhat impugned by the fact that Wilkes was at the time safely shut up in prison, and the two must have shouted their remarks over a distance of some miles.

Walpole continues: "This was his constant style; and though certainly conveyed to the mob, they still followed him—probably because they saw no man of whom they had a better opinion." It is just possible that the real explanation was a lesser degree of gullibility in the mob than in Horace Walpole. Wilkes was not "sick of his part", as the future was to show;

he was sick of a much more serious complaint—the unending folly of the King and his Ministers, which was breaking out as a terrible eruption in America.

(2)

Yet in March 1776, fifteen months or more after he had taken his seat, he suddenly moved to bring in a Bill "for a just and equal representation of the people of England in Parliament"— his whole scheme of reform. At first sight it seems as though he had thrown aside his scruples and after all was quite prepared to embarrass Government, now much more deeply entangled in the war. But incidents cannot be judged in isolation. The reason for this step, inexplicable in itself, becomes clear in the light of surrounding events.

Four months earlier Wilkes's term of office as Lord Mayor came to an end. Ever since his return to England he had proposed first to serve the various offices of the City, and then to secure one of the rich posts in the gift of the Corporation— there to live out his days. No very high ambition, perhaps. But he was in his forty-ninth year, and his life had been full of vicissitudes; parliamentary advancement he could not hope for; there were no further civic honours to gain—and he was still living on charity.

The particular post on which he had set his heart, both for its prestige and for its salary, was the Chamberlainship. It was now held by a friend, Sir Stephen Theodore Janssen, an aged baronet in poor health. During his mayoralty Wilkes had hinted that Janssen should retire at an appropriate moment, thus paving the way for Wilkes himself. On the 18th of November Wilkes jogged his memory, pointing out that no moment could be more favourable than the present, when "the City are almost unanimous in their approbation of the late Mayor". With his usual, wholly disarming frankness he gave his reasons. "In this favourable and full flow everything might be prosperous, but the ebb in the tide of the affairs of men is to be apprehended from the experience of all past times. . . . After being harassed for so many years, I cannot but earnestly desire to arrive in a safe port, and acquire an honourable independence by a continuance of services in the best way I am able."

Janssen turned the matter over, and resigned on the 6th of February, 1776. Unfortunately he could not nominate his successor, and two other candidates were forthcoming—Hopkins and Patterson, the latter, however, soon withdrawing. Hopkins had become an alderman two years before and was mainly remarkable for usury. He had never served as Sheriff or Lord Mayor, and though he had once represented the City in Parliament had refused to stand a second time. At first sight this was not a peculiarly striking record, but Hopkins, who was blessed either with an exceptionally keen sense of humour or a prodigious lack of it, managed to make it look well. "My endeavours", he declared in his manifesto, "have ever been exerted to promote, as much as in my power, the peace, harmony, and tranquillity of my fellow-citizens; with that in view I early declined giving the Livery of London any trouble on my account at the last General Election." For the rest he depended mainly on his money, on emphasizing Wilkes's poverty, and, of course, on all the influence which the Court could give. Both sides strained every nerve, and the poll was exceptionally large, the numbers being Hopkins 2,887, Wilkes 2,710. Wilkes had failed by 177 votes.

There is no doubt that this was one of the most serious blows that Wilkes ever received. It hurt him in pride, pocket, and prospects, and galled him with the thought that Hopkins had profited by a vacancy for which Wilkes had angled. Wilkes was a man who never admitted defeat, and his need and obstinacy now drove him into actions that were both peevish and silly. The Chamberlain was nominally elected for the year; but by an unwritten law he always retained office for life. Regardless of this fact, Wilkes declared his intention of standing again at the midsummer election.

Meanwhile it was his wretched lot to discover why on this

of all occasions he should have failed. It is possible that some
votes had been lost by the scandal of Mrs. Barnard, not yet
four months old—perhaps sufficient to turn the scale, a thought
more pleasing to moralists than accordant with the manners of
the age. A more likely cause was dissatisfaction with Wilkes's
parliamentary career. He had failed to satisfy those who
hankered after reform; he had definitely antagonized the rising
number of those who supported the American war. The latter
he must continue to offend, but what was there to prevent a
reforming motion, not intended seriously at the moment, but
at least giving proof of future *bona fides*?

There was nothing, and on the 21st of March Wilkes introduced his Bill. It was almost too easy to prove the need of
reform; elections were a drunken orgy and politics hopelessly
corrupt. A lesser man than Wilkes could have done all that
was necessary. Far more noticeable is the tone of his speech.
It was logical; it was unanswerable; but it wholly lacked the
fine seriousness of his American speeches. Instead, it was
pointed with wit. He chaffed the Scotch; he twitted the
Ministers: "The little town of Banbury," he remarked, looking
at North, "*petite ville, grand renom*, as Rabelais says of Chinon,
has, I believe, only seventeen electors, yet gives us here, a First
Lord of the Treasury and a Chancellor of the Exchequer. Its
influence and weight on a division, I have often seen overpower
the united force of the members for London, Bristol, and
several of the most populous counties." Then he turned to
Lord George Germaine, the Colonial Secretary, who, as Lord
George Sackville, had disgraced himself at the battle of Minden.
"East Grinstead too, I think has only about thirty electors,
yet gives a seat among us to that brave, heroic lord at the head
of a great civil department now very military, who has fully
determined to conquer America—but not in Germany"—
a palpable hit that was repeated with delight in every club.

The whole speech was full of banter. Only once did he
become serious, and that in an oblique manner: "It will be
objected, I foresee, that a time of perfect calm and peace

throughout this vast empire is the most proper to propose internal regulations of this importance; and that while intestine discord rages in the whole northern continent of America our attention ought to be fixed upon that most alarming object, and all our efforts employed to extinguish the devouring flame of a civil war." Thus he summed up his own deep convictions, and indirectly explained his previous silence. That he was not acting now of his own free accord becomes clear from his weak handling of the objection: "In my opinion, Sir, the American war is in this truly critical era one of the strongest arguments for the regulation of our representation, which I now submit to the House. . . . In our late disputes with the Americans, we have always taken it for granted that the people of England justified all the iniquitous, cruel, arbitrary, and mad proceedings of administration, because they had the approbation of the majority of this House." An argument of this type, as Wilkes very well knew, might justify a change of Ministry or a general election, but was no answer to the original objection.

Knowing that he had no intention of pressing his Bill, he contented himself with a brief sketch of his proposals. "I do not mean, Sir, at this time to go into a tedious detail of the various proposals. . . . I will at this time, Sir, only throw out general ideas; that every free agent in this kingdom should, in my wish, be represented in Parliament; that the Metropolis, which contains in itself a ninth part of the people, and the counties of Middlesex, York, and others, which so greatly abound with inhabitants, should receive an increase in their representation; that the mean and insignificant boroughs, so emphatically styled the rotten part of our Constitution, should be lopped off, and the electors in them thrown into the counties; and the rich, populous trading towns, Birmingham, Manchester, Sheffield, Leeds, and others, be permitted to send deputies to the great council of the nation."

North's reply was equally off-hand, and the matter dropped, not to be raised again.

It is, of course, conjecture to suppose that this speech was

merely a device in an electioneering campaign for the post of
Chamberlain. But it accounts for several puzzling points—
his long silence, the particular moment chosen, the changed
tone in his speech, and his subsequent neglect of the subject.
As though to emphasize the contrast, about a month later
Wilkes renewed his old attack on the Middlesex election, and
declared that "while I have a seat in this House, I pledge
myself to my country, that I will be firm and unwearied in my
endeavours, till every syllable on our Journals, which marks
the injustice done to the freeholders of Middlesex, and to
every elector in the island, be fully erased or obliterated"—
a vastly different attitude.

For all his efforts, perhaps because they were so half-hearted,
Wilkes was even less successful at the midsummer elections,
when the majority for Hopkins rose to over a thousand. Wilkes
was now fighting for his life, and having been beaten fairly
and squarely at the poll, attempted to unseat Hopkins on a
technical point. He entered a protest on the ground that by
an ancient Act of the Common Council no one could be
Chamberlain who had not served an apprenticeship of seven
years or obtained his freedom by patrimony—neither of which
conditions had been fulfilled in Hopkins's case. The Sheriffs
met this paltry quibble in a manner at once dignified and skilful,
They swore Hopkins in with the proviso that he should act
officially only "till a legal determination be had in a court of
law". Either Wilkes recognized the meanness of his protest
or the Sheriffs managed to put off the case; at all events it
never went to the courts. But Wilkes stood as candidate in the
normal course both in 1777 and 1778, on each occasion failing by
nearly a thousand votes.

(3)

His failure to obtain the post of Chamberlain left Wilkes in a
most precarious position. Nominally he had an income of £700
a year, but out of that, £200 went to his wife and £150 in an
annuity to creditors. He was left with £350 a year to support

himself and his daughter, and pay for his latest mistress, a sum that fell far short of his needs. Not that it would have helped him much to live within his income. As Lord Mayor, with his genius for entertaining and his determination to do things well, he had spent exactly £3,337 12s. 5½d. more than his salary, augmented as it was by various perquisites. He had hardly laid down office before his creditors began pressing for payment. While the prospects of the chamberlainship were still before him, Wilkes met the situation with a light heart, and, indeed, he relied as one of the main inducements for his election as Chamberlain on a promise to set aside a regular portion of his salary for paying his debts. When he failed, the position seemed desperate, and almost excuses his determination to break through precedent and fight Hopkins on every possible occasion. His second failure made matters still more desperate. After this he was definitely living on charity without the least idea how he could ever win through to independence. The position was not only galling—Wilkes must long since have learnt to pocket his pride—but extremely uncomfortable. His income was as variable as the weather. Sometimes, as Almon records, he was "distressed for a guinea". At others friends would send or lend him large sums. Cash still came dribbling in at intervals from the old Rockingham Ministers, and well-wishers dropped money upon him anonymously or otherwise. The friendship which he was able to excite is well displayed in a mysterious note which he received about this time from a certain Sam Petrie: "What is, and whatever was, between you and me, does now and always did, lay in my mind, as a gift, not a loan. Of course never in the light of a debt. This remark will need no explanation." That same evening Wilkes read in the *Gazette* that Petrie had been declared bankrupt. It is pleasant to record that later on Wilkes helped to support his old friend and benefactor.

In spite of his troubles Wilkes kept a brave face to the world, and retracted not one of his principles or promises. He maintained the same line in the House of Commons, and still

proved a cheerful companion in private life. It was in this year
—15th May, 1776—that the famous meeting took place between
Wilkes and Dr. Johnson at Mr. Dilly's in Poultry—a meeting
that Boswell has described once for all. The crusty old doctor
was won over. In 1763 he had told Boswell that Wilkes "is an
abusive scoundrel; and instead of applying to my Lord Chief
Justice to punish him, I would send half a dozen footmen and
have him well ducked", but some eighteen months after this
meeting he had revised his opinion. "Did we not hear so much
said of Jack Wilkes, we should think more highly of his conversation. Jack has a great variety of talk, Jack is a scholar, and
Jack has the manners of a gentleman. But after hearing his
name sounded from pole to pole, as the phœnix of convivial
felicity, we are disappointed in his company. He has always
been at *me*; but I would do Jack a kindness, rather than not.
The contest is over now." Before the contest began Jack had
done Johnson a kindness. In 1759 Johnson's black servant
was seized by the press-gang, and Smollett wrote to Wilkes
for his aid. Wilkes, who at that time had considerable influence,
secured the man's release.

There were other friends that Wilkes was making—friends
he might be proud to know. Most notable was the eccentric
Lord Effingham, who resigned from the Army at the outbreak
of the American war rather than fight his fellow-countrymen.
It was said of him that he was "the best of husbands, of fathers,
of masters, of friends". It is strange that the "libertine" Wilkes
should have gradually become intimate with the finest characters
of the age.

So 1776 dragged on with little comfort to Wilkes and less to
England. On the 4th of July the Colonies made their Declaration
of Independence, and when Parliament met in October Wilkes
told the Ministers that though they had prophesied this move,
they had no more reason to plume themselves on their fore-
sight than the Jesuits who had prophesied that Henri IV would
die within the year and then hired Ravaillac to murder him.
Government was to blame, and if they pursued their course

France and Spain would join the number of our enemies. "If we expect to save the Empire, to preserve even for a short period Canada or the West Indian Islands, or to recover any part of the immense territories we have lately lost, we must recall our fleets and armies, immediately repeal all the Acts injurious to the Americans passed since 1763, and restore their charters." Again his warnings fell on deaf ears.

(4)

The next year—1777—Wilkes's position was no better, but nothing daunted he began a new campaign, which was to have surprising results. In April Government were compelled to admit a deficit of £600,000 in the Civil List, and ask Parliament to pay the King's debts and increase his income. These debts were certainly not due to any extravagance in the King's private life—he lived in the utmost simplicity. How the money went can best be seen in a letter which the King wrote to North in 1774. It was the period of the General Election which returned Wilkes and his Twelve Apostles to Parliament. There seemed to be a danger that Wilkes would sweep the country— a disaster that justified any step. "Lord Falmouth", the King wrote, "must be told in as polite terms as possible that I hope he will permit me to recommend to three of his six seats in Cornwall. The terms he expects are two thousand five hundred pounds a seat, to which I readily agree." As a matter of fact Lord Falmouth held out for guineas, which the King, with a proper regard for public money, thought uncommonly shabby, but ultimately agreed to pay.

Wilkes knew all about debt. He examined the accounts with a practised eye, and readily picked out the makeshifts and evasions. Speaking from deep knowledge of all the tricks of the trade, he informed the House that "more loose, unsatisfactory, perplexed, and unintelligible no accounts can be. Their defectiveness and fallacy is highly culpable." No one knew how these debts had been contracted; there were no signs of luxury or profusion. "The nation, Sir, suspects that the regular Ministerial majorities in Parliament are bought by these very grants." In Wilkes's eyes nothing could be more despicable. Had the King lived in luxury, Wilkes might have felt some sympathy with a fellow-sinner; but to misuse public money went very much against the grain, especially at such a time. "There is, at present, Sir, a peculiar cruelty in thus endeavouring to fleece the people when we are involved in a most expensive as well as unnatural and ruinous civil war." He demanded an inquiry, which he did not get; but he had effectually raised the cry for economy, which the nation pondered for two years and then endorsed—emphatically.

Meanwhile, a fortnight later, prolific of new ideas as ever, he turned his attention to the British Museum, pleading that money should be granted for forming a library, that publishers should be required to send a bound copy of every book they produced, and that a picture-gallery should be built to house the nation's pictures. Publishers may perhaps be pardoned for agreeing that Wilkes is a worthless fellow, but it is not quite so clear why neither the British Museum nor the National Gallery has a modest inscription to his memory.

The next day, to show that he was persevering as well as prolific, he returned to the Middlesex election. His speech was short, but it contained one maxim that is not always popular: "The first great object is truth, and we ought to follow where it leads".

In May Chatham once more reappeared, once more unavailingly lifted up his voice, in thrilling accents and trembling eagerness. Peace with America, peace urgently and at once; peace from this mad war by which England was giving America to France "at the expense of twelve millions a year". And the method? In almost the words of Wilkes, Chatham explained his plan: "I wish for a repeal of every oppressive Act which your Lordships have passed since 1763."

In November Parliament met again, and again the two strangely assorted allies urged their proposals of peace—

Chatham pleading majestically in the Lords and Wilkes re-echo-ing his words and sentiments in the Commons. Both alike spoke in terms of pressing anxiety, as though by some mysterious means they sensed the overwhelming news even now upon the way, as though the shame of the future hung over their hearts and they felt its cold shadow. Vainly they poured out their argu-ments and entreaties. A cool and indifferent House ignored Chatham's solemn periods; a corrupt and mocking House laughed at Wilkes's urgent warnings. Less than a fortnight later a terrible rumour ran through England like a shudder— Burgoyne and his army had surrendered at Saratoga.

On December 5th Chatham urged the instant recall of our armies from America as the first step towards reconciliation. On the 10th Wilkes moved the repeal of the Declaratory Act as "the preliminary to peace" and declared that he meant after-wards to submit another motion "for the repeal of the whole system of new statutes and regulations since the year 1763".

North met the appeal of the one and the proposition of the other, backed as they were by confirmation of the ugly rumour, with a grudging promise. Parliament was to be adjourned for six weeks; after the holidays he would lay before the House a plan for treating with the Colonies. Wilkes, accustomed to delays, accepted the stingy sop; Chatham, with a sad presenti-ment, begged the Lords to remain in session, ending a noble speech with the words: "I am strongly inclined to believe that before the day to which the proposed adjournment shall arrive, the noble Earl who moved it will have just cause to repent of his motion." They were as nearly prophetic as words are likely to be. Parliament reassembled on the 20th of January, 1778. Seventeen days later a treaty of alliance between France and America was signed, and the chance of reconciliation had gone.

(5)

At this crisis of affairs the various factions in the Opposition began to draw together. But as the year drew to an end, fresh lines of cleavage appeared. Rockingham became suddenly convinced that the only course was to grant America independence. Chatham would have none of it. So at the most critical point the Opposition fell to pieces.

Parliament met; the Franco-American Alliance was signed, and eleven days later North redeemed his promise—too late. Briefly he proposed to renounce the alleged right to tax America, and to appoint five Commissioners with powers to suspend any or all of the Acts passed since 1763, and accept any terms of reconciliation short of independence.

The Ministerial party acquiesced in sullen silence; the Opposition flavoured their support with taunts. It was left to Wilkes to be constructive. He made his speech on March 2nd, and perhaps legitimately prefaced his proposals by pointing out that "it is not three months since I had the honour of submitting to the House a motion for the *repeal* of those very Acts which, in a less constitutional mode, Commissioners are now authorized to *suspend*. I made that motion, Sir, while America was still free to negotiate, still free from all foreign treaties, or solemn engagements as independent States, with any of the Great Powers of Europe." But facts had to be recognized; he did not believe the Government's Bills held out any real hope; he was not sure if they were intended to do more than shield the Ministers. But he was quite clear what was the proper course: "We ought to enter into a federal union with them, and endeavour to secure the advantages of the most important trade with America by a commercial treaty". In the meantime there should be an immediate cessation of arms, and the troops should be recalled: "It will do more than all your Commissioners can do without it. . . . It will give time for cooling on both sides. . . . It may save the fragments of this dismembered empire." The suggestion offered a half-way house where both sides of the Opposition, where the Government and America could all meet, and it faced the facts. Wilkes was always a realist, and always fertile in ideas. Unfortunately the others were not.

So one more opportunity, slender though it was, passed away, and by the middle of March England had broken with France, though war had not been definitely declared. Wilkes stepped forward again on the 2nd of April with proposals which, like the Sybilline books, the folly of others was steadily curtailing. "Since the affair of General Burgoyne, and the French acknowledgment of their independence, it cannot be supposed that the Americans will ever think of returning to a dependence on this country. The experiment, however, Sir, might be made, of endeavouring to detach the United States from France, by an acknowledgment of their independence and a league of more than amity and commerce, a treaty offensive and defensive with the Mother Country."

Here, at long last, Wilkes had gone farther than Chatham would allow. On the 7th of April the Duke of Richmond moved an address on the lines of Wilkes's proposal. Chatham, for whom the country was calling in this dark hour and for whom the King felt nothing but loathing—Chatham struggled to the House of Lords, and broke his heart protesting "against the dismemberment of this ancient and most noble monarchy".

CHAPTER XXV

THE PEACEFUL HAVEN

(1)

THIS crisis in the war coincided with a strange experience in Wilkes's own life. The adjournment over Christmas at which Chatham had protested, Wilkes spent at Bath. Penniless as he was, he was always welcome for his wit, and moved there in the best circles. On the 10th of January, 1778, he was introduced at a dinner-party to a certain Mrs. Stafford. The lady was passing through a troubled period; her husband had proved faithless, and not long before they had agreed to separate.

This Mrs. Stafford attracted Wilkes at first sight. But she seems to have done something more; she seems to have roused in him for the first and only time a genuine feeling of love. There can be no definite proof, and no one can be blamed for thinking it incredible that an experienced man of the world should have been fired with a deep emotion at the age of fifty-one. The fact that Wilkes called her "the most faultless woman in face, in form, in soul", means very little; the fact that he swore "you are the only person of your sex, either at home or abroad, who has inspired me with the wish even of an honourable and indissoluble union for life", may have been mere humbug; but it is an undeniable fact that Wilkes remained deeply attached to the lady for at least six years, and possibly for life, without obtaining any return and without any hope of it.

A long correspondence took place between them. It requires a strong flight of imagination to picture the type of letter which an elderly man, falling genuinely in love for the first time, and with a lady of gentle birth, might be expected to write. These letters are unlike any others from Wilkes's pen; they are frankly dull and anxious, with streaks of almost youthful extravagance and passages of great candour. They seem to reflect the turmoil of his mind, labouring under a new experience, and trying to walk in unaccustomed paths. Their curious tone, with the steadiness of his feelings, are the best and only proof that can be offered.

According to his own letters his views were entirely honourable, and he was pondering the best means of overcoming the obvious difficulties—his wife and her husband. Meanwhile he loaded her with gifts and deplorable verses. He also gave her very frankly, and with some dignity, the details of his past life—a record that is interesting as the only attempt he ever made to justify himself. "In my nonage, to please an indulgent father, I married a woman half as old again as myself, of a very large fortune; my own that of a gentleman. It was a sacrifice to Plutus, not to Venus. I never lived with her in the strict sense of the word, nor have I seen her near twenty years. I stumbled at the very threshold of the temple of Hymen.

> The god of love was not a bidden guest
> Nor present at his own mysterious feast.

Are such ties at such a time of life binding, and are schoolboys to be dragged to the altar? I have since often sacrificed to beauty, but I never gave my heart except to you, nor were any other impressions more lasting that the sight of the object."

When he first met her Wilkes had little time to spare, being due in London for the meeting of Parliament on the 20th. But he made the most of his opportunities, and immediately on his return home began to correspond. Mrs. Stafford was also attracted, or perhaps merely flattered; but her position was delicate, and therefore in a half-timid, half-reluctant fashion she begged him not to write, doubtful whether to accept his gifts, whether to answer, what to do. In fact, she drifted.

As soon as the House rose in April, Wilkes hurried to Bath to spend a happy week visiting his lady. Then his dreams were rudely shattered. On Saturday, April 18th, Wilkes called at her house to leave a concert ticket and some flowers. Mrs. Stafford was out, and before she returned an old friend arrived and saw the flowers on the hall table. This friend demanded a full account, which Mrs. Stafford gave reluctantly. Good advice followed in no measured terms. "I will own to you", Mrs. Stafford admitted to Wilkes, "that she has made me see it in a very different light from what I have hitherto viewed it, and I now wonder at my own want of discretion." She entreated him to shake off "this idle fancy", returned his ticket, and refused to see him alone. None the less, the correspondence continued, and so did the friendship. It did not even end when some eighteen months later the lady was reconciled to her husband and returned to live with him. Wilkes visited the couple on more than one occasion, and, as he told Polly, found the husband, not unnaturally, a "puppy", and more surprisingly, a "Wilkite". Little gifts passed between the two, Wilkes sending books, franked envelopes, and venison, the lady purses knitted with her own hands.

Maybe there was little in it; but when Wilkes told her that "I never gave my heart except to you", the first half was certainly true, and rather sad. If the last half was true, perhaps it was sadder. As Boswell once wrote to Wilkes, "Marriage is an excellent fruit when ripe. You have been unlucky enough to eat it green." It was some merit, though poor consolation, that he never allowed his teeth to be set on edge.

(2)

So with his love-story ended, his debts greater, and England no nearer peace, Wilkes reached the despondent close of 1778. For all his own troubles, he remained true to his task in Parliament. In the winter session he renewed his plea for peace, not only for the obvious reasons, but also to prevent "a future Spanish war"—a war that duly came some seven months later.

In the opening session of 1779, as though wearied of assailing deaf ears, he turned to a new subject—religious liberty—supporting a Bill to relieve dissenters. Wilkes's reputation as an atheist rests mainly on Chatham's sounding phrase. It was

merited only to the extent that Wilkes thought deeply about
tenets which most of his contemporaries accepted without
heed, without conviction, and certainly without applying them
to their everyday conduct, and because of his examination
rejected some of the orthodox views. Such a man was more
likely to understand the venom of religious persecution. So it
proved; and so it was that Wilkes was always at his best on
the point of religious liberty. "It is impossible, Sir," he cried,
"that toleration can create tumults and religious wars . . .
the spirit of toleration is conciliating, heals divisions, and
teaches men mutual forbearance, meekness, gentleness, and
universal benevolence." Because he believed this with his whole
soul, he would extend toleration to every form and shadow of
belief or disbelief. "I would not, Sir, persecute even the
atheist." To persecute was no part of pure religion and un-
defiled: "Religion should teach us the most refined humanity,
and all her ways should be peace". So, with a retort on his own
critics, as effective as it was mild, he exclaimed, "Upon my
word, Sir, the doctrine of some, who call themselves orthodox,
and deal out damnation so liberally, makes a humane man
tremble". His efforts, masterly and vigorous, earned him the
grateful thanks of the dissenters.

It was hardly surprising that Wilkes should have been
equally the champion of toleration for Roman Catholics. More
interesting, in the light of future events, was his angry scorn
at the pusillanimity of Government in bending to the Edin-
burgh mob and consequently refusing to Roman Catholics in
Scotland the relief which had been granted to their English
brethren.

If Wilkes for the moment despaired of peace with America
through his parliamentary efforts, he did not neglect the
matter altogether. While he was pleading for religious liberty
in the House, he was active for peace in the City. In March he
was engaged in drawing up a strong petition, which set out
the facts in a clear, forceful style, and besought the King to
take "such measures as may restore internal peace, and (as far

as the miserable circumstances into which the late destructive courses have brought us will permit) reunite the British nation in some happy, honourable, and permanent connection."

(3)

By this time Wilkes had reached the lowest limit of his misfortunes, and the tide was about to turn. He had flouted popular opinion, and the people in their anger had kept him depressed and in poverty. With their aid lacking, no one was likely to help him, and it must always remain a mystery how he managed to live, still more to preserve a cheerful countenance and a bold front. But time had proved Wilkes right and the people wrong; and now fate was to give the people a fleeting chance of showing their repentance—fleeting indeed, for while it was long enough to repair Wilkes's fortunes, it was not long enough to save England the depths of humiliation and a protracted parliamentary struggle.

At midsummer Wilkes did not stand for the post of Chamberlain because Hopkins was dangerously ill. He died towards the end of the year, and on the 22nd of November, 1779, at long last Wilkes was elected. The revulsion of feeling in his favour was reflected in the figures, Wilkes obtaining 2,343 votes and his opponent, William James, 371. At the moment of success Wilkes behaved with exemplary moderation. "I will have no enemies, gentlemen, but those of my country, of your rights and privileges. I wish to see all the members of this respectable corporation, all the natives of this free nation, united against our ancient, inveterate, insolent foes of France and Spain, in defence of our excellent Constitution, and in support of the rights and privileges of this great metropolis."

(4)

So much for Wilkes himself. Meanwhile the seed which he had sown in April 1777 had blossomed in the soil of continual disaster. Economy was the crying need when England stood alone against practically the whole world. At the end of 1779 there was a rising demand that the waste of corruption should be checked, the abuse of sinecures remedied. In December two motions for reform were brought before the House of Lords, one by Richmond and the other by Shelburne. At the same moment Burke gave notice in the Commons that he would introduce a Bill after the Christmas holidays. The efforts of the Opposition might well have failed, but that they called to mind the methods of Wilkes. The demand in Parliament would be reinforced a thousandfold, if it could be backed by petitions from the country. So a campaign was started, and the machinery once employed to thunder against Luttrell's election was now used to demand a measure of economic reform. The results were amazing. Associations and committees were set up throughout the length and breadth of England, and petitions, addresses, and remonstrances flowed in as though by magic.

Wilkes, the Chamberlain, was as ready to respond as Wilkes the outcast. It made no difference to him that now he was not the central figure, that now he was fighting as a soldier in the ranks rather than as a general. All his knowledge of popular feeling, all his skill in organization, were thrown into the scale, and gratefully accepted by those magnates who had been too righteous to consort with him before. Well might Walpole sneer: "It was curious to see Charles Fox, lately so unpopular a character, become the idol of the people. . . . It was no less curious to see Lord Cavendish acting so cordially with Wilkes, whom formerly he had been too nice to support."

The tide swept on with irresistible strength. Burke introduced his Bills in February 1780, but hardly had he done so before the associations and committees bethought themselves of their old champion and his wider plans of reform. Why be content merely with scotching corruption? Why not demand the full rights of representation? So in March they were adding to their petitions two further resolutions—one demanding

shorter parliaments and the other a system of equal representation. Borne along by this huge tide of popular feeling,
Dunning, one of Wilkes's old friends, moved a startling resolution in the House of Commons, and by a majority of eighteen
maintained that "the influence of the Crown has increased, is
increasing, and ought to be diminished". Everything seemed
set fair for the full realization of all Wilkes's plans, when in a
moment everything was overthrown.

In the past two years of cloud the people who had neglected
Wilkes had gone after strange gods. One, Lord George Gordon,
had taken upon himself to handle Jove's thunder, but without
Jove's skill. At this precise moment he led the mob on London,
and the mob, heated with his cry of "No popery", got out of
hand. For the first week of June London lay at the mercy of
the rioters, and was saved only by the exertions of two men—
George III and John Wilkes—so ironically does Fate work
out her masterpieces.

The Gordon Riots have a twofold interest in the story of
Wilkes's life—the interest of the actual part he played, and
the interest of the light they shed on his character. There are
some who half scornfully exclaim that Wilkes might have
headed a revolution in 1769, but for some inscrutable reason
lost his opportunity—an ineffective, half-hearted man. They
misunderstand him. Wilkes could never have led a revolution.
He had been brought up to believe in the English Constitution;
it never entered his head to resort to violence; he would have
been the first to bewail it, and more to the point, the first to
put it down. From beginning to end Wilkes was law-abiding
and honest; he saw certain anomalies in the Constitution, and
still more corruption in the political practice. All he wished to
do was to correct the one and abolish the other, aiding the
natural growth of the Constitution, and giving the people that
share in government which was theirs in everything but fact.
So he began a long, slow process of moral influence, keeping
the mob in order, and striving by moderation, by wit, by
logic, and by ridicule to persuade and win over, first the

electorate and then Parliament. He failed partly by the ill-luck of circumstances, and still more by the virulence of the King and the blindness of politicians. In tremendous contrast to Wilkes came the crazy Lord George Gordon, who whipped up his followers to frenzy, and was then half surprised, half gratified,· to find them out of hand. Gordon's failure is a measure, not only of Wilkes's moderation, but of his power and skill.

In the actual course of events Wilkes played an outstanding part. Government were completely paralysed at this sudden outbreak of force, and the City would have been laid in ruins but for the temporary bewilderment of the leaderless mob and the vigour of the King himself in calling out the troops. Suddenly the mob, giving way to its destructive instincts, swept across Blackfriars Bridge to attack the Bank. The Lord Mayor, a Court creature, trembled in the Mansion House, praying for his own safety; the officials caught the infection of his terror. It was Wilkes the Chamberlain who headed the forces of law and order, Wilkes the ex-militia colonel who commanded the guard which saved the Bank and rolled back the infuriated crowds.

Dr. Johnson, in a letter to Mrs. Thrale, described the conduct of his erstwhile enemy. "The public has escaped a very heavy calamity. The rioters attempted the Bank on Wednesday night, but in no great number; and, like other thieves, with no great resolution. Jack Wilkes headed the party that drove them away. . . . Jack, who was always zealous for order and decency, declares that, if he be trusted with the power, he will not leave a rioter alive." Jack, who was always zealous for order and decency! Five years earlier the learned doctor out of his profound ignorance wrote a pamphlet on the Middlesex election, called *The False Alarm*. In the course of this not uninteresting work, he remarked of Wilkes: "Lampoon itself would disdain to speak ill of him of whom no man speaks well. It is sufficient that he is expelled the House of Commons, and confined in jail as being legally convicted of sedition and impiety."

But Wilkes did much more than defend the Bank or patrol the City; unlike Government, he used his brains. On the 21st of June Charles Jenkinson, afterwards the Earl of Liverpool, and at this time a subordinate member of Government, wrote to Lord Amherst, the Secretary at War: "Mr. Wilkes has desired me to recommend to your Lordship that the guard of cavalry posted at Guildhall may be withdrawn. He says it is a great inconvenience to them . . . but he mentioned in confidence another reason, which is, that the election for Sheriffs is on Saturday at Guildhall, and if the guard is then there, it will be the foundation for clamour. For this last reason, which is, I think, a good one, and as I am persuaded that Mr. Wilkes is sincere in what he says, I earnestly recommend to your Lordship to order that guard for the present at least to be withdrawn." Rather gingerly the Secretary at War agreed to believe the sincerity of the man who had saved the City.

(5)

The effect of the Gordon Riots was a serious setback to the popular cause. It was impossible to suggest greater powers for the mob who had just been burning houses, breaking open prisons, and murdering honest citizens. The associations and committees hung their heads in silent shame, and a glorious irony flaunted itself—the City voted a loyal and gushing address to the King; peers and solid, respectable gentlemen waited in Wilkes's hall with votes of thanks; Government, which had been weak, corrupt, and trembling to a fall, plucked up heart of courage and took on a new lease of life. Even the war in America, which had been languishing, took a fresh turn, and victories were reported at Charlestown and Camden. It was a thousand pities, for this flash in the pan hardened the King's heart and stiffened North. Government moved a vote of thanks to the victorious generals, and practically ordered the vote to be unanimous. There was an awkward silence, and then Wilkes rose to protest. He would not thank generals for killing his fellow-subjects; he could not rejoice over victories that would merely prolong an impossible war and lead to fresh slaughter and more humiliation. Peace was the one necessity and peace on almost any terms. He poured scorn on the decision not to concede independence. "Whether it is granted or not by a British Parliament, *de jure*, seems to me of little moment or avail. It is merely an amusing, curious theme of speculation among a set of idle, listless, loitering, lounging, ill-informed gentlemen at Westminster, who remark the disorders of the State, to combat which they possess not vigour of mind or virtue." The war was unnatural, as this very motion proved, producing a conflict of different passions. The mover himself must be both sad and glad, and Wilkes entreated him to withdraw a motion "from every part of which I find it my duty to dissent, while I deeply lament that the lustre of such splendid victories is obscured and darkened by the want of a good cause, without which no war, in the eye of truth and reason, before God or man, can be justified".

It was a brave and honest speech, flung in the teeth of power and popular feeling.

As though to emphasize his words, the year ended with a declaration of war on Holland. There was already a League of Armed Neutrality among the northern nations, caused by England's claim to search neutral vessels, and thus England was truly isolated—at enmity with all the world.

The new war, the crushing burdens, the feeling of hopelessness, Wilkes's words, combined to revive the flagging spirit of the associations. They raised their heads again, timidly, one by one. Westminster came first with a vote of thanks to Wilkes for his speech. Yorkshire followed suit at the opening of 1781. In February Burke was encouraged to renew his Bill for reducing the Civil List, and maybe the insolence of Government in its treatment of the Bill served to inflame the spirit of exasperation. The second reading was deferred in order that honourable members might attend the benefit of Vestris, a favourite French dancer at the Opera.

Throughout the year feeling grew, quietly but none the less effectively, until in November England learnt of the surrender at Yorktown. North received the news "as he would have taken a cannon-ball in his breast". He paced up and down the room muttering again and again, "O God, it is all over!" and entreated the King to let him resign. But the King, whose courage was as magnificent as it was mad, bade him hold on. The people, however, were too deeply stirred. It was no time to mince words, and the City told the King the blunt and bitter truth: "Your armies are captured; the wonted superiority of your navies is annihilated; your dominions are lost." In Parliament a motion for peace was rejected by only one vote, and the Opposition began a series of furious attacks. It was only a question of time, and on the 20th of March, 1782, North resigned. A week later Rockingham was Prime Minister.

(6)

Peace was now a mere matter of negotiation, and the interest of the war had gone, leaving only the bitter taste of folly, bungling, and disaster. The preliminaries were signed in November 1782, and the definitive treaties ten months later.

More important, because more speculative, were the chances of reform. Wilkes had set two balls rolling—parliamentary reform and economic reform. In reality they were two sides of one question, neither of which was effective without the other. But for practical purposes they could very well be distinguished, and while those who were most whole-hearted adopted both with the emphasis on the first, those who were more timid confined themselves to the latter. Rockingham was, and always had been, timid; he rarely looked beyond the purest negative; and Rockingham was Prime Minister. As in his first administration, so now in his second, he wallowed in repeal. The official Bills were wholly negative—a Bill to reduce sinecures, a Bill to exclude contractors from Parliament, a Bill

to disfranchise revenue officers; measures that only reduced
the electorate, whatever effect they might have on the purity
of elections. Further than this Rockingham was most unwilling
to go. But there was a more active party among his followers,
including the Duke of Richmond and the younger Pitt. Wilkes,
as might be expected, belonged to this small band of enthu-
siasts. They had met at the Duke of Richmond's house towards
the end of the previous year to concert measures, and the
Duke had extorted a reluctant promise from Rockingham that
the matter should be considered. All was now ready, and as
a preliminary, on the 3rd of May, 1782, Wilkes for the last time
moved that the Middlesex election resolutions should be
expunged. Even Rockingham could support this wholly negative measure, and the long-drawn-out dispute was ended by a
vote of 115 to 47.

Wilkes at once issued a manifesto to his constituents, telling
them the great news, and adding, "I am happy, gentlemen, to
acquaint you that the appointment of a committee to examine
into the present state of the representation of the Commons of
Great Britain is on the eve of being moved in the House of
Commons by a gentleman of as great abilities, matured even
in youth, as this country has at any time produced. You long
ago suggested the idea of the propriety of such a measure, and
in pursuance of your instructions I had the honour, in March
1776, of moving the House of Commons for leave to bring in
a Bill for a just and equal representation of the people of
England in Parliament, but without success. The solemn
engagement between us in 1774, at a numerous county meeting,
in relation to this and other essential objects, I have never
lost sight of, and shall ever hold sacred. Some of the more
important particulars of that engagement, respecting the fair
and equal representation of the people in the House of Commons, and the shortening the duration of parliaments, are
among the grand objects, the striking features, of the intended
inquiry. You will always find me, gentlemen, uniformly pursuing the noble plan of liberty, which you early marked out

for my conduct, and above all endeavouring to enforce the clear right of the people to the free and frequent choice of their representatives." So for a second time he appeared to be on the verge of a strenuous and successful campaign. A second time he did precisely nothing. Why?

The answer is no less clear than before. Wilkes was once more defeated, not by weariness, insincerity, or lack of skill, but by circumstances. On the 7th of May, 1782, true to his promise, Pitt moved for a committee of inquiry, and was defeated. Eleven days later the little band of stalwarts met at the Thatched House Tavern in St. James's Street, and decided that "application should be made to Parliament by petition from the collective body of the people in their respective districts". It was too late to do anything that session, so there was to be a summer campaign among the people "in order to lay their petitions before Parliament early in the next session".

Alas for their hopes! Much was to happen before the next session arrived. As a first calamity, Rockingham died on the 1st of July. No proper arrangements had been made for his successor; jealousies broke out, and when Shelburne became Prime Minister Fox left the party in a huff, taking some members with him and shaking the loyalty of others. Worse than that, he began intriguing with North, and ultimately formed a Coalition with him that drove Shelburne from power. The session that was to have seen the beginning of reform found Government struggling even to secure the peace.

In February 1783 Shelburne fell, and in April the Coalition succeeded. With North in power there was no hope of reform, and Wilkes had perforce to wait. It is significant of his honesty, and perhaps of his clear sight, that he would have nothing to do with the Coalition, much as he respected Fox and admired his powers. Instead, he pinned his faith to the rising star of Pitt, the new champion of reform.

As it is a frequent taunt against Wilkes that he always fell out with his colleagues, it may be as well here, when he broke

with Fox, to point to the reason. There is practically no statesman or politician of the eighteenth century, except Wilkes,
who failed to turn his coat at least once. On almost every occasion that Wilkes fought with a colleague, that colleague had
first changed his principles, and so far as Wilkes was concerned,
the dispute was generally confined to the public stage. Speaking against Fox's East India Bill in December 1783, Wilkes
made a touching reference to his old friend, which well exem-
plifies his attitude: "I protest, Sir, I do not feel the least per-
sonality against either of the chief members of the Coalition."
Then, after praising the private, and deploring the public
character of Lord North, he continued: "With his colleague
I have acted against his Lordship for many years. I fought by
his side through the whole American war, and in all the spirited
struggles against the too great power of the Crown. I have
frequently been in rapture from the strains of his manly eloquence, the force of his reasoning, and the torrent of his
oratory. So perfect a parliamentary debater this House has
never known. I grieve when I recollect how unavailing all our
tedious struggles have been, and that so large a part of the
Empire has been torn away from us; but I am indignant when
I see the noble lord in one of the highest offices of the State,
brought back to power and caressed by the very man who
undertook to impeach him as the great criminal of the State,
the corrupter of Parliament, the author and contriver of our
ruin."

The Coalition was kicked out by the King himself on the
23rd of December, 1783, and Pitt became Prime Minister.
For the next year Pitt was consolidating his position, and then
on the 18th of April, 1785, renewed his plan of reform. He
failed, and according to Wilberforce was "terribly disappointed
and beat". Whether he would have tried again it is hard to
say. The overwhelming fact is that stern necessity soon made
it impossible. There were troubles in plenty on the Continent,
driving up too soon to the storm of the French Revolution.
But whatever Pitt might, or might not, have done, it was

hopeless for Wilkes in his sixtieth year to dream of starting another agitation—and unnecessary, seeing that the Prime Minister was at the time himself an ardent reformer.

(7)

There is little more to be told of Wilkes. Though he remained in Parliament till 1790, he realized that his work was over, and withdrew gradually from the turmoil. Throughout his career he had been an independent. It was his task to be the pioneer, tilling the ground and sowing the seed. When his ideas had once taken root, once been adopted by a political party, Wilkes was unnecessary. Neither by instinct nor by experience could this individualist work well in a party organization. The harvest was certain, and others must reap where he had sown. Moreover, the issues were no longer clear-cut. Following ever his twin stars of liberty and reform, he had inevitably thrown in his lot with Pitt against Fox, and many ignorant sneers were thrown at him for apostasy, for supporting the King's nominee. The best known came from Sheridan's pen:

> Johnny Wilkes, Johnny Wilkes,
> Thou greatest of bilkes,
> How changed are the notes you now sing!
> Your famed Forty-five
> Is Prerogative,
> And your Blasphemy "God save the King".

So Wilkes declined in popularity and usefulness. He made only one more great speech—in defence of Warren Hastings, inspired partly by friendship and still more by patriotism and a revival of the glowing memories of his youth, when English armies were triumphant and England's campaigns victorious. He would have liked "to have died in my gears", but a new generation had grown up who had already forgotten his great fight, and murmured at his support of Pitt's financial measures. Seeing the tide rise against him at the election of 1790, he declined a poll and quietly withdrew.

With the fading of his political importance he no longer found it necessary to rouse the City. More and more he retired from the dusty arena to the quiet duties of the Chamberlain, carrying out the routine work with his accustomed thoroughness, and the more public functions with the aplomb of a man who has suffered much and experienced more.

In private life relief from financial worries brought to light his essential moderation and spirit of independence. Slowly but steadily he cleared up his debts, and then with an honesty as admirable as it is rare turned his retentive memory to loans which friends had long since forgotten, pressing repayment upon them, and becoming a benefactor to those who had fallen by the wayside—a steady but masterful benefactor, content to give according to his means, but testy at the slightest assumption that the contributions would continue.

The straightening out of his own affairs added a measure of serenity to a wit and bonhomie perpetually green. As in his early days, so in his last, he became the admired centre of a brilliant group, chuckling with his contemporaries over the nuts and wine, and taking a delight in shocking priggish youngsters with tales of his wild past.

In all manner of odd corners, happy and amusing glimpses of him may be caught—Wilkes snubbing a pushful young journalist, and being duly handed down to posterity as irritable and passionate; Wilkes laughing at himself as an exploded volcano; Wilkes telling the King that he had never been a Wilkite; Wilkes silencing an old market-woman who raised the cry of "Wilkes and Liberty"; Wilkes voting at Westminster for his old enemy, Horne; Wilkes telling stories against himself—as that of the old lady looking up at the signboard of one of the numerous Wilkes's Head Taverns, and muttering, "Aye, he swings everywhere but where he ought."

But there are larger portraits worth recording. In May 1781 Boswell contrived a second dinner at Mr. Dilly's. An evening of wit and laughter was followed by a gift of *The Lives of the Poets*, with Johnson's compliments. Wilkes paid the old man a visit of thanks. "The company", says Boswell, "gradually dropped away; Mr. Dilly himself was called downstairs upon business; I left the room for some time; when I returned, I was struck with observing Dr. Samuel Johnson and John Wilkes, Esq., literally *tête-à-tête*; for they were reclined upon their chairs, with their heads almost close to each other, and talking earnestly, in a kind of confidential whisper, of the personal quarrel between George the Second and the King of Prussia. Such a scene of perfectly easy sociability between two such opponents in the war of political controversy as that which I now beheld would have been an excellent subject for a picture. It presented to my mind the happy days which are foretold in the scripture, when the lion shall lie down with the kid."

Less than a year later Wilkes delighted the Society of Beef Steaks with an excellent paper entitled "Remarks of the Earl of Effingham on a Late Excursion to Elysium". The eccentric Earl had retired some two years before to the country, and somehow the rumour had got abroad that he had been murdered in the Gordon Riots. On his return to London in 1782 Wilkes read this amusing little phantasy to the Society in the presence of the delighted Earl. "I shall first", ran the paper, "establish the fundamental point of belief, that the noble Earl was killed on Blackfriars Bridge the 6th day of June 1780." The proof involved much good-humoured chaffing. Effingham was notoriously a sloven in his dress, and accordingly his *valet de chambre* was made to depose that his master was on the fatal day attired as a perfect eighteenth-century fop. Having proved his death, Wilkes proceeded to prove his return to the world, and so, "having cleared away the rubbish of modern infidelity, I proceed to relate with the most scrupulous exactness in what manner his Lordship passed his time in the regions below". There followed a neat satire on political and religious controversies, full of imagination, wit, and good sense —one that deserves more publicity than the Manuscript Room of the British Museum.

Wilkes's old restlessness was disappearing, aided maybe by

the hand of death. In 1781 his mother died, and three years later his wife. Polly succeeded to her mother's money, and as she never married and remained devoted to her father, this increased wealth served to lighten his declining days. Meanwhile the besetting vice cooled, and Wilkes found himself more and more contented in the company of his last mistress, Amelia Arnold—a plain, country-bred woman of no pretensions and almost less beauty. He seems to have met her first about 1777, and she bore him a daughter, Harriet, in whom he found great pleasure. Later on he took a house for her in Kensington Gore, and used to dine alternately with Polly and his mistress. There is a story of her worth recording. On one occasion Wilkes found her depressed at some unkind remarks about her plain features. "You see, my dear," said Wilkes with tender wit, "there has never been *any difference* between us."

In 1788 he took a small house near Sandown in the Isle of Wight, where he spent his holidays, showing a keen interest in his garden and the breeding of birds. Here also he employed his spare time editing *Catullus* and the *Characters of Theophrastus*, both of which he printed privately and distributed among his friends—some of them men who had once been his bitterest enemies.

To the end he remained active and at work. On the 28th of November, 1797, it was his duty as Chamberlain to present the freedom of the City to Nelson, and on December 5th to Admiral Waldegrave. A few days later he was confined to his bed. On Boxing Day, late in the afternoon, he asked Polly for something to drink. She gave him a cup of water, and lifting it towards her, he drank to the health of his "beloved and excellent daughter". Shortly afterwards he was dead. His epitaph he wrote himself:

"A FRIEND OF LIBERTY".

CHRONOLOGICAL TABLE

1727	Birth of Wilkes.	Accession of George II.
1739	Wilkes at school.	War of the Austrian Succession.
1745	Wilkes at Leyden University.	Jacobite rising.
1747	Wilkes marries.	
1748	—	Peace of Aix-la-Chapelle.
1750	Birth of Polly.	
1754	Wilkes stands for Berwick-upon-Tweed; writes his parodies.	Death of Pelham; General Election.
1756	Separates from his wife.	Outbreak of the Seven Years War.
1757	Enters Parliament.	Pitt becomes Prime Minister.
1760	—	Accession of George III.
1761	—	Resignation of Pitt.
1762	*Observations. The North Briton.*	War with Spain. Peace of Paris.
1763	"No. 45."	Grenville becomes Prime Minister.
1764	Expelled from the House of Commons.	
1765	Wilkes in exile.	Stamp Act. Rockingham administration.
1766	Wilkes in exile.	Repeal of Stamp Act. Chatham administration.
1768	Middlesex election.	Massacre of St. George's Fields. Resignation of Chatham.
1769	Wilkes repeatedly expelled from the House; becomes an Alderman.	Letters of Junius. Reappearance of Chatham.
1770	Wilkes attacks Press Warrants.	North becomes Prime Minister; Burke's *Present Discontents.*
1771	Wilkes asserts the freedom of the Press; becomes Sheriff.	City challenges Parliament.

1774	Wilkes elected Lord Mayor.	Boston Tea-party; General Election.
1775	Wilkes returns to Parliament.	War with America.
1776	Fails at election for Chamberlain; introduces motion for parliamentary reform.	American Declaration of Independence.
1777	Wilkes initiates economic reform.	Surrender at Saratoga.
1778	—	Death of Chatham.
1779	Wilkes supports religious liberty; becomes Chamberlain.	War with Spain.
1780	—	Dunning's Motion; Gordon Riots; War with Holland.
1781	—	Cornwallis surrenders at Yorktown.
1782	Middlesex election resolutions expunged.	Rockingham's second administration; Shelburne's administration.
1783	—	Peace Treaties; Coalition Government.
1784	—	Pitt becomes Prime Minister.
1789	—	Beginnings of French Revolution.
1790	Wilkes retires from Parliament.	
1797	Death.	

BIBLIOGRAPHY

The following is a list of the more important works which have been consulted:

ALBEMARLE, Lord. Memoirs of Lord Rockingham.
ALMON, J. Anecdotes of the Earl of Chatham.
        Wilkes's Life and Correspondence.
        History of the Late Minority.
ANSON, W. Memoirs of the Duke of Grafton.
BATESON, M. A Narrative of the Changes in the Ministry 1765–67.
Bedford Correspondence.
BLEACKLEY, H. Life of John Wilkes.
BOSWELL, J. Life of Johnson.
        Letters.
BROUGHAM, Lord. Statesmen of the Time of George III.
BURKE, Edmund. Works and Letters.
Chatham Correspondence.
CHURCHILL, C. Poetical Works.
COOKE, G. W. History of Party.
DILKE, Sir C. Papers of a Critic.
DODINGTON, Bubb. Diary.
English Liberty.
FITZGERALD, P. Life of Wilkes.
FITZMAURICE, E. Life of Lord Shelburne.
FORTESCUE, J. Correspondence of George III.
Grenville Papers.
GRENVILLE, G. Speech of a Rt. Hon. Gentleman on the Motion for Expelling Mr. Wilkes.
GREENE, J. R. Short History of the English People.
GREEN, E. John Wilkes and his Visits to Bath.
        Some Bath Love Letters.
        Two Welsh Correspondents.
Hardwicke Papers. (British Museum.)
HARRIS, G. Life of Lord Hardwicke.
HARRISON, F. Chatham.
Hervey's Memoirs.
HITCHMAN, F. Eighteenth Century Studies.
JOHNSON, Dr. The False Alarm.
JOHNSTONE, C. Chrysal.
JUNIUS. Letters.
KILVERT, F. Unpublished Papers of W. Warburton.
LECKY, W. E. H. History of England in the 18th Century.
Liverpool Papers. (British Museum.)
MACAULAY, Lord. Essays.
MAHON, Lord. History of England.

Newcastle Papers. (British Museum.)
PERCY, Elizabeth. Diaries of a Duchess.
PRIOR, J. Life of Burke.
RAE, W. Fraser. Wilkes, Sheridan, and Fox.
RIKKER, F. W. Henry Fox, First Lord Holland.
SOMERVILLE, T. My Own Life and Times.
TASWELL-LANGMEAD. English Constitutional History.
THORNTON, W. The New History of London.
TOWNSHEND, C. A Defence of the Minority.
TRELOAR, Sir W. Wilkes and the City.
TREVELYAN, Sir G. O. Early History of Charles James Fox.
American Revolution.
VEITCH, G. S. Genesis of Parliamentary Reform.
WALDEGRAVE, Lord. Memoirs.
WALPOLE, H. Letters.
Memoirs of the Reign of George II.
Memoirs of the Reign of George III.
Journals.
WILKES, John Cæsar. The Weekly Magazine.
WILKES, John. Addresses to the Gentlemen of Middlesex.
Addresses to the Liverymen.
Complete Collection of Genuine Papers (1767).
Letters to and from Mr. Wilkes (1769).
Controversial letters of Wilkes and Horne (1771).
Essay on Woman.
Letters to his daughter.
Letter to a member of the Club in Albemarle Street.
Letter to the Rt. Hon. George Grenville.
Letter to Samuel Johnson.
Letter on the public conduct of Mr. Wilkes.
The North Briton.
Papers. (British Museum.)
Speeches.
WILLIAMS, A. F. B. Life of Lord Chatham.
WORTLEY, V. S. A Prime Minister and his Son.
WRIGHT, T. Caricature History of the Georges.

INDEX